AA004129

INFOCOMP 2019

The Ninth International Conference on Advanced Communications and Computation

July 28 – August 2, 2019

Nice, France

INFOCOMP 2019 Editors

Claus-Peter Rückemann, WWU Muenster and DIMF, Germany

Yerach Doytsher, Technion - Israel Institute of Technology - Haifa, Israel

Zlatinka Kovacheva – University of Mining and Geology, Sofia Bulgaria and Institute of Mathematics and Informatics, Bulgarian Academy of Sciences, Sofia, Bulgaria

Printed from e-media with permission by:

Curran Associates, Inc.
57 Morehouse Lane
Red Hook, NY 12571

Some format issues inherent in the e-media version may also appear in this print version.

International Academy, Research, and Industry Association (IARIA)
412 Derby Way
Wilmington, DE 19810

Phone: (408) 893-6407
Fax: (408) 527-6351

petre@iaria.org

Additional copies of this publication are available from:

Curran Associates, Inc.
57 Morehouse Lane
Red Hook, NY 12571 USA
Phone: 845-758-0400
Fax: 845-758-2633
Email: curran@proceedings.com
Web: www.proceedings.com

Table of Contents

INFOCOMP 2019

Forward

The Ninth International Conference on Advanced Communications and Computation (INFOCOMP 2019), held between July 28, 2019 and August 02, 2019 in Nice, France, continued a series of events dedicated to advanced communications and computing aspects, covering academic and industrial achievements and visions.

The diversity of semantics of data, context gathering and processing led to complex mechanisms for applications requiring special communication and computation support in terms of volume of data, processing speed, context variety, etc. The new computation paradigms and communications technologies are now driven by the needs for fast processing and requirements from data-intensive applications and domain-oriented applications (medicine, geoinformatics, climatology, remote learning, education, large scale digital libraries, social networks, etc.). Mobility, ubiquity, multicast, multi-access networks, data centers, cloud computing are now forming the spectrum of de factor approaches in response to the diversity of user demands and applications. In parallel, measurements control and management (self-management) of such environments evolved to deal with new complex situations.

The conference included academic, research, and industrial contributions. It had the following tracks:

- Biometry, security, access technologies, algorithms, and applications
- Modeling and simulations
- Advanced applications
- MATHNUM: Mathematical and numerical applications

We take here the opportunity to warmly thank all the members of the INFOCOMP 2019 technical program committee, as well as all the reviewers. The creation of such a high quality conference program would not have been possible without their involvement. We also kindly thank all the authors who dedicated much of their time and effort to contribute to INFOCOMP 2019. We truly believe that, thanks to all these efforts, the final conference program consisted of top quality contributions.

We also thank the members of the INFOCOMP 2019 organizing committee for their help in handling the logistics and for their work that made this professional meeting a success.

We hope that INFOCOMP 2019 was a successful international forum for the exchange of ideas and results between academia and industry and to promote further progress in the field of communications and computation. We also hope that Nice, France provided a pleasant environment during the conference and everyone saved some time to enjoy the charm of the city.

INFOCOMP 2019 Chairs

INFOCOMP Steering Committee

Claus-Peter Rückemann, Leibniz Universität Hannover / Westfälische Wilhelms-Universität Münster / North-German Supercomputing Alliance (HLRN), Germany [Chair]
Kei Davis, Los Alamos National Laboratory, USA
Malgorzata Pankowska, University of Economics, Katowice, Poland
Subhash Saini, NASA, USA

Hans-Joachim Bungartz, Technische Universität München (TUM) - Garching, Germany
Almadena Chtchelkanova, National Science Foundation - Arlington, USA

INFOCOMP Industry/Research Advisory Committee

Bernhard Bandow, Max Planck Institute for Solar System Research (MPS), Göttingen, Germany
Alfred Geiger, T-Systems Solutions for Research GmbH, Germany
Edgar A. Leon, Lawrence Livermore National Laboratory, USA
Lutz Schubert, Institute of Information Resource Management, University of Ulm, Germany
Walter Lioen, SURFsara, Netherlands
Huong Ha, School of Business, Singapore University of Social Sciences (SUSS), Singapore
Manfred Krafczyk, Institute for Computational Modeling in Civil Engineering (iRMB) - Braunschweig, Germany
Hans-Günther Müller, Cray, Germany

INFOCOMP Publicity Chair

Ustijana Rechkoska-Shikoska, University for Information Science and Technology "St. Paul the Apostle" - Ohrid, Republic of Macedonia

INFOCOMP 2019

Committee

INFOCOMP Steering Committee

Claus-Peter Rückemann, Leibniz Universität Hannover / Westfälische Wilhelms-Universität Münster / North-German Supercomputing Alliance (HLRN), Germany [Chair]
Kei Davis, Los Alamos National Laboratory, USA
Malgorzata Pankowska, University of Economics, Katowice, Poland
Subhash Saini, NASA, USA
Hans-Joachim Bungartz, Technische Universität München (TUM) - Garching, Germany
Almadena Chtchelkanova, National Science Foundation - Arlington, USA

INFOCOMP Industry/Research Advisory Committee

Bernhard Bandow, Max Planck Institute for Solar System Research (MPS), Göttingen, Germany
Alfred Geiger, T-Systems Solutions for Research GmbH, Germany
Edgar A. Leon, Lawrence Livermore National Laboratory, USA
Lutz Schubert, Institute of Information Resource Management, University of Ulm, Germany
Walter Lioen, SURFsara, Netherlands
Huong Ha, School of Business, Singapore University of Social Sciences (SUSS), Singapore
Manfred Krafczyk, Institute for Computational Modeling in Civil Engineering (iRMB) - Braunschweig, Germany
Hans-Günther Müller, Cray, Germany

INFOCOMP Publicity Chair

Ustijana Rechkoska-Shikoska, University for Information Science and Technology "St. Paul the Apostle" - Ohrid, Republic of Macedonia

INFOCOMP 2019 Technical Program Committee

Mohamed Riduan Abid, Al Akhawayn University, Morocco
Ayaz Ahmad, COMSATS University Islamabad, Wah Campus, Pakistan
Mehmet Aksit, University of Twente, Netherlands
Daniel Andresen, Kansas State University, USA
Andres Ignacio Avila Barrera, Universidad de La Frontera, Chile
Marc Baaden, Institut de Biologie Physico-Chimique, Paris, France
Raymond Bair, Argonne National Laboratory / University of Chicago, USA
Bernhard Bandow, Max Planck Institute for Solar System Research (MPS), Göttingen, Germany
Valeria Bartsch, Fraunhofer ITWM in Kaiserslautern, Germany
Karunakar R. Basireddy, University of Southampton, UK
Md Zakirul Alam Bhuiyan, Fordham University, USA
Tekin Bicer, Argonne National Laboratory, USA

Mauro Ianni, University of Rome, Italy
Sergio Ilarri, University of Zaragoza, Spain
Neena Imam, Oak Ridge National Laboratory, USA
Haziq Jeelani, Galgotias University, India
Jinlei Jiang, Tsinghua University, Beijing, China
Eugene B. John, The University of Texas at San Antonio, USA
Seifedine Kadry, Beirut Arab University, Lebanon
Izabela Karsznia, University of Warsaw, Poland
Nicolas Kemper Valverde, Universidad Nacional Autónoma de México, Mexico
Jinoh Kim, Texas A&M University-Commerce, USA
Alexander Kipp, Robert Bosch GmbH, Germany
Penporn Koanantakool, Google, USA
Stefanos Kollias, University of Lincoln, UK
Harald Köstler, Friedrich-Alexander Universität Erlangen-Nürnberg, Germany
Zlatinka Kovacheva, Institute of Mathematics and Informatics of the Bulgarian Academy of Sciences, Sofia, Bulgaria
Manfred Krafczyk, Institute for Computational Modeling in Civil Engineering (iRMB) – TU Braunschweig, Germany
Nane Kratzke, Lübeck University of Applied Sciences, Germany
Bettina Krammer, MoRitS, Bielefeld University & Bielefeld University of Applied Sciences, Germany
Rolf Krause, Università della Svizzera italiana, Switzerland
Herbert Kuchen, Westfälische Wilhelms-Universität Münster, Institut für Wirtschaftsinformatik, Germany
Kalyan Kumaran, Argonne Leadership Computing Facility, USA
Sonal Kumari, Robert BOSCH, Bangalore, India
Julian Kunkel, University of Reading, UK
Robert S. Laramee, Swansea University, UK
Stephen Leak, NERSC User Engagement, USA
Edgar A. Leon, Lawrence Livermore National Laboratory, USA
Yiu-Wing Leung, Hong Kong Baptist University, Kowloon Tong, Hong Kong
Elżbieta Lewańska, Poznan University of Economics and Business, Poland
Xin Li, Johns Hopkins University, USA
Yanting Li, City University of HongKong, China
Jaehan Lim, Kwangwoon University, South Korea
Walter Lioen, SURFsara, Netherlands
Iryna Lishchuk, Institut für Rechtsinformatik | Leibniz Universität Hannover, Germany
Maciej Liskiewicz, Universität zu Lübeck, Germany
Chin-Jung Liu, Michigan State University, USA
Jinwei Liu, University of Central Florida, USA
Piotr Luszczek, University of Tennessee, USA
Dionisio Machado Leite Filho, Federal University of Mato Grosso do Sul, Brazil
Sandeep Madireddy, Argonne National Laboratory, USA
Alessandro Margara, Politecnico di Milano, Italy
Antonio Martí-Campoy, Universitat Politècnica de València, Spain
Nikolaos Matsatsinis, Technical University of Crete, Greece
Kassiano Matteussi, Federal University of Rio Grande do SUL (UFRGS), Brazil
Artis Mednis, Akero Systems, Latvia
Roderick Melnik, MS2Discovery Interdisciplinary Research Institute | Wilfrid Laurier University (WLU),

Canada
Gabriele Mencagli, University of Pisa, Italy
Mariofanna Milanova, UA Little Rock, USA
Victor Mitrana, Polytechnic University of Madrid, Spain
Sangman Moh, Chosun University, Korea
Sébastien Monnet, University Savoie Mont Blanc - LISTIC, France
Hans-Guenther Mueller, Cray, Germany
Mithun Mukherjee, Guangdong University of Petrochemical Technology, China
Katsuhiro Naito, Aichi Institute of Technology, Japan
Syed Naqvi, Birmingham City University, UK
Duc Manh Nguyen, University of Ulsan, Korea
Lena Noack, Free University of Berlin, Germany
Ulrich Norbisrath, University of Applied Sciences Upper Austria (FH UA) Linz, Austria / George Mason University, USA
Morteza Noshad, University of Michigan, USA
Krzysztof Okarma, West Pomeranian University of Technology, Szczecin, Poland
Aida Omerovic, SINTEF ICT, Norway
Malgorzata Pankowska, University of Economics in Katowice, Poland
Vangelis Th. Paschos, LAMSADE | University Paris-Dauphine | CNRS, France
Giuseppe Patane', CNR-IMATI, Italy
Ripon Patgiri, National Institute of Technology Silchar, India
Prantosh Kumar Paul, Raiganj University, India
Daniela Pöhn, University Bundeswehr München, Germany
Simon Portegies Zwart, Leiden University, Netherlands
Jonas Posner, University of Kassel, Germany
Guillaume Puigt, ONERA, France
Giovanni Puglisi, University of Cagliari, Italy
Xin Qi, Microsoft, USA
Francesco Quaglia, DIAG - Sapienza Universita' di Roma, Italy
Elena Ravve, ORT Braude College, Israel
Barbara Re, University of Camerino, Italy
Carlos Reaño, Queen's University Belfast, UK
Ustijana Rechkoska-Shikoska, University for Information Science and Technology "St. Paul the Apostle" - Ohrid, Republic of Macedonia
Yenumula B. Reddy, Grambling State University, USA
Theresa-Marie Rhyne, Visualization Consultant, Durham, USA
Vincent Rodin, University of Brest, France
Claus-Peter Rückemann, Westfälische Wilhelms-Universität Münster / Leibniz Universität Hannover / North-German Supercomputing Alliance, Germany
Hakizumwami Birali Runesha, Research Computing Center | University of Chicago, USA
Julio Sahuquillo, Universitat Politecnica de Valencia, Spain
Subhash Saini, NASA, USA
Sebastiano Fabio Schifano, University of Ferrara / INFN, Italy
Lutz Schubert, Institute of Information Resource Management, University of Ulm, Germany
Saeed Seddighin, University of Maryland, College Park, USA
Mohamed Sedky, Staffordshire University, UK
Tapan K. Sengupta, IIT Kanpur, India
Rifat Shahriyar, Bangladesh University of Engineering and Technology, Bangladesh

Patrick Siarry, Université de Paris 12, France
Theodore Simos, Ural Federal University - Ekaterinburg, Russian Federation | University of Peloponnese - Tripolis, Greece
Christine Sinoquet, University of Nantes, France
Hari Sivaraman, VMware, USA
Estela Suarez, Juelich Supercomputing Centre - Forschungszentrum Juelich GmbH, Germany
Rolf Sperber, Consultant, Huawei European Research Centre Munich, Germany
Giandomenico Spezzano, CNR-ICAR & University of Calabria, Italy
Przemyslaw Stpiczynski, Maria Curie-Sklodowska University, Lublin, Poland
Mu-Chun Su, National Central University, Taiwan
Hongyang Sun, Vanderbilt University, USA
Javid Taheri, Karlstad University, Sweden
Mahmut Taylan Kandemir, Pennsylvania State University, USA
Cuong Ngoc Tran, Ludwig-Maximilians-Universität München (LMU), Germany
Miron Vinarskiy, Independent researcher, USA
Teng Wang, Oracle, USA
Xiaoyan Wang, Ibaraki University, Japan
Yunsheng Wang, Kettering University, USA
Zheng Wang, Lancaster University, UK
Xianglin Wei, Nanjing Telecommunication Technology Research Institute, China
Qiao Xiang, Yale University, USA
Rengan Xu, Dell EMC, USA
Qimin Yang, Harvey Mudd College, USA
Andrew J. Younge, Sandia National Laboratories, USA
Quan Yuan, The University of Texas of the Permian Basin,USA
Jie Zhang, Amazon AWS, USA
Na Zhang, VMware Inc., USA
Sotirios Ziavras, New Jersey Institute of Technology, USA
Jason Zurawski, Lawrence Berkeley National Laboratory / Energy Sciences Network (ESnet), USA

Copyright Information

Privacy by Design Approach for eHealthcare System Architecture

Malgorzata Pankowska
Department of Informatics
University of Economics in Katowice
Katowice, Poland
pank@ue.katowice.pl

***Abstract*—Privacy engineering has recently attracted attention from professionals; therefore, current literature includes methodologies to support privacy modelling and system design. However, in order to ensure appropriate and successful implementation of these methodologies, it is important to develop business and system analyses focusing on privacy and security issues. The paper aims to identify privacy engineering requirements and conditions and model them for further holistic system architecture development in the eHealthcare context. The results show the demand to strongly focus on business architecture development for further mapping the privacy requirements into security systems.**

Keywords-Privacy; Security; Privacy by Design; Business Architecture; System Architecture; ArchiMate.

I. INTRODUCTION

Protection of data privacy is becoming a key challenge for most business entities. The discussions are now very intensive, particularly because of the General Data Protection Regulation (GDPR) [1] introduced in 2016 in European Union (EU) member countries. However, due to the big data and information, the GDPR recommendations are becoming popular in the digital space. Therefore, identifying key indicators for patient configured privacy policy in relation to eHealthcare personalized services is also very important and valid. Taking into account the existing literature, it is necessary to mention that information privacy refers mostly to the right to exercise control over the use of personal information. However, in this paper, we emphasize the need to develop a holistic approach for privacy requirements specification and modelling. The privacy by design approach, as well as Information Boundary Theory (IBT), and Communications Privacy Management Theory are used in discussion for this development. The privacy paradox is explained and the business architecture and system architecture models are presented. The paper is organized as follows. Firstly, background information regarding the privacy concepts is provided. Next, in Section 2, the literature review on Privacy by Design (PbD) approach is discussed. Further, in Section 3, the eHealthcare issues are presented as a certain context of privacy issues. Then, models of business architecture and system architecture in ArchiMate language are considered. This is followed by the discussion of results of the models' analysis. The conclusions cover implications and limitations of the work presented.

II. PRIVACY VS. SECURITY

Any information about an individual maintained and processed by an agency, including data on the individual's identity, i.e., names, social security number, personal identification number, parents' names, or biometric records is personal information and as such is usually linked to other medical, educational, financial, and employment information. In this context, privacy is an ability to control this information, because individuals are interested in keeping some of their personal information hidden from others.

According to de Souza et al. [2] privacy is a fundamental right guaranteed by the Universal Declaration of Human Rights, proclaimed by the United Nations General Assembly. Reference [3] includes a classification of different types of privacy:

- Personal privacy concerning the privacy of personal attributes.
- Informational privacy involving the protection of unauthorized access to information.
- Institutional privacy referring to the administration of organizational private data as well as strategic business information.

Burgoon et al. [4] assume a multidimensional approach and define privacy as the ability to control and limit physical, interactional, psychological, and informational access to a social group or just to its entity. For Solove [5], privacy is valued contextually, and it includes practices of information collecting, processing, dissemination and invasion. Information Boundary Theory (IBT) was formulated to explain the psychological processes individuals use to control the flows of private information. The theory proposes that consumers form physical or virtual informational spaces around them. The boundaries around the spaces play important roles in their willingness to reveal private information or not. Any attempt by an external party to cross these boundaries is perceived as an invasion. According to Communications Privacy Management Theory (CPMT), disclosure of private information renders people vulnerable to opportunistic exploitation, because the disclosed private information becomes co-owned by other parties. The boundary management mechanisms are developed to help people maximize the benefits of revealing private information while simultaneously reduce the risks of opportunistic behavior resulting from intrusive access.

In general, privacy is determined by the context, i.e., business environment, the individual value system and confidence awareness, which may encourage people to reveal their personal information. The value system constructs social patterns of all aspects of human interactions. Sherif et al. [6] argue that shared patterns of behaviours and interactions, cognitive constructs, and affective understandings are learned through a process of socialization. Privacy culture and security culture are defined as ideas, customs, habits, and social behaviours that help individuals to survive as a community. Cavoukian and Chibba [7] argue that while information security concerns protecting personal data through confidentiality, integrity, and availability control, privacy is about unlinkability, transparency, and intervenability assurance. Security is about how information is protected, but privacy is on how it is maintained and used.

Literature review reveals principles of data privacy assurance. The principles are hidden in theories, standards, and various regulations. Particularly important standards are as follows:

- The ISO 9241-210:2010 Ergonomics of human-system interaction Part 210: Human-centered design for interactive systems, which, as a framework for human-centered design processes, integrates different designs and developments appropriate in a particular context [8].
- The ISO/IEC 25010:2011 SQuaRE Systems and Software Quality Requirements and Evaluation, which is a standard that defines the system and software quality, which is highly focused on system's quality of use [8].
- The ISO/IEC 27034-3:2018 Information Technology - Application Security- Part 3: Application security management process, which is a part of standard series assisting organization in integrating security into the life cycle of their applications by providing frameworks and processes at the organization [10].
- The ISO/IEC 29100:2011 Information Technology - Security Techniques - Privacy Framework, applicable to individuals and organizations involved in the specification, procurement, architecturing, designing, developing, testing, maintaining, administering, and operating information and communication technology systems and services, where privacy controls are required for the processing of Personally Identifiable Information (PII) [11].
- The ISO/IEC 29147 - Information Technology - Security Techniques - Vulnerability Disclosure, which is a standard providing requirements and recommendations to vendors on the disclosure of vulnerabilities in products and services [12].

According to the last standard, privacy preferences are to be confronted with privacy safeguarding controls. The privacy principles included there concern data subject's consent and choice, purpose legitimacy and specification, collection limitation, data minimization, data use, retention and disclosure limitation, data accuracy and quality, data openness, transparency and notice, data subject's individual participation and access, accountability, information security, and privacy compliance. In May 25, 2018 the GDPR came in effect mandating data controllers and processors to emphasize transparency, security, and accountability of processed data. The GDPR specifies seven data protection principles that business organizations are to follow when collecting, processing, transferring, and storing individuals' personal data (Table 1). The Organization for Economic Co-operation and Development (OECD) [13] provided principles similar to the GDPR work (Table I). The regulations discussed above do not concern Privacy by Design (PbD) approach.

TABLE I. PRIVACY PRINCIPLES.

Privacy Standards		
Cavoukian Principles	***OECD Principles***	***GDPR Principles***
Proactive not Reactive	Collection Limitation	Storage Limitation
Privacy as the Default Setting	Data Quality	Accuracy
Privacy embedded into Design	Purpose Specification and Openness of Data Handling	Data Lawfulness, Fairness, and Transparency
Full Functionality	Use Limitation	Purpose Limitation
End to End Security	Security Safeguards	Integrity and Confidentiality
Visibility and Transparency	Accountability	Accountability
Respect for User Privacy	Individual Participation	Data Minimization

In 2011, Cavoukian published her Privacy by Design principles [14], which for years have been treated as the de facto standard in privacy protection (Table I). In Article 29, Data Protection Working Party, the proposed principles that should be respected in PbD approach are as follows:

- Choice and consent principle defining that data controllers and processors should describe choices suitable to the data subjects to obtain appropriate consents.
- Legitimate data use purpose specification and use limitations.
- Personal information and sensitive information lifecycle management to ensure minimization of data collection and all its use, just to the strictly specified, documented purposes.
- Accuracy and quality of data that is processed and utilized.
- Providing clear, accessible, transparent and accurate details about business organization privacy management program on how information is processed.
- Development of procedures to allow data subjects to withdraw the consent to use their personal data at any time.
- Establishing the requirements for data protection officers' responsibilities and actions.

- Development of security policies and supporting procedures.
- Implementation of monitoring, measuring and reporting procedures to provide sufficient regular privacy and security control.
- Preventing harms, reducing risk, and protecting vital interests of data subjects.
- Documenting the management policies and control cooperation with third party vendors and security outsourcing companies.
- Elaboration of documented personal data breach policies and supporting procedures that include requirements for notifications of appropriate supervisory authorities.
- Development of procedures concerning implementation technologies and PbD protection.
- Maintaining the policies and procedures to contact the appropriate supervisory authorities.

Nowadays, the PbD issue seems to be increasingly important, particularly because people commonly use Internet of Things (IoT) applications. An exemplary list of devices includes baby monitors, smart home assistants, connected safety-relevant products such as smoke detectors and door locks, smart cameras, TVs and speakers, wearable health trackers, connected home automation and alarm systems. The devices should be safe and secured. Safety is assumed to be a situation, in which people are protected from injury, but security is identified with a condition, where individuals are protected against the consequences of malicious acts. Taking into account the IoT common usage, security and privacy should be embedded in the IoT software application development. Privacy and security by design mean that basic security features are to be built into products and the consumer should learn how to secure their devices. The PbD and security by design ideas require methodological approaches and good practices guidelines. The Code of Practice for Consumer IoT Security [15] covers the following guidelines: password idiosyncrasy, vulnerability disclosure policy implementation, software updating, credentials protection, remote control, software integrity, personal data protection, system resilience, monitoring telemetry data, and making personal data easy to delete. So, the suggested PbD methodological approach is expected to emphasize the principles of response to customer needs, monitoring, learning and anticipation.

III. Privacy by Design - Literature Review

At first glance, the idea of PbD can be recognized as an approach that promotes privacy and data protection compliance from the start of data collecting and processing and maintains such protection in the whole information system lifecycle. Beyond that, it is expected to increase the awareness of privacy and decrease human vulnerabilities. Literature review confirms this attitude. The fundamental reviews have been done using the following tools: 1) IEEEXplore Digital Library [16], 2) AIS (Association of Information Systems) eLibrary [17], 3) ScienceDirect.com [18], 4) Google Scholar [19], 5) Sage Journals [20], 6) Scopus [21], and 7) Web of Science (WoS) research paper repository [22]. The numbers of publications found in these repositories were impressive, but incomparable. The maximum number of publications were presented in GoogleScholar, i.e., 3 340 200 papers, and the smallest on IEEEXplore Digital Libery, i.e., 2791 papers. The reviewed papers include considerations on combining the Privacy by Design concept with information system development methodologies. According to information from the surveyed repositories, lately, authors are working on privacy issues in big data methodologies, as well as in Internet of Things (IoT) application design and implementation. However, in years 2009-2019 , the volume of publications in Google Scholar is going down. Evident increase of growth rates happened in 2012-2014 for WoS publications. The literature review has been done at the beginning of 2019, therefore the minor volume of publications for this year has been registered. However, taking into account further research work on PbD approach in eHealthcare system modelling, this huge volume of papers was reduced to the list of publications in Table II.

TABLE II. Privacy by Design for eHealthcare

No	Paper	Research Results
1	[23]	Privacy patterns for Information System design are proposed and compared to ISO 29100 Privacy Framework principles
2	[24]	Practical approaches in designing IoT for data collection and data sharing within the health domain
3	[25]	Novel data linkage and anonymisation infrastructure in clinical study on chronic diseases in Scotland
4	[26]	Formal methodology for designing privacy mechanisms in pervasive healthcare applications
5	[27]	Analysis of legal difficulties surrounding the use of social networking for healthcare applications
6	[28]	Demonstration of why the implementation of PbD is a necessity in a number of sectors, where specific data protection concerns arise (biometrics, e-health, and video-surveillance)
7	[29]	Examining technological limits, ethical constraints and legal conditions of privacy by design, so as to prevent some misapprehensions of the current debate
8	[30]	In personal health monitoring, PbD approach implies that in some contexts like medication assistance and monitoring of specific health parameters one single automatic option is legitimate
9	[31]	Providing a critical reflection of the perceived privacy risks associated with social media recruitment strategy and the appropriateness of the risk mitigation strategies. Alignment with PbD. Discussion of the following: What are the potential risks and who is at risk? Is cancer considered "sensitive" personal information? What is the probability of online disclosure of a cancer diagnosis in everyday life? What are the public's expectations for privacy online?
10	[32]	This paper presents an analysis of personal e-health systems and identifies privacy issues as a first step towards a 'privacy by design' methodology and practical guidelines.

The paper presented in Table II reveal that researchers focus on combining the PbD approach with the healthcare system development methodologies and applications. The PbD approach is applied to mitigate privacy risk in online information systems and it is considered as a way for protecting personal information. The reviewed research papers have revealed many questions for further investigation, particularly in social networks.

IV. eHealthcare Architecture Models including Privacy by Design

Information Communication Technology (ICT) is incorporated into healthcare management programs enabling care personalization to an individual's needs. The patient-physician relationship system with more virtual interactions is possible to better coordinate care. The relationship systems are developed as formal support of the medical services, as well as informal communication in social networks. The European Group on Ethics in Science and New Technologies (EGE) [33] published an opinion on the ethical implications of new health technologies and individual participation. Therein, they have identified a set of risks. Patients' group focusing on particular diseases take greater responsibility for their health. They are voluntary involved and openly manifest using the online forums their private problems and data. They share symptoms, advices, opinions, and diagnoses. They use social media and internet forums to verify the quality of the professional healthcare as well as for ranking services and physicians. Internet and mobile applications enable them to avoid traditional medical services and develop self-diagnosing and self-treatment. This behavior implies that in some contexts, like medication assistance and monitoring, specific health parameters are revealed and individuals lose control on them. Although in the technical design professionals think about privacy in the aspect of problems of data collecting and security, the social networks people consider the privacy effects of communication on humans and they are open to exchange views in their own individual interests. The need to help themselves and to help others strongly stimulates them to reveal private data. According to Yoo et al. [34], privacy paradox is a phenomenon whereby individuals present strong privacy concerns, but they disclose their personal information. Within an individual's borders, people want to be free to self-determine what they want to reveal. On the other hand, society also has impact on defining these borders by accepting, supporting, tolerating, mocking or punishing. Unfortunately, some people see only the informational aspect without perceiving the consequences of privacy revealing for social relationship development. eHealthcare architecture modelling with respect to the PbD approach can be considered as a privacy engineering issue. The system architecture models proposed below are embedded in a specific healthcare context, particularly they concern the eHealthcare self-treatment, which as such is strongly based on the use of wearable devices, human behaviour monitors and smart assistants. In this paper, system architecture models are presented in the ArchiMate language [35]. Therefore, as it is in The Open Group Architecture Framework (TOGAF) [36] four architecture layers are defined. In the aspect of privacy management, the motivation layer is the most important. Here, perceived privacy risks, principles, constraints, stakeholders, their requirements, goals and values are to be identified and considered (Fig. 1).

Privacy risk is defined as a loss resulting from the negative outcomes and the possibility of an opportunistic behaviour of other parties. Privacy risk includes the misuse of private personal information or unauthorized access and theft [37]. In literature, privacy is perceived from the point of view of reputation loss and identity theft [38]. However, in opposition to that interpretation, private personal data is perceived as necessary to self-promotion. Privacy revealing actions are considered as good investments for individual and organizational development. In Fig. 1, the fundamental concepts of TOGAF motivation layer for eHealthcare self-management are presented.

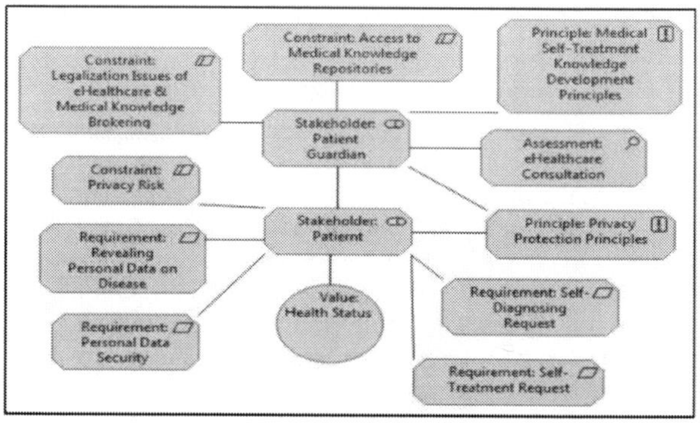

Figure 1. eHealthcare Self-Treatment Architecture Model: Motivation Layer in ArchiMate.

The next TOGAF layer is Archimate Business Layer, which includes the specification of fundamental business concepts, i.e., business partners, processes, services, functions, and objects (Fig. 2). Particularly, the process of control is to be embedded in most privacy regulations, so it is used to operationalize privacy.

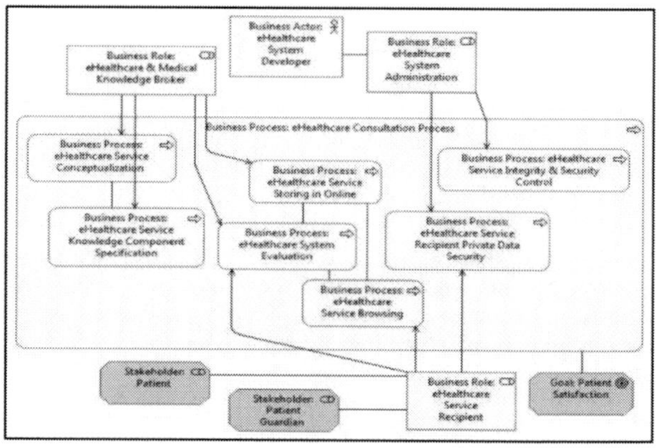

Figure 2. eHealthcare Self-Treatment Architecture Model: Business Layer in ArchiMate.

The eHealthcare consultation process comprises on the one side actions to reveal data, on the other side to hide and protect them. Therefore, basically, to prevent a privacy breach event the following activities are required [39]:

- Monitor of the event trigger generation.
- Notice of event triggers to privacy stakeholders.

- Blocking leakages to avoid personal data flows to the wrong hands.
- Security of delivery channel - encryption.

Anonymity, pseudonymization, unlinkability, and confidentiality prevent individual privacy from revealing i.e., breach of confidentiality. That process decomposition is presented in Fig. 3. Although in some cases "less identification means more privacy" [40], however, sometimes less data, but discovering critical data can lead to violation of privacy.

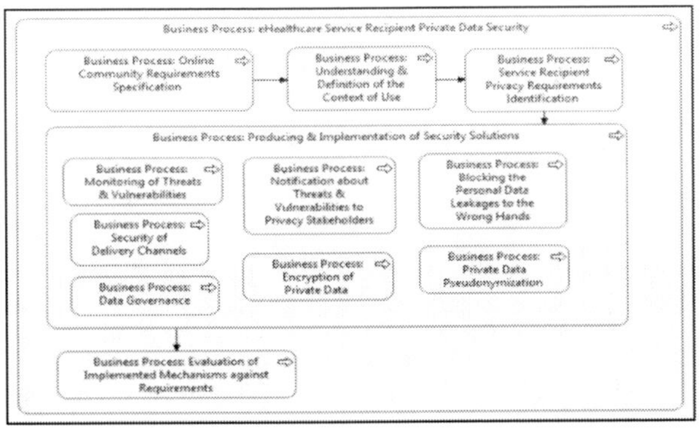

Figure 3. eHealthcare Self-Treatment Architecture Model: Recipient Private Data Security Process in ArchiMate.

The Data Governance process emphasized in Fig. 4 is assumed to include activities to appropriate data provenance, accuracy, lawfulness, fairness, transparency, integrity, and accountability. Implementation of all these processes is not common, however, it should be considered as obligatory. Even the knowledge broker's role is difficult, but in the interests of patients and their life protection, this role is needed. In the TOGAF framework, the next two layers cover software and hardware architecture modelling (Fig. 4).

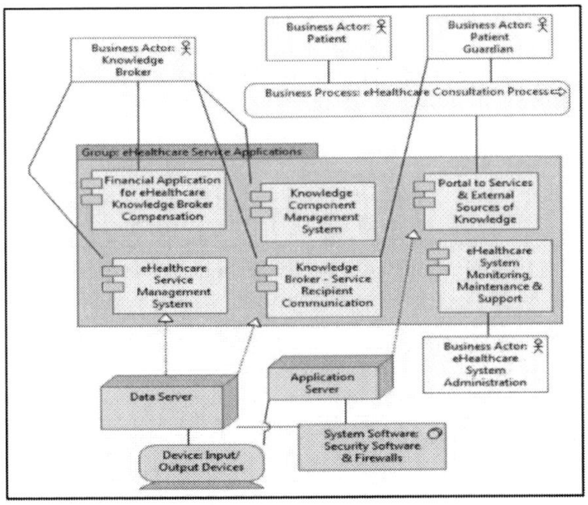

Figure 4. eHealthcare Self-Treatment Architecture Model: Software and Hardware Layers in ArchiMate.

Technologies like firewalls and access control filters are implemented to ensure the security of information assets, but they cannot provide enforcement of acceptable use policies, because of the users, who make decisions on the usage of confidential data and documents.

V. Conclusion

The Privacy by Design approach makes the application or information system more reliable from the personal data management point of view. Following literature review, we conclude that the PbD approach is implemented in software development methodologies. However, in this paper, the holistic approach to privacy management is proposed. Therefore, the system architecture modelling is presented. The TOGAF architecture models for motivation, business, software and hardware layers are included in Figures. The ArchiMate language and modelling tool were used. In this paper, privacy is discussed as a social category and issue, which is determined by personal data subjects. Beyond that, there are solutions developed for personal data protection. The fundamental processes of data security are also presented in ArchiMate language in this paper. The architecture modelling can be further considered as an introduction to application development. The limitation of the presented analysis results from the weaknesses of the applied tool, i.e., ArchiMate. On the one hand, it is suitable for modelling motivation and explaining preferences, but, on the other hand ArchiMate is not integrated with other software engineering tools.

References

[1] Regulation (EU) 2016/679 of the European Parliament and of the Council of 27 April 2016 and repealing Directive 95/46/EC (General Data Protection Regulation). [Online]. Available from: https://eur-lex.europa.eu/ 2019.07.20

[2] P. C. de Souza and C. Maciel, "Legal Issues and User Experience in Ubiquitous Systems from a Privacy Perspective," in Human Aspects of Information Security, Privacy, and Trust, T. Tryfonas and I. Askoxylakis, Eds. Cham: Springer, pp. 449-460, 2015.

[3] J. M. Kizza, Ethical and Social Issues in the Information Age. New York: Springer, 2013.

[4] J. K. Burgoon, R. Parrot, B. A. LePoire, D. L. Kelley, J. B. Walther, and D. Perry, "Maintaining and restoring privacy through communication in different types of relationship," Journal of Social and Personal Relationships, Volume 6, pp. 131-158, 1989.

[5] D. J. Solove, "Conceptualizing privacy," California Law Review, 90, pp. 1087-1156, 2002.

[6] E. Sherif, S. Furnell, and N. Clarke, "An Identification of Variables Influencing the Establishment of Information Security Culture," in Human Aspects of Information Security, Privacy, and Trust, T. Tryfonas and I. Askoxylakis, Eds. Cham: Springer, pp. 436-448, 2015.

[7] A. Cavoukian and M. Chibba, "Start with Privacy by Design in All Big Data Applications," in Guide to Big Data Applications, S. Srinivasan, Ed. Heidelberg: Springer, pp.29-48, 2018.

[8] International Organization for Standardization. *ISO 9241-210:2010 Ergonomics of human-system interaction, Part 210: Human-centered design for interactive systems.* [Online]. Available from: https://www.iso.org/ 2019.06.11

[9] International Organization for Standardization. *ISO/IEC 25010:2011 SQuaRE Systems and Software Quality Requirements and Evaluation.* [Online]. Available from: https://www.iso.org/ 2019.06.11

[10] International Organization for Standardization. *ISO/IEC 27034-3:2018 Information Technology - Application Security-Part 3: Application security management process.* [Online]. Available from: https://www.iso.org/ 2019.06.11

[11] International Organization for Standardization. *ISO/IEC 29100:2011 Information Technology -Security Techniques - Privacy Framework.* [Online]. Available from: https://www.iso.org/ 2019.06.11

[12] International Organization for Standardization. ISO/IEC 29147 - Information Technology - Security Techniques - Vulnerability Disclosure. [Online]. Available from: https://www.iso.org/ 2019.06.11

[13] S. Anderson, "Privacy by Design: An Assessment of Law Enforcement Drones," A thesis submitted to the Faculty of the Graduate School of Art and Sciences of Georgetown University, Washington, DC, 2014

[14] A. Cavoukian, "Privacy by design. The 7 foundational principles in Privacy by Design. Strong privacy protection—now, and well into the future, 2011. [Online]. Available from: https://www.ipc.on.ca/wp-content/uploads/Resources/7foundationalprinciples.pdf 2019.03.20

[15] Department for Digital, Culture, Media & Sport. *Code of Practice for Consumer IoT Security.* 2018 [Online]. Available from: https://www.gov.uk/government/publications/code-of-practice-for-consumer-iot-security 2019.06.11

[16] IEEEXplore Digital Library. [Online]. Available from: https://ieeexplore.ieee.org/Xplore/home.jsp 2019.03.10

[17] Association of Information Systems AIS eLibrary. [Online]. Available from: https://aisel.aisnet.org/ 2019.03.10

[18] ScienceDirect.com. [Online]. Available from: https://www.sciencedirect.com/ 2019.03.10

[19] GoogleScholar. [Online]. Available from: https://scholar.google.pl/ 2019.03.10

[20] Sage Journals. [Online]. Available from: https://journals.sagepub.com/ 2019.03.03

[21] Scopus [Online]. Available from: https://www.scopus.com/home.uri 2019.02.02

[22] Web of Science (WoS). [Online]. Available from: https://clarivate.com/products/web-of-science/ 2019.02.02

[23] M. Aljohani, K. Hawkey, and J. Blustein, "Proposed Privacy Patterns for Privacy Preserving Healthcare Systems in Accord with Nova Scotia's Personal Health Information Act," in Human Aspects of Information Security, Privacy, and Trust, T. Tryfonas, Ed. Cham: Springer, pp. 91-102, 2016

[24] Y. O'Connor, W. Rowan, L. Lynch, and C. Heavin, "Privacy by Design: Informed Consent and Internet of Things for Smart Health," The 7th International Conference on Current and Future trends of Information and Communication Technologies in Healthcare (ICTH2017), Procedia Computer Science, 113, 2017, pp. 653-658. [Online]. Available from: www.elsevier.com/locate/procedia 2019.02.20

[25] R. O. Sinnott, O. Ajayi, and A. J. Stell, "Data Privacy by Design: Digital Infrastructures for Clinical Collaborations," 2009. [Online]. Available from:
https://minerva-access.unimelb.edu.au/handle/11343/28791 2019.02.23

[26] S. Moncrieff and S. Venkatesh, "A framework for the design of privacy preserving pervasive healthcare," ICME 2009. [Online]. Available from: https://www.researchgate.net/publication/221262735 2019.02.20

[27] J. B. Williams and J. H. Weber-Jahnke, "Social networks for health care: Addressing regulatory gaps with privacy-by-design," Eighth International Conference on Privacy, Security and Trust, 2010, pp. 134-143. [Online]. Available from: https://ieeexplore.ieee.org/xpl/mostRecentIssue.jsp?punumber=5564352 2019.03.20

[28] A. Romanou, "The necessity of the implementation of Privacy by Design in sectors where data protection concern arise," Computer Law & Security Review, Volume 34, Issue 1, February 2018, pp. 99-110.

[29] U. Pagallo, "On the Principle of Privacy by Design and its Limits: Technology, Ethics and the Rule of Law," in European Data Protection: In Good Health? S. Gutwirth, R. Leenes, P. DeHert, Y. Poullet, Eds. Dordrecht: Springer, pp. 331-346, 2012.

[30] A. Nordgren, "Privacy by Design in Personal Health Monitoring," Health Care Analysis, 23, pp. 148-164, 2015.

[31] J. L. Bender, A. B. Cyr, L. Arbuckle, and L. E. Ferris, "Ethics and privacy implications of using the internet and social media to recruit participants for health research: A privacy-by-design framework for online recruitment," Journal of Medical Internet Research, Volume 19, Issue 4, April 2017, [Online]. Available form: https://www.ncbi.nlm.nih.gov/pmc/articles/PMC5399223/ 2019.03.20

[32] G. Drosatos, P. S. Efraimidis, G. Williams, and E. Kaldoudi, "Towards Privacy by Design in Personal e-Health System," Proceedings of the BIOSTEC 2016 Conference - Volume 5: HEALTHINF. SCITEPRESS – Science and Technology Publications, 2016. p. 472-477. [Online]. Available from: https://eprints.lancs.ac.uk/id/eprint/79489/ 2019.03.15

[33] European Group on Ethics in Science and New Technologies (EGE), The ethical implications of new health technologies and citizen participation, Opinion of the European Group on Ethics in Science and New Technologies to the European Commission, Brussels, 2015. [Online]. Available from: https://ec.europa.eu/research/ege/index.cfm?pg=reports 2019.03.18

[34] Ch. W. Yoo, H. J. Ahn, and H. R. Rao, "An Exploration of the Impact of Information Privacy Invasion," Thirty Third International Conference on Information Systems, Orlando 2012, AIS/ICIS, pp. 2260-2278. [Online]. Available from: https://www.semanticscholar.org/paper/An-Exploration-of-the-Impact-of-Information-Privacy-Yoo-Ahn/6569055fc719f57b2492b35531f987edfaa18cd8 2019.03.19

[35] Archi – Open Source ArchiMate Modelling. [Online]. Available from: https://www.archimatetool.com/ 2019.02.02

[36] W. Engelsman, H. Jonkers, and D. Quartel D. "Supporting Requirements Management in TOGAF and ArchiMate," February 2010. [Online]. Available from: http://www.opengroup.org 2015.03.01

[37] H. Xu, T. Dinev, H. J. Smith, and P. Hart, "Examining the Formation of Individual's Privacy Concerns: Toward an Integrative View," ICIS 2008 Proceedings, 6 2008. [Online]. Available from: http://aisel.aisnet.org/icis2008/6 2019.03.20

[38] K. E. Greenaway, Y. E. Chan, "Designing a Customer Information Privacy Program Aligned with Organizational Priorities," MIS Quarterly Executive, September, 12:3, pp. 137-150, 2013.

[39] S. Chen and A-M. Williams, "Grounding Privacy-by-Design for Information Systems" . PACIS 2013 Proceedings. 2013. [Online]. Available from: http://aisel.aisnet.org /pacis2013/107 2019.03.24

[40] G. Ben Ayed, Architecting User-Centric Privacy-as-a-Set-of-Services, Digital Identity-Related Privacy Framework, Cham: Springer, 2014.

New Method for Designing Binary 8×8 Matrices With Branch Number 5 Using Quasigroups

Vesna Dimitrova

Faculty of Computer Science
and Engineering
Ss. Cyril and Methodius
University, Skopje
Republic of N. Macedonia
email: vesna.dimitrova@finki.ukim.mk

Verica Bakeva

Faculty of Computer Science
and Engineering
Ss. Cyril and Methodius
University, Skopje
Republic of N. Macedonia
email: verica.bakeva@finki.ukim.mk

Zlatka Trajcheska

Faculty of Computer Science
and Engineering
Ss. Cyril and Methodius
University, Skopje
Republic of N. Macedonia
email: zlatka.trajcheska@gmail.com

***Abstract*—Quasigroups are algebraic structures, which are useful for application in cryptography and coding theory. Their specific properties and Boolean representations open a lot of scientific questions and new ideas for research. In this paper, we investigate the application of Boolean representation of quasigroups. We propose a new method for designing of binary matrices of order 8×8, which have the highest branch number.**

Keywords*–*quasigroup; Boolean functions; branch number; binary matrices.

I. INTRODUCTION

We start by providing definitions of quasigroups, their Boolean representation and their properties.

The groupoid $(Q, *)$, where $*$ is a binary operation, is called a quasigroup if it satisfies the following:

$$(\forall\, a, b \in Q)(\exists!\, x, y \in Q)(x * a = b \wedge a * y = b) \qquad (1)$$

meaning that the equations $x*a = b$ and $a*y = b$ have unique solutions for any $a, b \in Q$. These simple algebraic structures are suitable for application in cryptography, especially because of their large, exponentially growing number and their properties.

In this paper, we will consider the quasigroups of order 4. Their total number is 576, but not all of them are suitable for cryptographic purposes. Therefore, classifications of finite quasigroups are very important for choosing good quasigroups for designing cryptographic primitives. There are several classifications of quasigroups of order 4, for example, in [1][2].

Here, quasigroups are numbered according to their lexicographic ordering. Namely, this ordering is made such that each quasigroup is presented as an array of n^2 symbols, obtained by concatenation of the rows of the Latin square that represents the quasigroup operation. After that, the sorting of quasigroups is done by lexicographic ordering of the obtained arrays. Finally, a number is assigned to each quasigroup of the ordering starting with 1, and increasing by 1 sequentially until the last quasigroup is assigned a number.

Each quasigroup of order 2^n can be represented as a vector valued Boolean function [3][4]. It is done so that each element from the quasigroup $x \in Q$ can be represented as a binary vector $x = (x_1, x_2, ..., x_n) \in \{0,1\}^n$. In short, x is presented as a vector of n binary digits, which are its binary representation. Now, if we consider two elements from the quasigroup $x, y \in Q$ with their vector representations $x = (x_1, x_2, ..., x_n)$ and $y = (x_{n+1}, x_{n+2}, ..., x_{2n})$ the quasigroup operation can be presented as:

$$x * y \equiv f(x_1, ..., x_{2n}) = (f_1(x_1, ..., x_{2n}), ..., f_n(x_1, ..., x_{2n}))$$

where

$$f_i : \{0,1\}^{2n} \to \{0,1\}$$

are the components of the vector valued Boolean function f.

The quasigroups of order 4 are represented with pair of Boolean functions $(f_1(x_1, x_2, x_3, x_4), f_2(x_1, x_2, x_3, x_4))$.

A quasigroup $(Q, *)$ with Boolean representation

$$f(x_1, ..., x_{2n}) = (f_1(x_1, ..., x_{2n}), ..., f_n(x_1, ..., x_{2n})) \qquad (2)$$

is linear by Boolean representation if f_i is a linear Boolean polynomial for each $i = 1, 2, 3, ..., n$. The quasigroup is generally called nonlinear if there is at least one nonlinear f_i for $i = 1, 2, 3, ..., n$. The quasigroup is pure nonlinear if f_i is a nonlinear Boolean polynomial for each $i = 1, 2, 3, ..., n$.

A important property that we will strongly consider in the further text is the linearity by Boolean representation. The classification of order 4 by linearity was previously done in [5]. According to this, from 576 quasigroups of order 4, 144 are linear quasigroups and 432 are nonlinear quasigroups (144 of them are pure nonlinear).

Lets assume that binary matrices with suitable properties are also important for designing cryptographic primitives. There are several constructions of binary matrices with certain properties. In [6], the authors give an efficient way for generating circulant binary matrices with a prescribed number of ones which are invertible over $\mathbb{Z}_2$.

In [7], the authors investigate all binary matrices of order 8×8 and come to the conclusion that the Hamming weight of all matrices with branch number 5 varies from 33 to 44.

Our goal in this research is the construction of binary matrices of order 8×8 with linear and differential branch numbers 5 using Boolean representations of quasigroups, which have the maximal Hamming weight.

The rest of the paper is organized as follows. In Section II, we give definitions of linear and differential branch number. The new method for designing of branch number is given in Section III. Section IV presents the conclusions and ideas for future work.

II. Branch Number

In this paper, we give a new method for constructing 8×8 nonsingular matrices with branch number 5. In [8], Kang has proved that the branch number of any 8×8 invertible binary matrix is less than or equal to 5, so the 8×8 binary matrices with branch number 5 are optimal. It is known that the diffusion layers of Camellia in [9] and E2, which are 8×8 binary matrices, have branch number 5. Kanda et al. in [10] found 10080 8×8 binary matrices with branch number 5 by using a searching algorithm, and for all candidate matrices, the total Hamming weight was 44 with 4 column (row) vectors with Hamming weight 6 and 4 column (row) vectors with Hamming weight 5.

At first, we give some definitions and principles in order to introduce the branch number of matrices.

Confusion in cryptography is a principle that indicates the lack of clarity in the relation between the plaintext and ciphertext. In the ciphers, this means that the key is not related to the ciphertext in a simple manner. It is usually made by substitution. Blocks that are used in ciphers for substitution are S-boxes. S-boxes are transformation units, which take m bits as input and give n bits as output. They are usually implemented with a lookup table [11][12].

Diffusion in cryptography means that, by changing of a single bit in the plaintext, approximately half of the bits in the ciphertext should be changed. It is usually implemented with a permutation of symbols.

Ciphers that have confusion and diffusion layer are called Substitution-Permutation Networks (SPNs). We are interested in the diffusion layer in order to apply quasigroups there.

Definition 1: [13] If a block cipher has n S-boxes in its structure, where each S-box has input and output of m bits, then the diffusion layer can be represented as:

$$A : (\{0,1\}^m)^n \longrightarrow (\{0,1\}^m)^n \quad (3)$$

or with this linear transformation:

$$A(x) = A \cdot x^T = \begin{bmatrix} a_{11} & a_{12} & \dots & a_{1n} \\ a_{21} & a_{22} & \dots & a_{2n} \\ \vdots & \vdots & \ddots & \vdots \\ a_{n1} & a_{n2} & \dots & a_{nn} \end{bmatrix} \cdot \begin{bmatrix} x_1 \\ x_2 \\ \vdots \\ x_n \end{bmatrix}, \quad (4)$$

where $a_i \in \{0,1\}^m$, $x = (x_1, x_2, ..., x_n)$, $x_i \in \{0,1\}^m$, $i = 1, 2, ..., n$.

From this point on, we will only consider binary matrices and binary vectors.

The Hamming weight of a binary vector x is denoted by $wt(x)$ and represents the number of non-null components in x.

There are two different branch numbers – linear and differential. As their names indicate, one represents the resistance to the linear, and the other to the differential cryptanalysis.

Definition 2: Let A be a binary matrix of order $n \times n$.

i) The linear branch number of A is defined by:

$$\beta_l(A) = \min\{wt(x)+wt(A^T \cdot x^T) | x \in \{0,1\}^n,\ x \neq 0\}. \quad (5)$$

ii) The differential branch number of A is defined by:

$$\beta_d(A) = \min\{wt(x)+wt(A \cdot x^T) | x \in \{0,1\}^n,\ x \neq 0\}. \quad (6)$$

The design blocks in the ciphers should have good linear and differential properties, which means that the values of both branch numbers are high.

In our research, we consider only nonsingular binary matrices since the encryption and decryption are inverse processes.

Example 1: Let us calculate the branch number of the matrix $A = \begin{bmatrix} 0 & 1 \\ 1 & 1 \end{bmatrix}$. We consider all not-null binary vectors of order 2:

$$x_1 = (0,1), \quad x_2 = (1,0), \quad x_3 = (1,1).$$

Their Hamming weights are, respectively:

$$wt(x_1) = 1, \quad wt(x_2) = 1, \quad wt(x_3) = 2.$$

The products $y_i = A \cdot x_i^T$, $i = 1,2,3$ are

$$y_1 = (1,1), \quad y_2 = (0,1), \quad y_3 = (1,0),$$

whose Hamming weights are

$$wt(y_1) = 2, \quad wt(y_2) = 1, \quad wt(y_3) = 1,$$

respectively. The values of $\beta_i^{(d)} = wt(x_i) + wt(y_i)$, $i = 1,2,3$ are

$$\beta_1^{(d)} = 3, \quad \beta_2^{(d)} = 2, \quad \beta_3^{(d)} = 3.$$

The minimal value of $\beta_i^{(d)}$ $(i = 1,2,3)$ is the differential branch number, in this case $\beta_d(A) = 2$.

The linear branch number is calculated similarly.

III. Constructing Binary Matrices 8×8 with Branch Number 5

Our goal in this research is the construction of binary matrices of order 8×8 with linear and differential branch numbers 5 using Boolean representations of quasigroups. Namely, the maximal branch number for a binary matrix of order 8×8 is 5. These matrices are important in block ciphers and they are used in the design of a few ciphers in the lightweight cryptography, for example Camellia.

Before explaining the method of construction, we will divide the linear quasigroups into subclasses. Firstly, we choose a quasigroup that is linear by Boolean representation and take the algebraic normal forms of their Boolean functions. Since the quasigroup is linear by Boolean representation, the Boolean functions are also linear, i.e.,

$$f_j(x_1, x_2, x_3, x_4) = a_{j0} + a_{j1}x_1 + a_{j2}x_2 + a_{j3}x_3 + a_{j4}x_4,$$

where $a_{ji} \in \{0,1\}$, $i = 0,1,2,3,4$, $j = 1,2$. Firstly, we discard the constants a_{j0} and obtain two linear polynomials of the Boolean representation

$$f_j(x_1, x_2, x_3, x_4) = a_{j1}x_1 + a_{j2}x_2 + a_{j3}x_3 + a_{j4}x_4,$$

for $j = 1,2$. This way, the class of 144 linear quasigroups can be divided into 36 subclasses, each containing 4 quasigroups whose Boolean representations differ only by a constant $(const = 1)$:

- $Q_i(f_1, f_2)$
- $Q_j(f_1 + const, f_2)$
- $Q_k(f_1, f_2 + const)$
- $Q_l(f_1 + const, f_2 + const)$

In each subclass, all 4 quasigroups produce the same binary matrix. Therefore, the constants a_{j0} do not have influence on the final results and can be discarded. Further on, we will use one representative quasigroup from each subclass. The lexicographic numbers of quasigroups in each subclass and corresponding representative are given in Table I.

TABLE I. SUBCLASSES OF LINEAR QUASIGROUPS AND REPRESENTATIVE.

No.	Quasigroups in the subclass	Representative
1	1, 172, 405, 576	1
2	4, 169, 408, 573	4
3	11, 189, 388, 566	11
4	14, 192, 385, 563	14
5	21, 179, 398, 556	21
6	24, 182, 395, 553	24
7	26, 147, 430, 551	26
8	27, 146, 431, 550	27
9	37, 163, 414, 540	37
10	40, 166, 411, 537	40
11	43, 157, 420, 534	43
12	46, 160, 417, 531	46
13	51, 246, 331, 526	51
14	54, 243, 334, 523	54
15	57, 259, 318, 520	57
16	60, 262, 315, 517	60
17	70, 252, 325, 507	70
18	71, 253, 324, 506	71
19	77, 272, 305, 500	77
20	80, 269, 308, 497	80
21	82, 284, 293, 495	82
22	83, 285, 292, 494	83
23	92, 274, 303, 485	92
24	93, 275, 302, 484	93
25	100, 197, 380, 477	100
26	101, 196, 381, 477	101
27	110, 212, 365, 467	110
28	111, 213, 364, 466	111
29	113, 203, 374, 464	113
30	116, 206, 371, 461	116
31	126, 223, 354, 451	126
32	127, 222, 355, 450	127
33	132, 234, 343, 445	132
34	133, 235, 342, 444	133
35	138, 228, 349, 439	138
36	139, 229, 348, 438	139

Let us explain the method of construction of the binary matrices. We choose two linear quasigroups by Boolean representation from different subclasses. Then, we take the corresponding linear polynomials based on the algebraic normal form of the four (two by two) Boolean functions that represent the chosen quasigroups. Let us denote these linear polynomials provided from the first quasigroup by $Q_1 : f_1$ and $Q_1 : f_2$, and from the second quasigroup by $Q_2 : f_1$ and $Q_2 : f_2$. Firstly, we fill two matrices A_1 and A_2 of order 8×4 and after that we form the matrix A (of order 8×8) as concatenation by rows. In the following, we give the method of construction.

- For each not-null a_{1i} in $Q_1 : f_1$, the cell in the row 1 and column i in A_1 is filled with 1, and for each null a_{1i} the corresponding cell is filled with 0 ($i \in \{1, 2, 3, 4\}$). Then, we fill the third row in A_1 by shifting the bits from the first row on left with offset 1, the fifth row by shifting the bits from the third row on left with offset 1 and the seventh row by shifting the bits from the fifth row on left also with offset 1.

- For each not-null a_{1i} in $Q_2 : f_1$, the cell in the row 2 and column i in A_1 is filled with 1, and for each null a_i the same cell is filled with 0 ($i \in \{1, 2, 3, 4\}$). Then, we fill the fourth row by shifting the bits from the second row on left with offset 1, the sixth row by shifting the bits from the fourth row on left with offset 1 and the eight row by shifting the bits from the sixth row on left also with offset 1.

- The same method is applied for construction of matrix A_2 using the polynomials $Q_1 : f_2$ (for odd rows) and $Q_2 : f_2$ (for even rows).

- We form the matrix $A = [A_1|A_2]$.

This construction will be denoted as $Q_1f_1 - Q_1f_2 - Q_2f_1 - Q_2f_2$, referring to the order of the Boolean functions that are used in the construction. A graphical presentation of the explained construction using the quasigroups with lexicographic numbers 4 and 14 is given in Figure 1.

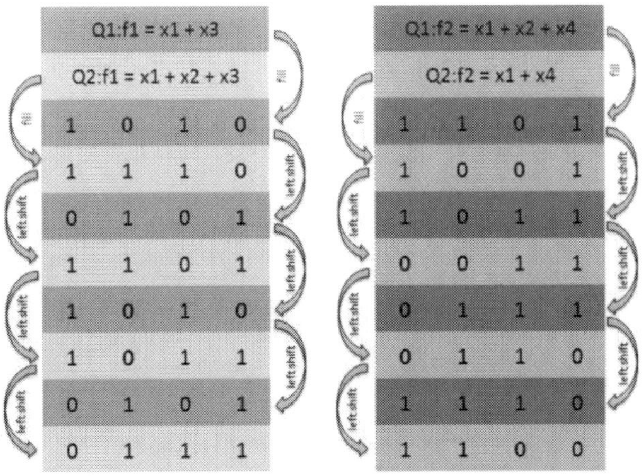

Figure 1. An example of binary matrix constructed using the Boolean function obtained from quasigroups 4 and 14.

Using this method, we obtain 384 nonsingular matrices such that:

- 160 matrices have branch number 3
- 192 matrices have branch number 4 and
- 32 matrices have branch number 5.

All 32 matrices with branch number 5 obtained by our method have the Hamming weight of 44, which is the maximal weight according to [7].

In our investigation, we consider a similar construction where the right shift is used instead of the left shift. The results were very similar and the distribution of matrices based on their branch number was the same. Also, the construction $Q_1f_1 - Q_2f_1 - Q_1f_2 - Q_2f_2$ was analyzed, either using left and right shift, and the results also were the same.

The complete results can be found in [14].

IV. CONCLUSION

Quasigroups are algebraic structures, which are useful for application in cryptography and coding theory. In this paper, using quasigroups of order 4, we propose a new way of constructing binary matrices of order 8×8 with branch number 5. These matrices are very useful for designing cryptographic primitives, especially in the field of lightweight cryptography.

Our research opens some questions that will be subjects for future investigation. Some of them are the following:

- Check if there is something specific and try to find a pattern in the matrices, which would lead to better understanding of their design or simplifying their generation.

- Check all possible combinations of the constructions and try to find a theoretical dependency between them. It is very important to check why all constructions lead to the same results and if these results depend on the quasigroup properties in some way.

ACKNOWLEDGMENT

This research was partially supported by Faculty of Computer Science and Engineering at "Ss Cyril and Methodius" University in Skopje, Republic of N. Macedonia.

REFERENCES

[1] V. Dimitrova and S. Markovski, "Classification of Quasigroups by Image Patterns", Proceedings of 5th International Conference for Informatics and Information Technology, Bitola, Macedonia, pp. 152–160, 2007.

[2] V. A. Artamonov, S. Chakrabarti and S. K. Pal, "Characterization of polynomially complete quasigroups based on Latin squares for cryptographic transformations", Discrete Applied Mathematics, vol. 200, pp. 5–17, 2016.

[3] D. Gligoroski, V. Dimitrova and S. Markovski, "Quasigroups as Boolean functions, their equation systems and Groebner bases", In: Groebner Bases, Coding, and Cryptography, Springer 2009, pp. 415-420, 2009.

[4] I.S.M. Sala, "An algebraic description of Boolean functions", Proceedings of WCC07, pp. 343–349, 2007.

[5] S. Markovski, V. Bakeva, V. Dimitrova and A. Popovska-Mitrovikj, "Representation of algebraic structures by Boolean functions and its applications", In: D. Trajanov, V. Bakeva (eds.): ICT-Innovations 2017, Data-Driven Innovation, Communications in Computer and Information Science Series (CCIS) Vol.778, Springer, Cham, pp. 229–23, 2017.

[6] T. Fabsic, O. Grosek, K. Nemoga and P. Zajac, "On generating invertible circulant binary matrices with a prescribed number of ones", Cryptography and Communications, vol. 10, no. 1, pp. 159–175, 2018.

[7] Y. Gao and G. Guo, "Unified approach to construct 8x8 binary matrices with branch number 5", In: Proceedings of the 2010 First ACIS International Symposium on Cryptography, and Network Security, Data Mining and Knowledge Discovery, E-Commerce and Its Applications, and Embedded Systems, CDEE '10, IEEE Computer Society, Washington, DC, USA, pp. 413–416, 2010.

[8] J. Kang, "Practical and provable security against differential and linear cryptanalysis for substitution-permutation networks", ETRI journal, vol. 23, no. 4, pp. 158-167, 2001.

[9] K. Aoki et al., "Camellia: A 128-bit block cipher suitable for multiple platforms - design and analysis", In: D. R. Stinson, S. Tavares (eds.) SAC 2000. LNCS, vol. 2012, Springer, Heindelberg, pp. 39–56, 2001.

[10] M. Kanda, Y. Takashima, T. Matsumoto, K. Aoki and K. Ohta, "A strategy for constructing fast round functions with practical security against differential and linear cryptanalysis", Selected Areas in Cryptography, LNCS 1556, pp. 264–279, 1999.

[11] I. Vergili and M. Yucel, "Avalanche and bit independence properties for the ensembles of randomly chosen $n \times n$ S-boxes", Turkish Journal of Electrical Engineering and Computer Sciences, vol. 9, no. 2, pp. 161–176, 2001.

[12] D. Loebenberger and M. Nsken, "A family of 6-to-4-bit S-boxes with large linear branch number", Cryptology ePrint Archive, Report 2013/188, pp. 1–11, 2013.

[13] D. Kwon, S. H. Sung, J. H. Song and S. Park, "Design of block ciphers and coding theory", Trends in Mathematics", Information Center for Mathematical Sciences, vol. 8, no. 1, pp. 13–20, 2005.

[14] https://goo.gl/vbtvuM, Last access: 22.07.2019

A DRM Solution for Online Content Using Blockchain - A Music Perspective

Ahmed Gomaa
Operations and Information Management Department,
University of Scranton
Scranton, USA
email: ahmed.gomaa@scranton.edu

Abstract—**The amount of piracy in the streaming and static digital content in general and the music industry specifically is posing a challenge to digital content owners. This paper proposes a Digital Rights Management (DRM) framework to monetize, track, and control online content across platforms. The system addresses the need to lower the barriers of entry for music bands, content reconciliation for royalty payments, and control the content after dissemination. The paper benefits from the current advances in Blockchain and cryptocurrencies. Specifically, the paper presents a digital currency (Asset Assertion (AA) token) on a permission-based Blockchain to enable the secure dissemination and tracking of the digital content. The proposed framework provides the content owner the ability to control the flow of information even after he/she releases it, by creating a secure, self-installed, cross-platform reader located on the digital content file header.**

Keywords-Blockchain; Cryptocurrency; Digital Rights Management; Public Key; Private Key.

I. Introduction

Online music streaming in the United States has been increasing in the past several years. It currently accounts for 65% of the online music market share [1]. This multibillion-dollar industry is continuously faced with intellectual rights infringement. For instance, in January 2018, Wixen Music Publishing Inc. sued Spotify, a music streaming company, for allegedly using thousands of songs, without a license and compensation to the music publisher [2].

There are two main music royalty-collecting societies in the USA: the American Society of Composers, Authors, and Publishers (ASCAP) and, Broadcast Music Inc. (BMI), with hundreds of thousands of members each. If two artists collaborated on the same music album, but are members of different royalty collecting societies, they will receive different royalties, a fact that shows the discrepancy in how different organizations counts played streams. As of 2016, ASCAP and BMI alone collect and disburse payments in the range of $1.8 billion annually on behalf of hundreds of thousands of musicians for royalties around the world. It is not the actual value of the market [3] [4]. According to the Institute for Policy Innovation (IPI) 2007 report [5], it costs the US economy more than $12 Billion US dollars due to sound recording piracy in the US. In 2017, ASCAP and BMI announced the creation of a new comprehensive musical works database to increase ownership transparency in performing rights licensing that is expected to roll out at the end of 2018 [6].

The problem becomes more challenging when considering the online radios and the Disk Jockeys (DJs) who are mixing music live and streaming it online with an audience listening around the world. The sale and distribution of media content using a digital medium provides flexible and straightforward production, consumption, and transmission of such content. However, it also reduces the efforts needed for unauthorized usage of this data. Thus, digital media content is more easily copied, distributed, or used in a manner not allowed by law or license agreement.

The paper is organized as follows. In Section 2, the paper presents an overview of the current solutions and their problems. Section 3 presents the problem statement. Section 4 presents the proposed solution overview, and Section 5 presents the conclusion and future work.

II. Current Solutions and Their Problems

Lawmakers recognized the growing need to protect digital media and enact the US Digital Millennium Copyright Act (DMCA) to protect property rights. One approach to curbing the proliferation of illegal activity surrounding digital media content is to incorporate a form of Digital Rights Management (DRM) into the digital content.

Traditionally, the business model has the content owner, licensing its content to several distributors. The distributors package the content to distribute on satellite or cable to different channels and sell those channels or pay per view- for the popular event- to the content viewers.

The barriers to entry for content owners, as well as distributors and channels, are high as the cost to running a channel that is capable of creating its programming and Electronic Programming Guide (EPG) and program it to potential customers is not very trivial. Companies combine content to sell channel subscriptions and optimize their profitability. For instance, one may find the same song presented on several different radio stations, where each distribution channel is trying to maximize its audience numbers. Currently, from the content owners' perspective, they are interested in one aspect: monetizing content consumptions. The major content owners are faced with the challenge of the content streamed online, without any compensation, on shady platforms. The small content creators need aggregators and distribution partners to be able to monetize their content. From the content viewer perspective, they are forced to subscribe to channel bundles and deal with the distribution channels such as online radio stations, where they only need to listen/watch a subset of streams that is relevant to them.

Current research attempts to use Blockchain to facilitate the compensation of the content creators using different techniques. In [7], the author uses the Blockchain and Web crawling to help the content owners to identify their online work and use the Blockchain as a proof of ownership.

More similar to this paper concept is [8], where the authors encode the software to be activated based on the Blockchain information in a system that addresses the software license. On the same school of thoughts is [9], which introduces the notion of including verification information with the file metadata to enforce the digital rights within a 4k video on a multilayer Blockchain solution.

In addition to the research efforts in the area of Blockchain and DRM, several start-ups turned to Blockchain in an attempt to address this need, to assert their rights, and to prevent unauthorized usage. For instance, Swarm, an Ethereum layer for distributed storage, along with Livepeer, are infrastructures for distributed transcoding of live video. Tokit is a crowdfunding platform where artists can issue tokens and share revenues with fans, while JAAK is a framework for decentralized content licensing and metadata handling. Furthermore, SOUNDAC, previously known as Muse, is the technology behind peerTracks, a platform that allows monetizing music when distributed across predefined distribution channels using Blockchain technology. Also, Sony published a recent patent [10] where each user claims their rights on the Blockchain. Those solutions benefit from the Blockchain technology to provide monetization tools for content creators as well as possible privacy solutions to support anonymity.

There are three distinct issues this paper addresses, namely the monetization of the content, the tracking of the content, and the protection of the content. In contrast with the current literature, this paper argues that without having a solution that takes into account those three dimensions, the solution will not be complete. Hence, the paper promotes encoding with the streamed content, an embedded payment gateway and player that is activated based on validation from the Blockchain. This format would enforce digital rights, track the usage, and monetize the content.

Figure 1 shows a stream that is encoded in as an Asset Assertion (AA) format, which includes the stream content player, the payment gateway, and the content itself in a secure AA file format.

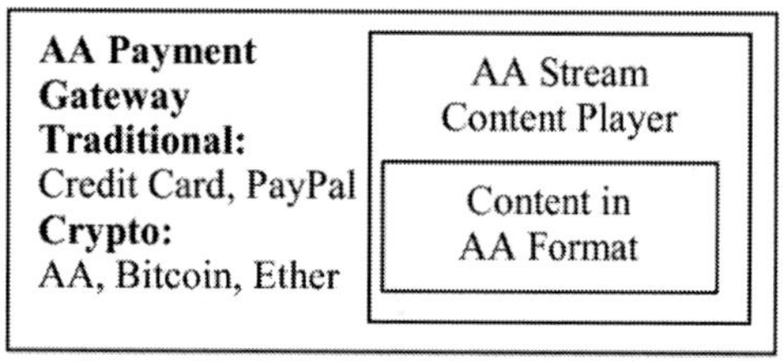

Figure 1. AA File Architecture

In this paper, an integral part of the framework is to have with each content its player to enforce the digital rights, even after disseminating the content, which is different from the proposition in [10], where the content owner is the cornerstone of the Blockchain DRM solution. Besides, the paper fulfills the required future work mentioned in [9] where a discussion of the business model is included by compensating the listeners.

The paper presents a framework that embeds the access control policy within the file header. The access control policy validates the credentials, after checking the Blockchain posted information. When validated, the embedded player retrieves the file required codec to render the content from a separate file system, tracks and posts the usage to the Blockchain and compensates the content constituents accordingly. This process prevents the information silo and reconciliation issue existing in the industry since all constituents' exchange tokens and the transactions are recorded on the Blockchain. Furthermore, the framework presented has the ability to eliminate the content, if needed, after dissemination.

III. Problem Statement

Given the current state of piracy in the online music industry and the current advancement in Blockchain platforms, this paper proposes a DRM framework for the stated problems using Blockchain and cryptocurrency technology. The incentive to use Blockchain in DRM is to address three specific challenges in the current systems, namely, barriers of entry, reconciliation, and content control after dissemination.

A. *Barriers of Entry*

The framework should lower the barriers of entry for digital content owners, where compensation should be an option even for unpopular items, in contrast to the most widely used advertising compensation system, such as YouTube where content owners start to be compensated when the masses view their content.

B. *Reconciliation*

The framework should enable automatic reconciliation of content consumption. This is very hard to achieve with the current tracking frameworks since each tracking mechanism is working in a silo from each other. The framework should allow all constituents to view the same truth. To achieve this, all constituents (fans, radio stations, and content owners) should be involved in the same transaction. Using Blockchain and cryptocurrencies, the system is providing a reward mechanism to the fans to participate in the proposed eco-system to close the loop of discrepancy and to enable the additional system objective of simple reconciliation. It is worth noting that this paper uses the Blockchain after adjusting the supply chain within the content dissemination and compensates the content consumer to prevent tracking issues of content usage, especially when aggregators are introduced into the business model.

C. Content Control after Dissemination

The framework should allow content owners to control the access to their files even after dissemination. Content usage for a particular time is challenging to control after dissemination. A mechanism to control content usage after dissemination would address this challenge.

IV. PROPOSED SOLUTION OVERVIEW

In the proposed framework, after receiving AA tokens from the content owner to encode the original content in the AA file format and embed the content with a player and a payment gateway, the file header includes the digital rights possible as the access control policy. When a content consumer satisfies the access control policy constraints, usually by paying AA tokens, as depicted on the content smart contract, the content player uses the content consumer digital wallet tokens. All framework constituents exchange tokens when creating sending, retrieving, and consuming content. All token exchanges are recorded on the Blockchain, creating a single source of truth about the content. In contrast to the Sony patent [10], the Blockchain stores information from the content perspective, rather than the content creator perspective. This allows for a more straightforward reconciliation process when payments are distributed between multiple constituents.

In contrast with [9], our solution uses smart contracts to distribute the royalties, instead of using the public key encryption. One of the advantages of using smart contracts is the ability to have multiple constituents' requirements satisfied instead of having only two involved parties. This accommodates a more complex business model. The framework constituents send all transactions to the Blockchain nodes, that is, a decentralized peer-to-peer network. When the nodes reach a consensus, the transaction is then added to the Blockchain.

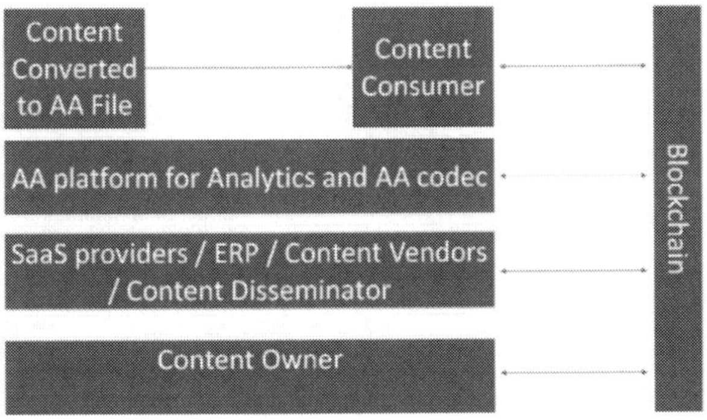

Figure 2. AA Framework

Figure 2 shows that the relation can be direct between the viewer and the content creator with the help of the AA platform in converting the content into AA format and make the file accepting payment as an independent object while ensuring the content owner's digital rights. If the viewers or the content creators would like to gain insights about the interactions with the object, they can do this with the AA platform for analytics. The framework might reward the viewers if they opted to share their interaction information with other interested parties. The usage of Blockchain allows for having a variation of the business model, including SaaS providers, Enterprise partners, independent content vendors, or disseminators.

A. Use Case: Buying Digital Content Rights Using the Blockchain

The permission-based Blockchain provides an open ledger solution to address the discrepancy in monetizing, tracking, and controlling online streams. It is a change in the music industry. It provides music professionals with an environment where they release their music with the confidence that their high-quality original content will be traced all the time. The transaction, once validated using the Blockchain consensus mechanism, is recorded to the Blockchain and there is no longer any confusion or debate as to the transaction and reconciliation.

The proposed Blockchain, in its purest form, is effectively a white list of legitimate online music disseminators and retailers. The smart contract assesses if the song is played on a domain as validated by its record on the Blockchain. Once the played stream is validated, the smart contract clears the transaction, and the AA token passes from the content disseminator to the content wallet, which is controlled by the content owner. If the played stream cannot be validated, it is presumed that the played stream is invalid and the AA token does not move. The outcome is recorded and provable and any potential debate over reconciliation disappears between content owners and content disseminators. Since transactions are validated in a short period of time, the Blockchain creates another change for the music industry. Payment cycles can be shortened to the time it takes the smart contract to complete. If both parties desire that, payment is nearly instantaneous. The option of reducing payment cycles from a few months to minutes is possible. The tracking agency collects a royalty, payable in AA tokens, on these transactions. These commissions are charged as a percentage of the transaction value.

B. Use Case: Blockchain to Compensate Listeners

Listeners of songs are drawn to pirated content to save money. The system can compensate them if they are enjoying a higher quality song from their preferred bands. The Blockchain gives the content consumer ownership on how to use their tracked information, if any. The Blockchain lets the listeners receive compensation. Upon consuming a digital asset, listeners receive AA tokens as a reward. These tokens can be used for many purposes within the ecosystem ranging from free ad blocking to promotional offers from similar bands.

When the transaction related to the digital asset consumption engages all involved parties in the same permission-based ledger, the value circle is closed. This allows for a single point of truth; hence, all engaged parties save on transaction reconciliation, costs and allows for new business models.

V. CONCLUSION

In summary, the paper presents a DRM framework focusing on the secure delivery of digital assets. The framework allows for generating, monetizing, tracking, and controlling access to copy-protected media files after dissemination. The system is allowing content owners, content distributors and content consumers, the freedom to pursue new business models, by making the digital content the focal point that connects all system constituents using a typical traceable transaction located on the Blockchain. This creates a single truth, rather than having information silos.

Future work includes more elaboration on the AA token, the content player, and the file format, in addition to presenting the model notation and information schematic on the information flow. Also, tracking subsections used in streamed online content and how to create a valuation model for the content disseminated and the fans using their information and influential relationships within the ecosystem are needed.

REFERENCES

[1] C. Micames, "Sprotify hit with $1.6 billion copyright infringement lawsuit," 18 April 21018. [Online]. Available: http://www.ipbrief.net/2018/04/18/spotify-hit-with-1-6-billion-copyright-infringement-lawsuit/. [Accessed June 2019].

[2] L. I. C. Nevins and L. Fischer, "ASCAP & BMI Announce Creation Of A New Comprehensive Musical Works Database To Increase Ownership Transparency In Performing Rights Licensing," ASCAP, 26 07 2017. [Online]. Available: https://www.ascap.com/press/2017/07-26-ascap-bmi-database. [Accessed June 2019].

[3] E. Christman, "BMI Again Tops $1 Billion in Collections, Breaks Record for Royalty Distributions," *Billboard.com,* Septemeber 2016.

[4] The American Society of Composers, Authors and Publishers (ASCAP), "2016 Annual Report," ASCAP, New York, 2016.

[5] S. E. Siwek, "The true cost of sound recording piracy to the US economy," IPI, 2007.

[6] A. Gomaa, "The Creation of a Cryptocurrency to Support Disintermediation," *Operations Management Education Review,* vol. 12, pp. 63-100, 2018.

[7] M. McConaghy, G. McMullen, G. Parry, T. McConaghy and D. Holtzman, "Visibility and digital art: Blockchain as an ownership layer on the Internet," *Strategic Change,* vol. 26, no. 5, pp. 461-470, 2017.

[8] A. Litchfield and J. Herbert, "ReSOLV: Applying Cryptocurrency Blockchain Methods to Enable Global Cross-Platform Software License Validation," *Cryptography,* vol. 2, no. 10, pp. 1-24, 2018.

[9] J. Kishigami, F. Shigeru, W. Hiroki, N. Atsushi and A. Akihiko, "The blockchain-based digital content distribution system," in *IEEE Fifth International Conference on Big Data and Cloud Computing*, 2015.

[10] E. Diehl, "Blockchain-based digital rights management". US Patent 15/458,807, 26 April 2018.

[11] Paratii, "The State of Decentralised Video Q4 2017: Tubes and Flixes will never be the same. Here's why.," 18 December 2017. [Online]. Available: https://medium.com/paratii/the-state-of-decentralised-video-q4-2017-42663ff94b28. [Accessed June 2019].

[12] G. Muthoni, "How Blockchain Impacts the Music Industry," Sepember 2018. [Online]. Available: https://blocktelegraph.io/soundac-using-blockchain-solve-major-problem-music-industry/. [Accessed June 2019].

Topological Reduction of Gas Transport Networks

Anton Baldin(1), Tanja Clees(1,2), Barbara Fuchs(1), Bernhard Klaassen(1),
Igor Nikitin(1), Lialia Nikitina(1), Inna Torgovitskaia(1)

(1) Fraunhofer Institute for Algorithms and Scientific Computing, Sankt Augustin, Germany
(2) University of Applied Sciences Bonn-Rhein-Sieg, Sankt Augustin, Germany
Email: Name.Surname@scai.fraunhofer.de

Abstract—**The paper presents the topological reduction method applied to gas transport networks, using contraction of series, parallel and tree-like subgraphs. The contraction operations are implemented for pipe elements, described by quadratic friction law. This allows significant reduction of the graphs and acceleration of solution procedure for stationary network problems. The algorithm has been tested on several realistic network examples. The possible extensions of the method to different friction laws and other elements are discussed.**

Keywords–modeling of complex systems; topological reduction; globally convergent solvers; applications; gas transport networks.

I. Introduction

The physical modeling of gas transport networks is comprehensively described in works [1]–[3]. The element equations for pipes vary from the simplest quadratic form to more complex formulae by Nikuradze, Hofer and Colebrook-White. In our paper [4], we have shown how to continue these formulae to the whole domain of model variables, in order to achieve a global convergence for non-linear solvers. Further, in paper [5] we have constructed a universal translation algorithm, capable of formulating network problems for non-linear solvers with arbitrary problem description language. In paper [6], we presented theoretical foundations of topological reduction methods for generic stationary network problems.

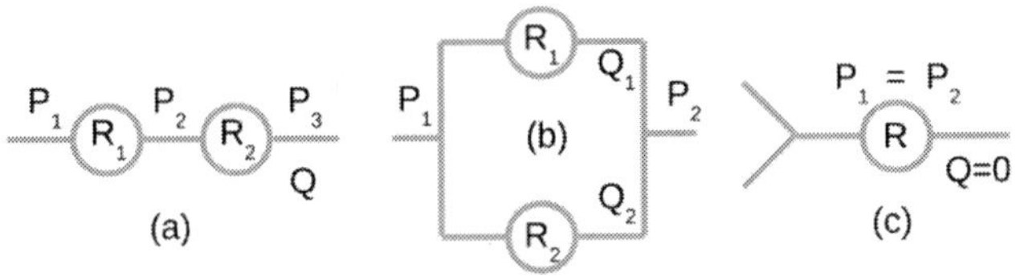

Figure 1. Main operations in GSPG reduction: series (a), parallel (b) connections to be reduced, contraction of a leaf (c).

In this paper, we continue the development of topological reduction methods in application to gas transport networks. Our motivation is to accelerate solution procedure for stationary gas network problems. The goal is to perform significant reduction of the graphs, preserving the accuracy of the modeling. The main idea is to reduce the series and parallel connections of elements in the network, with the operations, known in the theory of Series-Parallel Graphs (SPG) [7]. These operations can also be extended by contraction of a leaf, which after recurrent application contracts tree-like subgraphs, leading to Generalized Series-Parallel Graphs (GSPG) [8]. Such elementary operations are shown in Figure 1. In paper [6], we have estimated the efficiency of this method and shown on realistic gas transport networks that high reduction factors can be achieved. In our current work, we perform an actual implementation of the topological reduction for pipes, which form a considerable part of the networks.

In Section II, we present the details of a topological reduction procedure for pipes, modeled by quadratic friction law. In Section III, the results of numerical experiments with estimation of reduction factors and acceleration rates are given. In Section IV, we perform a comparison of our method with [9], which is also based on graph theory but using a different approach. In Section IV, we also discuss possible extensions of our method.

The described algorithms are implemented in the software MYNTS (Multi-phYsics NeTwork Simulator) [10], developed in our group.

II. Topological Reduction Algorithm for Pipe Networks

For the equations representing the pipes, one can use the simplest quadratic friction law from [1][9]:

$$P_{in}|P_{in}| - P_{out}|P_{out}| = RQ|Q|, \quad (1)$$

where $P_{in,out}$ are the input and output pressures and Q is the mass flow through the pipe. R is a resistance coefficient, depending on the pipe length L, diameter D, roughness parameter k, universal gas constant R_{gas}, temperature T, compression factor z and molar mass μ:

$$R = 16L/(\pi^2 D^5)/(2\log_{10}(D/k) + 1.138)^2 \\ \times R_{gas}Tz/\mu \cdot 10^{-10}. \quad (2)$$

All parameters are given in SI units (French, Système International), except of pressures, given in bar, hence the scale factor at the end of the formula. The structure of the term $Q|Q|$ ensures the symmetry of the equation when reversing the flow direction $Q \to -Q$. The similar structure of P-terms has a very special reason: it provides a monotonic continuation of the equation to the non-physical domain $P < 0$.

It was shown in [4] that, as a result of such continuation, the solver maintains stability also in the non-physical domain, where it can occasionally wander during the iterations. In addition, with such an extension, the system describing the stationary state of the network has a unique solution, even if the problem was set infeasibly. The simplest example of such an infeasible setting is to take a real network, such as shown in Figure 2, require a large throughput from suppliers to consumers, but at the same time switch off all the compressors. This problem, obviously, will not have a solution. On the other hand, if one uses the techniques from [4], the solution will exist and will be unique even in this case, but it will be located in the nonphysical domain $P < 0$. Thus, in this approach, one has a necessary and sufficient *feasibility indicator*, lacking for other solvers, for which the infeasible statement of the problem is indistinguishable from the occasional divergence.

Let us consider the above described GSPG elementary operations for pipe networks.

The series connection is (see Figure 1a):

$$P_1|P_1| - P_2|P_2| = R_1Q|Q|, \quad (3)$$
$$P_2|P_2| - P_3|P_3| = R_2Q|Q|.$$

From here, we add the 2 formulas to get:

$$P_1|P_1| - P_3|P_3| = R^s_{12}Q|Q|,\ R^s_{12} = R_1 + R_2. \quad (4)$$

The inverse reconstruction of the eliminated variable P_2 is:

$$P_2|P_2| = P_1|P_1| - R_1Q|Q|. \quad (5)$$

The parallel connection is (see Figure 1b):

$$P_1|P_1| - P_2|P_2| = R_1Q_1|Q_1| = R_2Q_2|Q_2|, \quad (6)$$
$$Q = Q_1 + Q_2.$$

From here, we solve this system for $Q_{1,2}$ to get:

$$P_1|P_1| - P_2|P_2| = R^p_{12}Q|Q|, \quad (7)$$
$$R^p_{12} = \left(R_1^{-1/2} + R_2^{-1/2}\right)^{-2}.$$

The inverse reconstruction of the eliminated variables $Q_{1,2}$ is:

$$Q_1 = Q/((R_1/R_2)^{1/2} + 1), \quad (8)$$
$$Q_2 = Q/((R_2/R_1)^{1/2} + 1).$$

Contracting the leaf, see Figure 1c, in the simplest case of zero flow results in the removal of P_2, Q variables. The inverse reconstruction consists of the setting $Q = 0$ and copying $P_2 = P_1$.

It should be noted that there are two types of source/sink nodes in gas networks. Q_{set} is the node in which the flow is set. P_{set} is the node where the flow is not fixed, but the pressure is set. For parallel connections, nodes of this type at the ends do not pose a problem. For series connections, the presence of such specifiers in the intermediate node leads to deviations from Kirchhoff's law and represents an obstacle to the reduction. Next, we discuss a special algorithm that allows to move the Q_{set} specifiers over the network. In combination with it, the reduction can be continued.

For contraction of the leaf, the P_{set} specifier represents an obstacle, because when shifting to the neighboring node, the P_{set} specifier gets an unfixed pressure value that depends on the flow. To contract a leaf with the Q_{set} specifier, two options are possible. First, block contracting leafs with a nonzero Q_{set}. As a result, the reduction will be incomplete, but the end Q_{set} nodes will be intact, which is convenient for formulating scenarios with different values of Q_{set} and for controlling the feasibility condition $P > 0$ at endpoints. Second, allow such leafs to be moved, with Q_{set} moving to the other side and summing it up with another Q_{set} that may be located there. For the inverse reconstruction, the value of Q_{set} must be saved, after that the inverse operations can be performed. The pressure at the free end is not determined by simple copying, but is found from the equation of the element:

$$P_2|P_2| = P_1|P_1| - RQ_{set}|Q_{set}|. \quad (9)$$

III. THE RESULTS

We have implemented GSPG reduction algorithm with fixed Qsets and tested it on three realistic networks. The simplest network N1 is shown in Figure 2. It includes 4 compressors (2 stations with 2 compressors each), 2 Psets (shown by rhombi n56, n99) and 3 Qsets (triangles n76, n80, n91). Originally (level0), the network contains N=100 nodes and E=111 edges, including P=34 pipes. Then (level1), a topological cleaning algorithm from [6] is used, removing (if any) parts of the graph, disconnected from pressure suppliers, as well as contracting superconducting edges, such as shortcuts, open valves and short pipes ($D = L = 1$ m). This operation is absolutely necessary for the stability of the solver, since disconnected parts possess undefined pressure and loops of superconducting edges have undefined circulating flow. This level of reduction looks similar to level0, just some valves, shortcuts and internals of stations are removed. The total count on this level is N=39, E=40, P=34.

TABLE I. PARAMETERS OF TEST NETWORKS

network	compressors	regulators	Psets	Qsets
N1	4	0	2	3
N2	7	18	4	64
N3	25	54	6	290

TABLE II. NODES:EDGES:PIPES COUNT FOR DIFFERENT REDUCTION LEVELS

network	level0	level1	level2	level3
N1	100:111:34	39:40:34	13:14:8	8:9:3
N2	973:1047:500	528:541:479	198:208:146	126:134:72
N3	4721:5362:1749	1723:1814:1666	705:755:607	296:332:184

TABLE III. TIMING FOR TWO REDUCTION LEVELS*

network	level1		level2	
	filter	solve	filter	solve
N1	0.006	0.044	0.009	0.02
N2	0.063	0.5	0.09	0.196
N3	0.243	2.103	0.371	0.944

* in seconds, for 3 GHz Intel i7 CPU 8 GB RAM workstation; 'filter' includes removing disconnected parts and superconductive elements (for level1,2) and GSPG reduction (for level2); 'solve' includes translation procedure, actual solving and extracting the result; the actual solving is performed with IPOPT.

After that (level2), GSPG reduction with fixed Qsets is applied, leaving N=13, E=14, P=8 elements. This corresponds to the reduction factor 2.9. Then, we have implemented all necessary GSPG operations described by the formulae above. For the solution procedure, after the reduction, we obtain the acceleration factor 2.2. The solution on level2 is identical with level1 up to the solver tolerance (set to tol=10^{-5} in our numerical experiments).

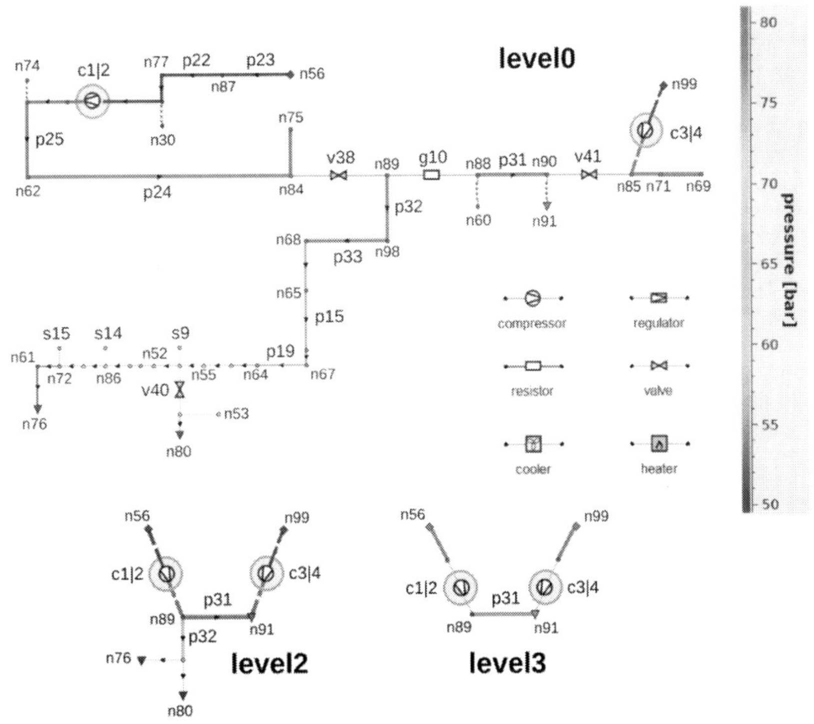

Figure 2. Realistic gas transport network N1 at different reduction levels: level0 = original network; level2 = GSPG reduction with fixed Qsets; level3 = GSPG reduction with moving Qsets. (Not shown: level1 = removing disconnected parts and superconductive elements, looking similar to level0.)

For GSPG reduction with moving Qsets (level3), we have implemented the formal reduction algorithm, sufficient for the estimation of the reduction factor. On this level, we have N=8, E=9, P=3 elements, comprising the reduction factor 1.6 relative to the previous level. The numerical counterpart of the algorithm has not been implemented yet, that is why the reduced network for level3 on Figure 2 does not have pressure data. In the next section, we will discuss the details of Qset movement algorithm necessary for this level.

The same tests have been performed on more complex networks N2 and N3, provided by our industrial partners for benchmarking. The parameters of the networks and the results of the reduction are presented in Tables I-III. The obtained level1/level2 reduction factors vary in the range 2.4-2.9, while acceleration factors solve1/solve2 are 2.2-2.6. The 'filter' step in Table III includes the necessary preprocessing and reduction of the networks. The 'solve' step includes translation of the network to the form suitable for the solver and the solution procedure itself, which share the timing in 1:1 proportion. Currently, our system uses the universal translation algorithm from [5]. It allows to plug in generic non-linear solvers with an arbitrary problem description language, requiring only to adjust a translation matrix in the algorithm. In particular, we have experimented with IPOPT (Interior Point OPTimizer) [11], Mathematica [12], MATLAB (MATrix LABoratory) [13] and a Newton solver, developed in our group. The best results for our type of problems have been obtained with IPOPT and Newton, while these two solvers among themselves have comparable performance. The details of the implementation of the Newton solver will be published elsewhere.

The solution procedure involves a multiphase workflow, described in [5]. Although global convergence from an arbitrary starting point for stationary network problems is guaranteed theoretically [4], the multiphase procedure is still empirically faster. This procedure gradually increases the complexity of the modeling and uses the result of the previous phase as a starting point for the next one. In our numerical experiments, a 3-phase procedure is used, relevant to the modeling of compressors and regulators in the network. In the first phase, compressors and regulators have enforced goals, e.g., $P_{out} = Const.$ Then, they are set to a simplified universal *free model* and, finally, to the individually calibrated *advanced model* [6]. The timing in Table III presents the sum over 3 phases.

IV. Discussion

At first, we perform a comparison with paper [9], where a different approach for topological reduction was taken. Then, we describe possible generalizations of our topological reduction algorithm.

a) Comparison with paper [9]: in this paper, the stationary problem in gas transport networks was studied, where subgraphs consisting of pipes only were considered. The pipes were modeled by the expressions of type (1) and the 2nd Kirchhoff law was consistently applied, by summing this expression over independent cycles in the subgraph. As a result, P-variables drop off from such sums and a system of smaller size depending only on Q-variables remains, for which the existence and uniqueness of the solution is proven.

Although the approach looks promising, for its practical implementation, some problems exist.

This approach does allow to reduce the dimension of the system by extracting from it a subsystem that depends only on Q-variables. The dimension of the subsystem is equal to the number of independent cycles in the subgraph. The subsystem has a unique solution for which, however, it is generally impossible to obtain an analytic expression. Thus, it should be solved numerically, for example, by Newton's method. The remaining variables in the subgraph are obtained by an unambiguous analytical reconstruction procedure. The problem appears when this subgraph is considered in the context of a complete graph containing other elements than pipes, for example, compressors. The solution of the complete problem is usually also found by the Newton's method. For the subgraph, this means that the solution must be found many times, with variable boundary conditions. In this case, a combination of two Newton's methods, external and internal, will require from the subgraph not only a solution, but also its derivatives with respect to the boundary conditions. Such a combination is in any case not an efficient way to solve the system.

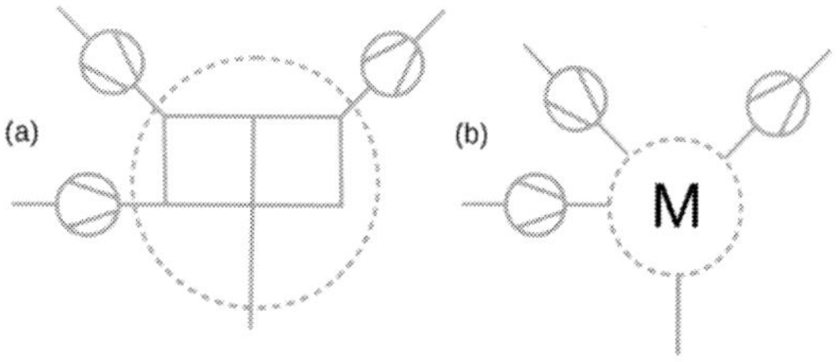

Figure 3. Shrinking a subgraph (a) creates a generalized network element with a fixed number of pins (b), a multipin (M).

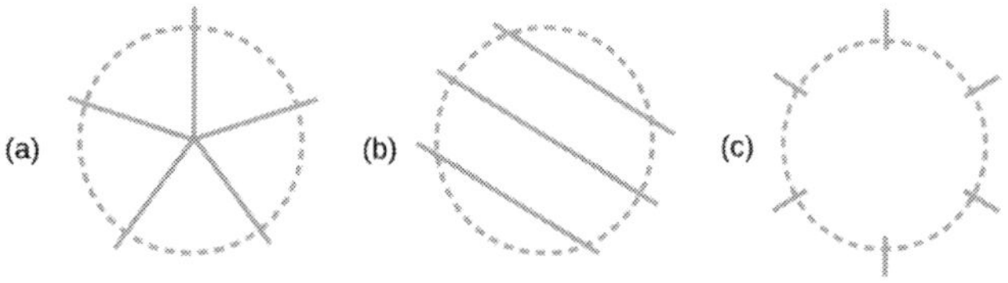

Figure 4. Particular examples: (a) 5-pin star; (b) 6-pin with 3 parallel connections; (c) empty 6-pin. In all cases, the number of equations describing the multipin is equal to the number of pins.

Another problem is that, according to [9], a pure pipe subgraph, contained in a general graph, can be shrunk to a single point. We cannot agree with this statement, since a subgraph can have many boundary points in which nodal P-variables are different, see Figure 3. The subgraph is not shrunk to a point, but to a generalized element containing N_b boundary points, or *pins* like in a microchip. We refer to such a generalized element further as *multipin*. As we show below, this element introduces not one, but N_b equations.

Without loss of generality, we can consider a connected subgraph for which the pins have definite flows serving as source/sink boundary conditions for the subgraph, as well as N_b nodal P-variables. One condition necessary for the stationary problem is the annulation of the sums of boundary flows. Here, for definiteness, we place all external sources/sinks in the subgraph, including Q_{set} and P_{set} nodes, on separate pins. Further, considering one of the boundary nodes as a point with a given pressure, the procedure from [9] uniquely reconstructs all other N_b-1 boundary pressures in terms of the first pressure and the boundary flows. The conditions for the equality of the reconstructed pressures to the given boundary pressures are the equations presenting the multipin for the external graph, totaling N_b equations.

In principle, it seems possible to precompute these N_b functions on a grid in the space of parameters and use fast interpolation algorithms to represent the multipin. The problem is the rapid increase of the grid data volume with the increasing dimension of N_b. In our approach, we have restricted our calculations to 2-pins, $N_b = 2$, which generally allows 2D tabulation (the pixel buffer from [6]). In this paper, we concentrate on the quadratic pipe model (1), which allows to encapsulate all the characteristics in one R-parameter and to perform all calculations analytically, without tabulated functions. Below, we consider also an intermediate case, where 1D-tabulation by splines is used. Thus, we avoid *curse-of-dimensionality* problems existing for general multipins and are still capable to reduce the dimension of the problem considerably.

In the remainder of this subsection, we consider in more detail an interesting question, why the multipin, regardless of its structure, is described by the same number of equations. Indeed, the number of equations external to the excluded subgraph is the same and does not depend on the topology of the subgraph. After eliminating the subgraph, the system must remain closed, meaning that the subgraph introduces the same number of equations. To calculate this number, it is enough to consider a specific configuration.

In Figure 4a, the star-like multipin is considered. One equation is the zero sum of the flows into the multipin. The Kirchhoff law in the center is equivalent to this equation. There is one P-variable in the middle, but there are also N_b conditions relating it to the boundary P_b and Q_b. In total, N_b-pin is equivalent to N_b equations on the boundary P and Q. Figure 4b shows the case when N_b is even and N_b-pin represents $N_b/2$ conditions for equality of incoming and outgoing flows, as well as $N_b/2$ of element equations. In total, we obtain N_b equations. In fact, even the connectivity of the graph is not important here. In Figure 4c, the case of an empty subgraph is considered, when all pins hang freely. Then, $Q_b = 0$ in all of them, comprising N_b equations.

b) Possible generalizations of friction laws: in the equations of the element, a general power dependence can be used, as was done in [9]. The consideration is quite similar. The element equation, series and parallel connections are described by:

$$P_{in}|P_{in}| - P_{out}|P_{out}| = RQ|Q|^{\alpha-1}, \ \alpha \geq 1, \qquad (10)$$
$$R_{12}^{s} = R_1 + R_2,$$
$$R_{12}^{p} = \left(R_1^{-1/\alpha} + R_2^{-1/\alpha}\right)^{-\alpha}.$$

The quadratic law (1) corresponds to $\alpha = 2$.

Contraction of the leaf and reverse reconstruction are done in the same way.

Consider a more general case:

$$F(P_{in}) - F(P_{out}) = G(Q), \qquad (11)$$

where F, G are monotonously increasing functions, every element has an own G, while F is the same for all elements (strictly speaking, it is enough if F is the same in a connected component of the graph).

For series connections, the equations can be combined as before:

$$F(P_1) - F(P_3) = G^s_{12}(Q), \quad (12)$$
$$G^s_{12}(Q) = G_1(Q) + G_2(Q).$$

If the original functions were monotonic, then their sum will also be. The inverse reconstruction is:

$$P_2 = F_{inv}(F(P_1) - G_1(Q)), \quad (13)$$

where by subscript *inv* we denote the inverse 1D-function, so as not to be confused with the algebraic inversion: $x^{-1} = 1/x$.

For parallel connections, the equations can be combined analogously:

$$F(P_1) - F(P_2) = G^p_{12}(Q), \quad (14)$$
$$G^p_{12} = (G_{1,inv} + G_{2,inv})_{inv}.$$

Proof:

$$F(P_1) - F(P_2) = x = G_1(Q_1) = G_2(Q_2),$$
$$Q_1 = G_{1,inv}(x),\ Q_2 = G_{2,inv}(x),\ Q =$$
$$Q_1 + Q_2 = G_{1,inv}(x) + G_{2,inv}(x) = G^p_{12,inv}(x),$$
$$x = G^p_{12}(Q) = (G_{1,inv} + G_{2,inv})_{inv}(Q). \blacksquare$$

It can be seen that the resulting G-function is also monotonic. The structure of the formulas for quadratic and α-power resistance is also clear: the inverse of the power function is also a power function. Thus, the inverse reconstruction is:

$$Q_1 = G_{1,inv}(G^p_{12}(Q)),\ Q_2 = G_{2,inv}(G^p_{12}(Q)). \quad (15)$$

To store 1D functions $y(x)$, one can use lists of tabulated values (x_n, y_n) and interpolate between them using cubic splines. Outside the working area $|P| \leq 150$ bar, $|Q| \leq 1000$ Nm^3/h, the data can be extended by linearly growing functions, similar to [4]. Such a representation is convenient for inverting the functions, for which it suffices to swap $(x_n, y_n) \to (y_n, x_n)$ and reconstruct the splines [14]. The accuracy of this procedure is controlled by the smoothness of the function and the density of subdivision. The computational complexity is proportional to the number of tabulated values, $O(N)$.

In the problems we are considering, the functions are odd: $y(-x) = -y(x)$. This means that it is enough for them to construct splines in the region $x \geq 0$ and use the symmetry for complete reconstruction. In addition, the functions have a vanishing derivative at zero, for example, $y = x|x| = x^2 \operatorname{sgn} x$, which leads to a non-smooth root dependence for inverse functions $x = \sqrt{|y|} \operatorname{sgn} y$. This leads to problems for representing such functions by cubic splines. In fact, as noted in [4], vanishing of the derivative also leads to instability of the solver. The case $Q = 0$ can occur in large regions of the network in the absence of a flow in them. This leads to zeroing of the derivative of the function $Q|Q|$ and entails the degeneration of the Jacobi matrix of the complete system. To overcome this problem, the laminar term $Q|Q| + \epsilon Q$ must be added to this function; similar regularizing terms must also be added to the P-functions. After this, the problem with the zero derivative disappears and does not hinder the spline inversion.

c) Precise friction laws: better precision can be achieved by Nikuradze and Hofer formulae [2][3]. These differential formulae can be analytically integrated under assumption of slow variation of temperature and compression factor over the pipe. If needed, the long pipes can be subdivided into smaller segments to achieve the necessary precision of the modeling. This piecewise integration approach is similar to the *finite element method* in modeling of flexible materials, flow dynamics, etc. The resulting formulae have the same quadratic form (1), with the resistance $R(Q, P_1, P_2)$ weakly (logarithmically) dependent on the flow and the pressures. Direct comparison between the quadratic and Hofer pipe laws on our test networks shows the difference on the level of 7-10%. The practical use of calculations with the approximate quadratic formula is a rapidly computable starting point for the subsequent refinement iterations with the precise formula. The gravitational term, available in the precise formula and taking into account the profile of the terrain, can be also embedded in the quadratic formula:

$$P_1|P_1|(1+\gamma) - P_2|P_2|(1-\gamma) = ... \quad (16)$$
$$\gamma = \mu g(H_1 - H_2)/(R_{gas}Tz),$$

where the dots denote the flow-dependent right part, in any form that we have considered. The dimensionless hydrostatic factor γ is determined by the gravitational acceleration g, the height difference $H_1 - H_2$ and the usual gas parameters. In real problems, the parameter γ is small, $|\gamma| \ll 1$, so the factors $(1 \pm \gamma)$ do not change the signature of the terms in the equation.

d) Inverse reconstruction: for practical purposes, it is enough to solve the problem on the reduced graph, the topological skeleton. The users are mainly interested in the values of flows and pressures at the end points of pipe subgraphs, where they are connected to active elements such as compressors and regulators or directed to the end consumers. One also needs to control the feasibility indicator $P > 0$. As we now show, it is enough to control this indicator at the endpoints.

Consider GSPG operations in the presence of nodes with negative pressure. For parallel connection, in the presence of negative pressure in the end node, it remains there after the reduction. For series connection, if there is negative pressure at the intermediate node, it will also be negative at the end node downstream. Indeed, considering the most general case with gravity corrections,

$$P_3|P_3|(1-\gamma) = P_2|P_2|(1+\gamma) - R_2Q|Q|, \quad (17)$$

since the factors $(1 \pm \gamma), R_2$ are positive, for $P_2 < 0$, $Q \geq 0$, we get $P_3 < 0$. Only contraction of a leaf with $Q_{set} > 0$ can be a problem, since this procedure can hide a negative pressure node downstream. As we have already explained, there is an option to block contracting leafs with nonzero Q_{set}. In this case, it suffices to check $P > 0$ at the end nodes of the pipe graph.

On the other hand, the data recovery in reduced elements is a straightforward analytical procedure. For this, a complete reduction history with all intermediate parameters and/or tabulated functions must be recorded. Then, the above-described inverse operations can be applied. On the graph obtained, it is possible to monitor the fulfillment of the condition $P > 0$ or the enhanced condition $P > 1$ bar or any other inequality on pressures and flows.

e) Level 3, Q_{set} movement algorithm: consider the two graphs depicted in Figure 5. Assuming that the central element is described by the general equation $F(P_1, P_2, Q)$, we require the equivalence of solutions, connecting these equations with the shift transformation of the argument:

$$F_b(P_1, P_2, Q) := F_a(P_1, P_2, Q + Q_{set}), \qquad (18)$$
$$F_a(P_1, P_2, Q) = 0 \Rightarrow F_b(P_1, P_2, Q - Q_{set}) = 0.$$

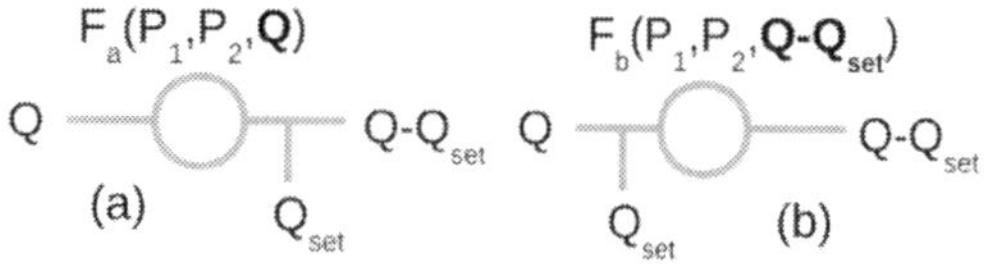

Figure 5. Q_{set} movement algorithm.

As a result, it is possible to move the Q_{set} specifier along a graph to an arbitrary place. For example, all Q_{set} specifiers can be moved to the P_{set} node, which should be present in each connected component of the graph. In this case, the undefined flow in this node will be shifted by the total Q_{set} in the subgraph. Alternatively, one can move all Q_{set} specifiers into one main consumer, who will represent all consumers in the subgraph. Note that such transformations change the distribution of flows in the graph, representing only a virtual distribution, that is visually unsimilar, but mathematically equivalent to the original one. To represent the result, of course, all the displaced Q_{set} specifiers must return to their places using inverse transformations. Note also that the argument shifts change the position of zero and violate the oddness of the functions. This requires to modify the tabulation algorithms; the easiest way is to consider all dependencies as monotonic functions of general form.

f) Not only pipes, combining 2D characteristic maps: after all pipe subgraphs are reduced to 2-pins, the functions can be transformed to a more general representation, in one of the equivalent forms:

$$Q = F(P_1, P_2), \; P_1 = F(P_2, Q), \; P_2 = F(P_1, Q). \quad (19)$$

All other elements, such as compressors and regulators, can be represented in the same way. Such a representation can use the 2D-tabulation (pixmaps) algorithms described in [6], as well as piecewise linear monotone extensions outside of the working region. As a result, GSPG reduction can be continued at the level of 2D functions. Thus, our proposed strategy is to keep the low-dimensional representations as long as possible, such as quadratic equations or 1D-splines for pipes, and then, after the network is strongly reduced, proceed to pixmaps.

V. CONCLUSION

In this paper, the topological reduction method for gas transport networks has been presented. The method uses a contraction of series, parallel and tree-like subgraphs, containing the pipes, described by quadratic friction law. This way, we achieve the goal of significant lossless reduction of the graphs and we accelerate solution procedure correspondingly. Several realistic network examples of different complexity have been used for the benchmarking of the method. Comparing with the original network (level0), the elimination of superconductive elements and disconnected parts (level1) brings the reduction factor into the range 1.9-2.9, further GSPG reduction with fixed Qsets (level2) multiplies it by the factor 2.4-2.9, then GSPG reduction with moving Qsets (level3) gives a projected multiplicative factor 1.6-2.3. We have done performance comparison between the numerically implemented levels 1, 2. While level1 is absolutely necessary for the convergence, level2 brings the acceleration factor 2.2-2.6 for the solution procedure, with a little overhead for GSPG pre-filtering.

The possible extensions of the method include a power law and generic monotone formula for pipes, iterative schemes for Nikuradze and Hofer formulae, rapid inverse reconstruction of data in reduced subgraphs, Qset movement algorithm for deeper reduction and the extension of the reduction methods to other elements using 2D tabulation (pixmaps). The implementation of these extensions is on the way. The question of the optimality of the proposed reductions will also be studied.

VI. ACKNOWLEDGMENT

The work has been supported by the German Federal Ministry for Economic Affairs and Energy, project BMWI-0324019A, MathEnergy: Mathematical Key Technologies for Evolving Energy Grids and by the German Bundesland North Rhine-Westphalia using fundings from the European Regional Development Fund, grant Nr. EFRE-0800063, project ES-FLEX-INFRA. The authors thank Kira Konich and Kevin Reinartz for proofreading the paper.

REFERENCES

[1] J. Mischner, H.G. Fasold, and K. Kadner, System-planning basics of gas supply, Oldenbourg Industrieverlag GmbH, 2011 (in German).

[2] M. Schmidt, M. C. Steinbach, and B. M. Willert, "High detail stationary optimization models for gas networks", Optimization and Engineering, vol. 16, 2015, pp. 131-164.

[3] T. Clees, "Parameter studies for energy networks with examples from gas transport", Springer Proceedings in Mathematics & Statistics, vol. 153, 2016, pp. 29-54.

[4] T. Clees, I. Nikitin, and L. Nikitina, "Making Network Solvers Globally Convergent", Advances in Intelligent Systems and Computing, vol. 676, 2017, pp. 140-153.

[5] A. Baldin et al., "Universal Translation Algorithm for Formulation of Transport Network Problems", in Proc. SIMULTECH 2018, vol. 1, pp. 315-322.

[6] T. Clees, I. Nikitin, L. Nikitina, and Ł. Segiet, "Modeling of Gas Compressors and Hierarchical Reduction for Globally Convergent Stationary Network Solvers", Int. J. On Advances in Systems and Measurements, IARIA, vol. 11, 2018, pp. 61-71.

[7] D. Eppstein, "Parallel recognition of series-parallel graphs", Information and Computation, vol. 98, 1992, pp. 41-55.

[8] N. M. Korneyenko, "Combinatorial algorithms on a class of graphs", Discrete Applied Mathematics, vol. 54, 1994, pp. 215-217.

[9] R. Z. Rios-Mercado, S. Wu, L. R. Scott, and E. A. Boyd, "A Reduction Technique for Natural Gas Transmission Network Optimization Problems", Annals of Operations Research, vol. 117, 2002, pp. 217-234.

[10] T. Clees et al., "MYNTS: Multi-phYsics NeTwork Simulator", In Proc. SIMULTECH 2016, SCITEPRESS, pp. 179-186.

[11] A. Wächter and L. T. Biegler, "On the implementation of an interior-point filter line-search algorithm for large-scale nonlinear programming", Mathematical Programming, vol. 106, 2006, pp. 25-57.

[12] Mathematica, Reference Manual, http://reference.wolfram.com [retrieved: June, 2019].

[13] MATLAB, https://de.mathworks.com/products/matlab.html [retrieved: June, 2019].

[14] T. Clees, I. Nikitin, L. Nikitina, and S. Pott, "Quasi-Monte Carlo and RBF Metamodeling for Quantile Estimation in River Bed Morphodynamics", Advances in Intelligent Systems and Computing, vol. 319, 2014, pp. 211-222.

Model Reduction in the Design of Alkaline Methanol Fuel Cells

Tanja Clees(1,2), Bernhard Klaassen(2), Igor Nikitin(2), Lialia Nikitina(2), Sabine Pott(2), Ulrike Krewer(3), Theresa Haisch(3)

(1) University of Applied Sciences Bonn-Rhein-Sieg, Sankt Augustin, Germany
(2) Fraunhofer Institute for Algorithms and Scientific Computing, Sankt Augustin, Germany
Email: Name.Surname@scai.fraunhofer.de
(3) Institute of Energy and Process Systems Engineering, Technical University, Braunschweig, Germany
Email: {u.krewer, t.haisch}@tu-braunschweig.de

Abstract—**In this paper, it is shown that the electrochemical kinetics of alkaline methanol oxidation can be reduced by setting certain fast reactions contained in it to a steady state. As a result, the underlying system of Ordinary Differential Equations (ODE) is transformed into a system of Differential-Algebraic Equations (DAE). We measure the precision characteristics of such transformation and discuss the consequences of the obtained model reduction.**

Keywords–modeling of complex systems; observational data and simulations; advanced applications; mathematical chemistry.

I. Introduction

In this short paper, we continue our research [1] on mathematical modeling of alkaline methanol oxidation, a process relevant for the design of efficient fuel cells. The considered reaction network is shown in Figure 1 left. It connects 6 reagents θ_i by 12 reactions r_j. The kinetics is described by the system of Ordinary Differential Equations (ODE):

$$\alpha_i d\theta_i/dt = F_i = \textstyle\sum_j C_{ij} r_j, \qquad (1)$$

where α_i are constant coefficients, for the case of ODE set to $\alpha_i = 1$; $\theta_i \in [0, 1]$ are surface coverages for the reagents; C_{ij} is a structural matrix relating production rates F_i and reaction rates r_j. The reaction rates are polynomial functions of θ_i, whose coefficients depend on the applied voltage $\eta(t)$. The voltage is a function of time, set in these experiments to a saw-like profile. The explicit form of all functions can be found in [1]. Here, only the structure of this system is important. Note that some reactions in Figure 1 are deselected (grayed out) by setting the corresponding matrix entries to zero. We have also reassigned normalization factors between F_i and r_j, so that both are measured in the same units (s^{-1}).

The experimental measurements are performed using the technique of Cyclic Voltammetry (CV) [2]), in a setup shown in Figure 1 right. The measured quantity is a cell current, in the model given by the expression:

$$I_{cell} = FAC_{act}F_7, \; F_7 = \textstyle\sum_j C_{7j} r_j, \qquad (2)$$

where F – Faraday constant, A – geometric electrode area, C_{act} – a surface concentration of Pt catalyst. Here, we add the 7th row in the structural matrix and omit the practically vanishing capacitance term $C_{dl} d\eta/dt$. The described mathematical model fits the experimental data well, as shown in Figure 3 left. Further improvements of the method are described in Section II and the results are discussed in Section III.

II. Improvements of the Method

In this paper, we draw attention to Figure 2, which depicts the evolution of production and reaction rates. It is visible that some r_j compensate each other, resulting in almost zero F_i. This common property, also noted in [3], means that some of the reactions proceed so fast that they are almost permanently in equilibrium. One production rate is not in equilibrium. It is also characterized by the presence of only one reaction: $F_6 = r_{12}$. Thus, in the equations, one can switch off the dynamic terms for all reagents except for the 6th, so that $\alpha_i = \delta_{i6}$. As a result, the ODE system is replaced by an equivalent system of Differential-Algebraic Equations (DAE). Mathematica v11 can be used to solve DAE systems with the same efficiency as ODE.

III. Discussion

After the replacement by DAE, the CV plot in Figure 3 left changes slightly, as well as the detailed evolution of θ_i, shown in Figure 3 center. An interesting property that immediately catches the eye is the temporal asymmetry of the profiles for some reagents. Since the voltage is an even periodic function, if all reactions were in equilibrium, all θ_i would be even periodic. They would behave like red or black lines, corresponding to OH_{ad} and free Pt in Figure 3. Deviation from this behavior for magenta and brown, that is, $COOH_{ad}$ and PtO, is a purely dynamic effect. The consequence of this effect is the observed mismatch (hysteresis) for the increasing and decreasing branches of the CV plot. In line with this work, it is important that DAE provides the same profiles as ODE. Figure 3 right measures the deviation between the DAE and ODE, for θ_i, in the same colors, as well as the deviation of I_{cell} relative to its maximum, shown in gray. As a result, the transition from ODE to DAE results in 0.8% maximal variation for θ_i and 2.5% for I_{cell}, proving a good accuracy of the DAE representation.

IV. Conclusion

The advantage of the DAE formulation obtained in this paper is that only one degree of freedom θ_6 remains in the system, to which the evolution of other reagents is strictly coupled. The model is reduced and still describes the same effects as the complete system. In particular, it explains the dynamic hysteresis of volt-ampere characteristics of the cell.

V. Acknowledgement

The work has been partially supported by the German Federal Ministry for Economic Affairs and Energy, grant BMWI-0324019A, project MathEnergy and by the German Bundesland North Rhine-Westphalia, the European Regional Development Fund, grant Nr. EFRE-0800063, project ES-FLEX-INFRA.

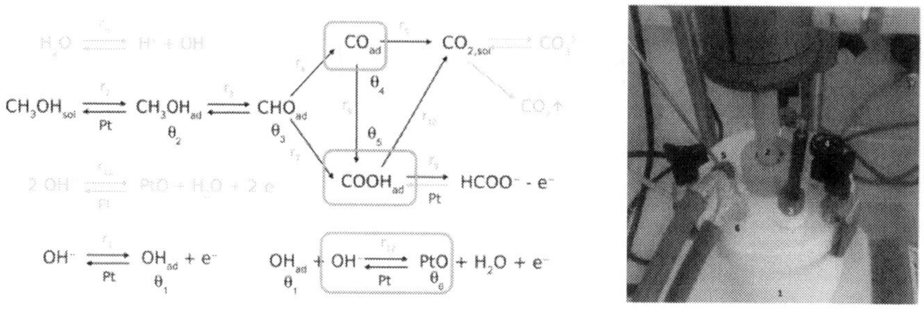

Figure 1. On the left: the chemical reactions network, the orange boxes show the reactions potentially responsible for the hysteresis effect on the CV plot. On the right: the experimental setup, consisting of a teflon cell (1) under deep vacuum, the rotating working electrode (2), the counter electrode (3), the reference electrode (4), the temperature sensor (5) and argon blow supply (6).

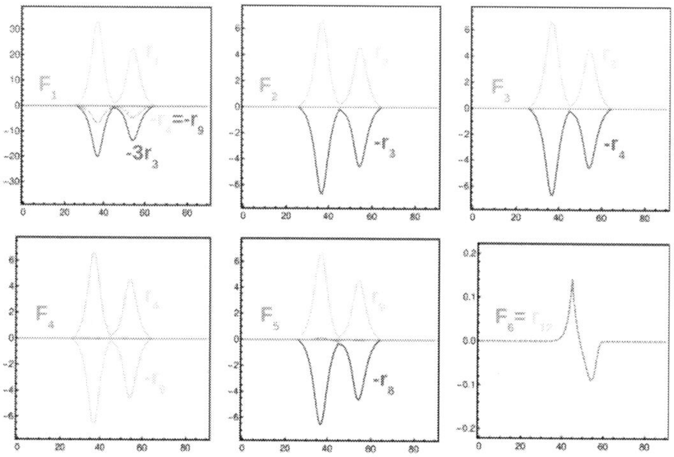

Figure 2. The plots of production rates F_i and reaction rates r_i. All production rates except F_6 show an approach to equilibrium. The horizontal axes show the time in seconds, the vertical axes: F_i and r_i in s^{-1}.

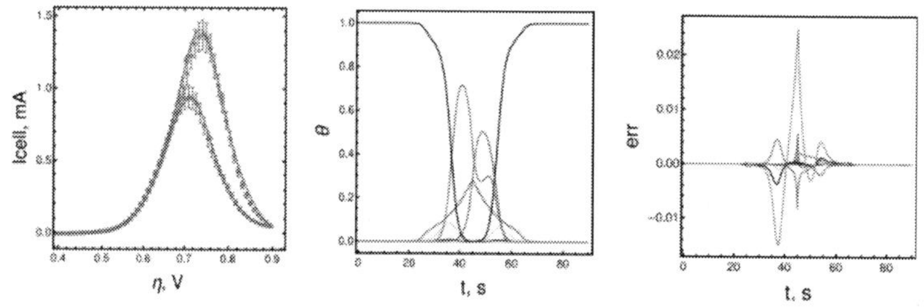

Figure 3. On the left: CV plot, blue points with error bars – the experiment, red line – the model. In the center: evolution of surface coverages, the colors (red, green, blue, cyan, magenta, brown) encode sequential θ_i, black shows the free Pt surface. On the right: ODE→DAE variations for θ_i (the same colors), relative variation for I_{cell} (in gray).

References

[1] T. Clees, I. Nikitin, L. Nikitina, S. Pott, U. Krewer, and T. Haisch, "Parameter Identification in Cyclic Voltammetry of Alkaline Methanol Oxidation", in Proc. SIMULTECH 2018, July 29-31, 2018, Porto, Portugal, pp. 279-288, ISBN: 978-989-758-323-0.

[2] A. J. Bard and L. R. Faulkner, Electrochemical Methods: Fundamentals and Applications, Wiley 2000, ISBN: 978-0-471-04372-0.

[3] A. N. Gorban, "Model reduction in chemical dynamics: slow invariant manifolds, singular perturbations, thermodynamic estimates, and analysis of reaction graph", Current Opinion in Chemical Engineering, vol. 21, 2018, pp. 48-59, DOI: 10.1016/j.coche.2018.02.009.

Periodic Solution of a Discretized Age-Dependent Model with a Dominant Age Class

Zlatinka Kovacheva
University of Mining and Geology and
Institute of Mathematics and Informatics
Bulgarian Academy of Sciences
Sofia, Bulgaria
e-mail: zkovacheva@hotmail.com

Valéry Covachev
Institute of Mathematics and Informatics
Bulgarian Academy of Sciences
Sofia, Bulgaria
e-mail: vcovachev@hotmail.com

Abstract—**A delay differential equation for the population size is derived from an age-dependent model with a dominant age class. This equation is provided with impulse conditions and its discrete-time counterpart is constructed using the semi-discretization method. Sufficient conditions for the existence of a periodic solution of the resulting difference problem are found by Mawhin's continuation theorem.**

Keywords-age-dependent model; impulse effect; discrete-time equation; periodic solution.

I. INTRODUCTION

Many evolutionary processes in nature are characterized by the fact that at certain instants of time they experience a rapid change of their states. This leads to the investigation of differential equations and systems with discontinuous trajectories, or with impulse effect, called for brevity impulsive differential equations and systems [1][2]. The theory of the impulsive differential equations is one of the attractive branches of differential equations which has extensive realistic mathematical modelling applications in physics, chemistry, engineering, and biological and medical sciences.

A classical problem of the qualitative theory of differential equations is the existence of periodic (or almost periodic) solutions. Numerous references on this matter concerning differential equations with delay and impulsive differential equations can be found in [3].

In [4], an age-dependent model with a dominant age class was considered. In a special case the total population size satisfies a delay differential equation. Sufficient conditions for the existence of a periodic solution of this equation satisfying appropriate impulse conditions were presented.

A brief survey is given in Section II of the present paper. In Section III, we obtain a discrete counterpart of the problem using the semi-discretization method. Finally, in Section IV, we find sufficient conditions for the existence of a periodic solution of the resulting discrete problem using Mawhin's continuation theorem [5, p. 40].

II. PRELIMINARIES

The following model is described in the papers of T. Kostova [6], T. Kostova and F. Milner [7], where the existence of oscillatory solutions is proved.

For two fixed ages σ_1, σ_2 such that $0 \le \sigma_1 < \sigma_2 < \infty$, the age distribution $u(a,t)$ of a population is considered, where a is the age and t the time, with dynamics described by the following integro-differential equation with age-boundary condition in integral form,

$$\begin{cases} \dfrac{\partial u}{\partial a} + \dfrac{\partial u}{\partial t} = -\delta(a,Q)u(a,t), & a,t > 0, \\ u(0,t) = \displaystyle\int_0^\infty \beta(a,Q)u(a,t)\,da, & t \ge 0, \\ u(a,0) = u_0(a), & a \ge 0, \end{cases} \tag{1}$$

where

$$Q = Q(t) = \int_{\sigma_1}^{\sigma_2} u(a,t)\,da$$

is the *dominant age cohort* size and $\delta(a,Q)$ and $\beta(a,Q)$ are, respectively, the age-specific death rate and birth modulus when the dominant age group is of size Q. It is assumed that δ, β and u_0 are nonnegative, and that u_0 is integrable (so that the initial population is finite). This model is a generalization of the classical one of Gurtin and MacCamy [8], which is obtained by setting $\sigma_1 = 0$ and $\sigma_2 = \infty$.

Further on, in [6][7], the special case

$$\beta(a,Q) = \begin{cases} \beta(Q), & a \in [\sigma_1, \sigma_2], \\ 0 & \text{otherwise}, \end{cases}$$

is considered. This means that the dominant age class is the only one capable of having offspring, i.e., births are possible only in the age interval $[\sigma_1, \sigma_2]$ and the fertility rate depends just on the size of the dominant age group itself (and not on the age within the group). Moreover, $\beta(Q) \in C^1(\mathbb{R}_+, \mathbb{R}_+)$ and the mortality rate $\delta > 0$ is assumed constant.Then, for the total population size,

$$P(t) = \int_0^\infty u(a,t)\,da,$$

the equation

$$\dot{P} + \delta P = \beta(Q)Q \tag{2}$$

is derived, where

$$Q(t) = P(t-\sigma_1)e^{-\sigma_1\delta} - (t-\sigma_2)e^{-\sigma_2\delta} \quad (3)$$

for $t > \sigma_2$. Thus, for $t > \sigma_2$, $P(t)$ satisfies a nonlinear scalar delay equation (2) with Q given by (3), while for $t \in [0,\sigma_2]$ $Q(t)$ and eventually $P(t)$ can be expressed in terms of the initial function $u_0(a)$ of the age-dependent model (1). Thus we find the initial function $P_0(t), t \in [0,\sigma_2]$ of the above mentioned delay equation.

We fix a number $\omega > 0$ much larger than the age σ_2, and try to obtain an ω -periodic regime of the population size by means of impulsive perturbations for a suitably chosen initial function u_0. More precisely, suppose that at certain moments t_k such that $t_{k+p} = t_k + \omega$ for all $k \in \mathbb{Z}$, the population size $P(t)$ is abruptly changed, while (2) with (3) is assumed to hold for all $t \in \mathbb{R}, t \neq t_k$. We normalize the quantities in (2) as follows:

$$s = \frac{t}{\omega}, \quad \Pi(s) = P(\omega s), \quad D = \omega\delta, \quad B(Q) = \omega\beta(Q).$$

Henceforth, we write again t, δ and β instead of s, D and B, respectively, x instead of Π, and $h = \sigma_2/\omega$ will be the small parameter, while the still smaller quantity σ_1/ω will be assumed 0, for the sake of simplicity. We suppose that the time interval between two successive abrupt changes (impulse effects) $t_{k+1} - t_k$ is large in comparison with the "age" h for all $k \in \mathbb{Z}$, and look for 1--periodic solutions of the problem

$$\dot{x}(t) = -\delta x(t) + R\big(x(t), x(t-h)\big), \quad t \neq t_k, \quad (4)$$
$$\Delta x(t_k) = -B_k x(t_k) + a_k, \quad k \in \mathbb{Z}, \quad (5)$$

where $\Delta x(t_k) \equiv x(t_k+0) - x(t_k-0)$ is the magnitude of the impulse effect at the moment t_k, $x(t_k) \equiv x(t_k - 0)$, a_k, B_k are positive constants satisfying $a_{k+p} = a_k$, $B_{k+p} = B_k \quad (k \in \mathbb{Z})$, $R\big(x(t), x(t-h)\big) = \beta\big(Q(t)\big)Q(t)$, $Q(t) = x(t) - x(t-h)e^{-h\delta}$, $0 = t_0 < t_1 < \cdots < t_{p-1} < t_p = 1$. We can consider (4) for $t > 0$, the impulse conditions (5) for $k \geq 0$, with initial condition

$$x(s) = \phi(s) \quad \text{for} \quad s \in [-1, 0], \quad (6)$$

where the initial function $\phi(s)$ is piecewise continuous with possible points of discontinuity of the first kind at t_{-p+1}, t_{-p+2}, ... , t_{-1}. To find a 1-periodic solution of problem (4), (5) means to determine the initial function $\phi(s)$ so that the solution of the initial value problem (4), (5), (6) is 1-periodic.

III. Statement of the Problem

We suppose that the period ω has been chosen so that $\omega = N\sigma_2$ for a positive integer N, thus $h = 1/N$. We assume N so large that

$$h < \min_{k=\overline{1,p}} (t_{k+1} - t_k).$$

Then, each interval $[nh, (n+1)h]$ contains at most one instant of impulse effect t_k.

For convenience, we denote $n = [t/h]$, the greatest integer in t/h, and $n_k = [t_k/h]$. Clearly, we will have $n_{k+p} = n_k + N$ for all $k \in \mathbb{Z}$.

Let $n \in \mathbb{Z}$, $n \neq n_k$. This means that the interval $[nh, (n+1)h]$ contains no instant of impulse effect t_k. We approximate the differential equation (4) on the interval $[nh, (n+1)h]$ by

$$\dot{x}(t) + \delta x(t) = R\Big(x(nh), x\big((n-1)h\big)\Big).$$

We multiply both sides of this equation by $e^{\delta t}$ and integrate over the interval $[nh, (n+1)h]$. Thus we obtain

$$x\big((n+1)h\big) - x(nh) = -\big(1 - e^{-\delta/N}\big)x(nh) + \frac{1 - e^{-\delta/N}}{\delta} R\Big(x(nh), x\big((n-1)h\big)\Big). \quad (7)$$

Henceforth, by abuse of notation, we write $x(n) = x(nh)$ and redefine $\Delta x(n) = x(n+1) - x(n) \quad (n \in \mathbb{Z})$. Now, (7) takes the form

$$\Delta x(n) = -\big(1 - e^{-\delta/N}\big)x(n) + \frac{1-e^{-\delta/N}}{\delta} R\big(x(n), x(n-1)\big). \quad (8)$$

Next, for $n = n_k$, the interval $[nh, (n+1)h]$ contains the instant of impulse effect t_k. On this interval, we approximate the impulse conditions (5) by

$$\Delta x(n_k) = -B_k x(n_k) + a_k, \quad k \in \mathbb{Z}. \quad (9)$$

The difference system (8), (9) can be written in operator form as

$$\Delta x = Hx, \quad (10)$$

where

$$(Hx)(n) = -\big(1 - e^{-\delta/N}\big)x(n) + \frac{1 - e^{-\delta/N}}{\delta} R\big(x(n), x(n-1)\big), \quad n \neq n_k, \quad (11)$$
$$(Hx)(n_k) = -B_k x(n_k) + a_k, \quad k \in \mathbb{Z}.$$

We can consider the system (10) for $n \geq 0$, with initial conditions

$$x(\ell) = \phi(\ell) \quad \text{for} \quad \ell = 0, -1, \ldots, -N, \quad (12)$$

where $\phi(\ell)$, $\ell = 0, -1, \ldots, -N$, is a given initial vector. To find an N -periodic solution of system (10) means to determine the initial vector $\phi(\ell)$ so that the solution of the initial value problem (10), (12) is N -periodic.

IV. Main Result

First, we introduce some notations:

$$A := \sum_{k=0}^{p-1} a_k, \quad B := \sum_{k=0}^{p-1} Ba_k, \quad D := (N-p)\left(1 - e^{-\frac{\delta}{N}}\right),$$
$$I_N := \{0,1,\dots,N-1\}, \qquad \Im_N := I_N \backslash \{n_k\}_{k=0}^{p-1}.$$

Next, we formulate some assumptions:

A1. There exists a constant $K > 0$ such that $|\beta(Q)| \le K$ for any $Q \in \mathbb{R}$.

A2. $$D + B - \frac{2DK}{\delta} - (D+B)\left(D + B + \frac{2DK}{\delta}\right) > 0.$$

Remark 1. Assumption **A2** may seem quite complicated. We show that it is easy to satisfy. If we denote $y = D + B$, $z = \frac{2DK}{\delta}$, then assumption **A2** takes the form

$$y - z - y^2 - yz > 0, \text{ i.e., } z < \frac{y(1-y)}{1+y}.$$

The right-hand side of the last inequality is positive for $0 < y < 1$, it achieves its maximum value $3 - 2\sqrt{2} \approx 0.18$ for $y = \sqrt{2} - 1 \approx 0.41$. Thus, it suffices to choose $D + B = 0.41$ and $\frac{2DK}{\delta} < 0.18$.

Remark 2. The inequality

$$D + B - \frac{DK}{\delta}\left(1 - e^{-\frac{\delta}{N}}\right) > 0 \tag{13}$$

follows from assumption **A2**. In fact,

$$D + B - \frac{DK}{\delta}\left(1 - e^{-\frac{\delta}{N}}\right) > D + B - \frac{DK}{\delta}$$
$$= \left[D + B - \frac{2DK}{\delta} - (D+B)\left(D + B + \frac{2DK}{\delta}\right)\right]$$
$$+ \left[\frac{DK}{\delta} + (D+B)\left(D + B + \frac{2DK}{\delta}\right)\right] > 0.$$

Now, we can state our main result as the following theorem.

Theorem 1. *Suppose that assumptions* **A1**, **A2** *hold. Then,* (10) *has at least one N-periodic solution.*

Proof. We shall prove Theorem 1 using Mawhin's continuation theorem [5, p. 40]. To state this theorem, we need some preliminaries (see [9][10]).

Let $\mathbb{X}, \mathbb{Y}$ be real Banach spaces, $L: \operatorname{Dom} L \subset \mathbb{X} \to \mathbb{Y}$ be a linear mapping, and $H: \mathbb{X} \to \mathbb{Y}$ be a continuous mapping. The mapping L will be called a Fredholm mapping of index zero if $\dim \operatorname{Ker} L = \operatorname{codim} \operatorname{Im} L < +\infty$ and $\operatorname{Im} L$ is closed in $\mathbb{Y}$. If L is a Fredholm mapping of index zero and there exist continuous projectors $P_1: \mathbb{X} \to \mathbb{X}$ and $P_2: \mathbb{Y} \to \mathbb{Y}$ such that $\operatorname{Im} P_1 = \operatorname{Ker} L$, $\operatorname{Ker} P_2 = \operatorname{Im} L = \operatorname{Im}(I - P_2)$, then the mapping $L|_{\operatorname{Dom} L \cap \operatorname{Ker} P_1}: (I - P_1)\mathbb{X} \to \operatorname{Im} L$ is invertible. We denote the inverse of this mapping by K_{P_1}. If Ω is an open bounded subset of $\mathbb{X}$, the mapping H will be called L-compact on $\bar{\Omega}$ if $P_2 H(\bar{\Omega})$ is bounded and $K_{P_1}(I - P_2)H: \bar{\Omega} \to \mathbb{X}$ is compact. Since $\operatorname{Im} P_2$ is isomorphic to $\operatorname{Ker} L$, there exists an isomorphism $J: \operatorname{Im} P_2 \to \operatorname{Ker} L$.

Now, Mawhin's continuation theorem can be stated as follows.

Lemma 1. *Let L be a Fredholm mapping of index zero, let* $\Omega \subset \mathbb{X}$ *be an open bounded set, and let* $H: \mathbb{X} \to \mathbb{Y}$ *be a continuous operator, which is L-compact on* $\bar{\Omega}$. *Assume that the following conditions hold:*
(a) for each $\lambda \in (0,1)$, $x \in \partial\Omega \cap \operatorname{Dom} L$, $Lx \ne \lambda Hx$;
(b) for each $x \in \partial\Omega \cap \operatorname{Ker} L$, $P_2 Hx \ne 0$;
(c) $\deg(JP_2H, \Omega \cap \operatorname{Ker} L, 0) \ne 0$, *where* $\deg(\cdot)$ *is the Brouwer degree.*

Then, the equation $Lx = Hx$ *has at least one solution in* $\bar{\Omega} \cap \operatorname{Dom} L$.

Before we proceed further, we shall recall the definition of Brouwer degree [11].

Suppose that M and N are two oriented differentiable manifolds of dimension n (without boundary), with M compact and N connected, and suppose that $f: M \to N$ is a differentiable mapping. Let $Df(x)$ denote the differential mapping at the point $x \in M$, that is, the linear mapping $Df(x): T_x M \to T_{f(x)} N$. Let sign $Df(x)$ denote the sign of the determinant of $Df(x)$. That is, the sign is positive if f preserves orientation, and negative if f reverses orientation.

Definition 1. Let $y \in N$ be a regular value, then we define the *Brouwer degree* (or just *degree*) of f by

$$\deg f = \sum_{x \in f^{-1}(y)} \operatorname{sign} Df(x).$$

It can be shown that the degree does not depend on the regular value y that we pick, so that $\deg f$ is well defined.

Note that this degree coincides with the degree as defined for maps of spheres.

Let us choose

$$\mathbb{X} = \mathbb{Y} = \{x(n): x(n+N) = x(n), n \in \mathbb{Z}\}.$$

If we define $\|x\| = \max_{n \in I_N} |x(n)|$, then $\mathbb{X}$ is a Banach space with the norm $\|\cdot\|$. For $x \in \mathbb{X}$, let Hx be defined by (11), $Lx = \Delta x$ and $P_1 x = P_2 x = \frac{1}{N}\sum_{n=0}^{N-1} x(n)$. Then, $\operatorname{Ker} L = \{x \in \mathbb{X}: x = c \in \mathbb{R}\}$ (independent of n), $\operatorname{Im} L = \{x \in \mathbb{X}: \sum_{n=0}^{N-1} x(n) = 0\}$ is a closed set in $\mathbb{X}$, and $\operatorname{codim} L = 1$. Thus, L is a Fredholm mapping of index zero. It is easy to see that P_1 and P_1 are continuous projectors and $\operatorname{Im} P_1 = \operatorname{Ker} L$, $\operatorname{Im} L = \operatorname{Ker} P_2 = \operatorname{Im}(I - P_2)$, and H is L-compact on $\bar{\Omega}$ for any bounded set $\Omega \subset \mathbb{X}$. Moreover, in condition (*c*) of Lemma 1 the isomorphism J can be taken as the identity operator I.

Now, we will derive some estimates for the solutions x of the operator equation $Lx = \lambda Hx$ for $\lambda \in (0,1)$, that is,

$$\Delta x(n) = \lambda(Hx)(n), \quad n \in I_N.$$

First, from (11) for $n \neq n_k$, we obtain

$$|\Delta x(n)| \le \left(1 - e^{-\frac{\delta}{N}}\right)|x(n)| + \frac{1 - e^{-\frac{\delta}{N}}}{\delta}|\beta(Q)|\,|Q|$$
$$\le \left(1 - e^{-\frac{\delta}{N}}\right)\left\{\|x\| + \frac{K}{\delta}\left|x(n) - x(n-1)e^{-\delta/N}\right|\right\}$$
$$\le \left(1 - e^{-\frac{\delta}{N}}\right)\left(1 + \frac{2K}{\delta}\right)\|x\|.$$

Similarly, for $n = n_k$, we have

$$|\Delta x(n_k)| \le B_k\|x\| + a_k.$$

From the above inequalities, we obtain

$$\sum_{n=0}^{N-1}|\Delta x(n)| \le (N-p)\left(1 - e^{-\frac{\delta}{N}}\right)\left(1 + \frac{2K}{\delta}\right)\|x\|$$
$$+\sum_{k=0}^{p-1} B_k\|x\| + \sum_{k=0}^{p-1} a_k,$$

or

$$\sum_{n=0}^{N-1}|\Delta x(n)| \le \left[D\left(1 + \frac{2K}{\delta}\right) + B\right]\|x\| + A. \tag{14}$$

Adding together all equations of (8), (9) for $n \in I_N$, we obtain

$$\left(1 - e^{-\frac{\delta}{N}}\right)\sum_{n\in\Im_N} x(n) + \sum_{k=0}^{p-1} B_k x(n_k)$$
$$= \frac{1 - e^{-\frac{\delta}{N}}}{\delta}\sum_{n\in\Im_N} R\big(x(n), x(n-1)\big) + \sum_{k=0}^{p-1} a_k.$$

Then, as above, we obtain

$$\left|\left(1 - e^{-\frac{\delta}{N}}\right)\sum_{n\in\Im_N} x(n) + \sum_{k=0}^{p-1} B_k x(n_k)\right|$$
$$\le D\frac{2K}{\delta}\|x\| + A. \tag{15}$$

Now, we shall use the following lemma (see [12] [13]).

Lemma 2. *Let $v: \mathbb{Z} \to \mathbb{R}$ be N-periodic, i.e., $v(n + N) = v(N)$ for any $n \in \mathbb{Z}$. Then, for any fixed $\nu_1, \nu_2 \in I_N$ and any $n \in \mathbb{Z}$, we have*

$$v(\nu_2) - \sum_{k=0}^{N-1}|v(k+1) - v(k)| \le v(n)$$
$$\le v(\nu_1) + \sum_{k=0}^{N-1}|v(k+1) - v(k)|.$$

According to Lemma 2, for arbitrary $n, \nu_1, \nu_2 \in I_N$, we have

$$x(\nu_2) - \sum_{n=0}^{N-1}|\Delta x(n)| \le x(n) \le x(\nu_1) + \sum_{n=0}^{N-1}|\Delta x(n)|.$$

We multiply these inequalities by $1 - e^{-\delta/N}$ for $n \neq n_k$ or B_k for $n = n_k$, and sum up over I_N to obtain

$$(D+B)x(\nu_2) - (D+B)\sum_{n=0}^{N-1}|\Delta x(n)|$$
$$\le \left(1 - e^{-\frac{\delta}{N}}\right)\sum_{n\in\Im_N} x(n) + \sum_{k=0}^{p-1} B_k x(n_k)$$
$$\le (D+B)x(\nu_1) + (D+B)\sum_{n=0}^{N-1}|\Delta x(n)|.$$

From the last two inequalities, we deduce

$$-x(\nu_1) \le -\frac{\left(1 - e^{-\frac{\delta}{N}}\right)\sum_{n\in\Im_N} x(n) + \sum_{k=0}^{p-1} B_k x(n_k)}{D+B}$$
$$+\sum_{n=0}^{N-1}|\Delta x(n)|,$$
$$x(\nu_2) \le \frac{\left(1 - e^{-\frac{\delta}{N}}\right)\sum_{n\in\Im_N} x(n) + \sum_{k=0}^{p-1} B_k x(n_k)}{D+B}$$
$$+\sum_{n=0}^{N-1}|\Delta x(n)|.$$

Let $|x(\nu_0)| = \|x\| = \max_{n\in I_N}|x(n)|$. If $x(\nu_0) \ge 0$, we choose $\nu_2 = \nu_0$. Then,

$$(D+B)\|x\| = (D+B)x(\nu_2)$$
$$\le \left|\left(1 - e^{-\frac{\delta}{N}}\right)\sum_{n\in\Im_N} x(n) + \sum_{k=0}^{p-1} B_k x(n_k)\right|$$
$$+(D+B)\sum_{n=0}^{N-1}|\Delta x(n)|.$$

If $x(\nu_0) < 0$, we choose $\nu_2 = \nu_0$,

$$
\begin{aligned}
(D+B)\|x\| &= -(D+B)x(\nu_1) \\
&\le -\left(\left(1-e^{-\frac{\delta}{N}}\right)\sum_{n\in\Im_N} x(n) + \sum_{k=0}^{p-1} B_k x(n_k)\right) \\
&\quad +(D+B)\sum_{n=0}^{N-1}|\Delta x(n)| \\
&\le \left|\left(1-e^{-\frac{\delta}{N}}\right)\sum_{n\in\Im_N} x(n) + \sum_{k=0}^{p-1} B_k x(n_k)\right| \\
&\quad +(D+B)\sum_{n=0}^{N-1}|\Delta x(n)|.
\end{aligned}
$$

Thus, in both cases, we have

$$
\begin{aligned}
(D+B)\|x\| \le &\left|\left(1-e^{-\frac{\delta}{N}}\right)\sum_{n\in\Im_N} x(n) + \sum_{k=0}^{p-1} B_k x(n_k)\right| \\
&+(D+B)\sum_{n=0}^{N-1}|\Delta x(n)|.
\end{aligned}
$$

Making use of the estimates (14) and (15), we obtain

$$
\begin{aligned}
(D+B)\|x\| &\le D\frac{2K}{\delta}\|x\| + A \\
&+(D+B)\left\{\left[D\left(1+\frac{2K}{\delta}\right)+B\right]\|x\| + A\right\} \\
&= \left\{D\frac{2K}{\delta} + (D+B)\left[D\left(1+\frac{2K}{\delta}\right)+B\right]\right\}\|x\| \\
&+A(1+D+B),
\end{aligned}
$$

or

$$
\begin{aligned}
\left\{D+B-D\frac{2K}{\delta}-(D+B)\left(D+B+D\frac{2K}{\delta}\right)\right\}\|x\| \\
\le A(1+D+B).
\end{aligned}
$$

By virtue of assumption **A2**, the number

$$
C^* := \frac{A(1+D+B)}{D+B-D\frac{2K}{\delta}-(D+B)\left(D+B+D\frac{2K}{\delta}\right)} > 0,
$$

and each solution x of the operator equation $Lx = \lambda Hx$ for $\lambda \in (0,1)$ satisfies the inequality $\|x\| \le C^*$.

Now, we take $\Omega = \{x \in \mathbb{X}: \|x\| < C\}$, where $C > C^*$ will be chosen later. For $x \in \partial\Omega \cap \operatorname{Dom} L$, we have $\|x\| = C$, thus x cannot be a solution of $Lx = \lambda Hx$ for $\lambda \in (0,1)$. Obviously, Ω satisfies condition (a) of Lemma 1.

Now, let $x \in \partial\Omega \cap \operatorname{Ker} L = \partial\Omega \cap \mathbb{R}$, i.e., x is a constant in $\mathbb{R}$ with $|x| = C$. For such x,

$$
NP_2Hx = D\left[-x+\beta(x)x\left(1-e^{-\delta/N}\right)\right] - Bx + A,
$$

and

$$
N\|P_2Hx\| \ge \left[D+B-\frac{DK}{\delta}\left(1-e^{-\frac{\delta}{N}}\right)\right]C - A.
$$

By inequality (13), we can choose $C > C^*$ so large that

$$
\left[D+B-\frac{DK}{\delta}\left(1-e^{-\frac{\delta}{N}}\right)\right]C > A.
$$

Hence, for $x \in \partial\Omega \cap \operatorname{Ker} L$, we have $N\|P_2Hx\| > 0$ and $P_2Hx \ne 0$, that is, condition (b) of Lemma 1 is satisfied.

To prove (c), we define the mapping

$$
(P_2H)_\mu : \operatorname{Dom} L \times [0,1] \to \mathbb{X}
$$

by

$$
(P_2H)_\mu = \mu P_2\widetilde{H} + (1-\mu)P_2H,
$$

where the operator $\widetilde{H}$ is defined by

$$
\begin{aligned}
(\widetilde{H}x)(n) &= -\left(1-e^{-\frac{\delta}{N}}\right)x(n), \quad n \ne n_k, \\
(\widetilde{H}x)(n_k) &= -B_k x(n_k), \quad k \in \mathbb{Z}.
\end{aligned}
$$

For $x \in \partial\Omega \cap \operatorname{Ker} L$, we have

$$
\begin{aligned}
N(P_2H)_\mu x = D\left[-x+(1-\mu)\beta(x)x\left(1-e^{-\delta/N}\right)\right] \\
-Bx + (1-\mu)A.
\end{aligned}
$$

As above, we obtain

$$
N\|(P_2H)_\mu x\| \ge \left[D+B-\frac{DK}{\delta}\left(1-e^{-\frac{\delta}{N}}\right)\right]C - A > 0.
$$

This means that $(P_2H)_\mu x$ for $x \in \partial\Omega \cap \operatorname{Ker} L$ and $\mu \in [0,1]$. From the homotopy invariance of the Brouwer degree, it follows that

$$
\begin{aligned}
&\deg(P_2H, \Omega \cap \operatorname{Ker} L, 0) \\
&= \deg\left(P_2\widetilde{H}, \Omega \cap \operatorname{Ker} L, 0\right) = -1 \ne 0.
\end{aligned}
$$

According to Lemma 1, (10) has at least one N-periodic solution. This completes the proof of Theorem 1. ∎

V. CONCLUSIONS

In the present paper, we derived a delay differential equation for the population size from an age-dependent model with a dominant age class. We provided this equation with impulse conditions and constructed its discrete-time counterpart using the semi-discretization method. We found sufficient conditions for the existence of a periodic solution of the resulting difference problem, in the form of assumptions **A1** and **A2**, by Mawhin's continuation theorem. **A1** assumes boundedness of the birth modulus, while **A2** is a not too complicated algebraic equation. Similar methods can be used to find conditions for the existence of periodic solutions of equations arising in physics and chemistry.

REFERENCES

[1] V. Lakshmikantham, D. Bainov, and P. Simeonov, Theory of Impulsive Differential Equations, Series in Modern Applied Mathematics, vol. 6, Singapore: World Scientific, 1989, ISBN: 978-9971-5-0970-5 (hardcover), 978-981-4507-26-4 (ebook), 978-981-281-275-9 (institutional ebook).

[2] A. M. Samoilenko and N. A. Perestyuk, Impulsive Differential Equations, World Scientific Series on Nonlinear Science Series A, vol. 14, Singapore: World Scientific, 1995, ISBN: 978-281-02-2416-5 (harcover), 978-981-4499-82-8 (ebook), 978-981-279-866-4 (institutional ebook).

[3] D. D. Bainov and V. C. Covachev, "Periodic solutions of impulsive systems with a small delay," J. Phys. A: Math. Gen., vol. 27, pp. 5551–5563, 1994, ISSN: 0305-4470 (print), 1361-6447 (online).

[4] V. Covachev, "Periodicity of the population size of an age-dependent model with a dominant age class by means of impulsive perturbations," Int. J. Appl. Math. Comput. Sci., vol. 10, pp. 147–155, 2000, ISSN: 2083-8492.

[5] R. E. Gaines and J. L. Mawhin, Coincidence Degree and Nonlinear Differential Equations, Lecture Notes in Mathematics, vol. 568, Berlin: Springer, 1977, ISBN: 978-3-540-08067-1 (softcover), 978-3-540-37501-2 (ebook).

[6] T. Kostova, Oscillations in an Age-Dependent Model with a Dominant Age Class, Sofia: Institute of Mathematics and Informatics, Bulgarian Academy of Sciences, Preprint No. 5 (March 1995).

[7] T. Kostova and F. Milner, "An age-structured model of population dynamics with dominant ages, delayed behavior, and oscillations," Math. Popul. Stud., vol. 5, pp. 359–375, 1995, ISSN: 0889-8480.

[8] M. E. Gurtin, R. C. MacCamy, "Nonlinear age-dependent population dynamics," Arch. Ration. Mech. Anal., vol. 54, pp. 281–300, 1974, ISSN: 0003-9527 (print), 1432-0673 (online).

[9] H. Akça, V. Covachev, Z. Covacheva, and S. Mohamad, "Global exponential periodicity for the discrete analogue of an impulsive Hopfield neural network with finite distributed delays," Funct. Differ. Equ., vol.16, pp. 53–72, 2009, ISSN: 0793-1786.

[10] Y. Li, L. Zhao, and X. Chen, "Existence of periodic solutions for neural type cellular neural networks with delays," Appl. Math. Model., vol. 36, pp. 1173–1183, 2012, ISSN: 0307-904X.

[11] J. W. Milnor, Topology from the Differentiable Viewpoint, Princeton Landmarks in Mathematics, Princeton University Press, 1997, ISBN-13: 978-0691048338, ISBN-10: 0691048339.

[12] M. Fan and K. Wang, "Periodic solutions of a discrete time nonautonomous ratio-dependent predator-prey system," Math. Comput. Model., vol. 35, pp. 951–961, 2002, ISSN: 0895-7177.

[13] R. Xu, L. Chen, and F. Hao, "Periodic solutions of discrete-time Lotka-Volterra type food-chain model with delays," Appl. Math. Comput., vol. 171, pp. 91–103, 2005, ISSN: 0096-3003 (print), 1873-5649 (online).

Derivation of Some Analytical Expressions in a Model of Overall Telecommunication System with Queue

Velin Andonov
Institute of Mathematics and Informatics
Bulgarian Academy of Sciences
Sofia, Bulgaria
Email: velin_andonov@math.bas.bg

Stoyan Poryazov
Institute of Mathematics and Informatics
Bulgarian Academy of Sciences
Sofia, Bulgaria
Email: stoyan@math.bas.bg

Emiliya Saranova
Institute of Mathematics and Informatics
Bulgarian Academy of Sciences
Sofia, Bulgaria
Email: emiliya@math.bas.bg

***Abstract*—In this paper, we consider a conceptual model in which, for the first time, a queuing system is included in an overall telecommunication system including users' behavior. On the basis of this model, analytical expressions for some of the important parameters of the model are derived. The results obtained allow definitions of new overall performance indicators of human-cyber-physical-systems, including interaction among human users, telecommunication network (including its protocols and management rules) and the nature-socio-economic environment.**

Keywords–Network performance modeling; Overall telecommunication system; Queuing systems; Conceptual modeling; Human-computer interaction.

I. INTRODUCTION

The classical model of overall telecommunication system is described in [1] and developed in more detail in [2]. It considers users' behavior, finite number of homogenous users and terminals, losses due to abandoned and interrupted dialing, blocked and interrupted switching, unavailable intent terminal, blocked and abandoned ringing and abandoned communication. The traffic of the calling (denoted by A) and the called (denoted by B) terminals and user's traffic are considered separately, but in their interrelation.

At the bottom of the structural model presentation, we consider base virtual devices that do not contain any other virtual devices.

The parameters of a base virtual device named x are the following (see [3] for terms definitions): Fx - intensity or incoming rate (frequency) of the flow of requests (i.e., the number of requests per time unit) to device x; Px - probability of directing the requests towards device x; Tx - service time (duration of servicing of a request) in device x; Yx - traffic intensity [Erlang]; Vx - traffic volume [Erlang - time unit]; Nx - number of lines (service resources, positions, capacity) of device x.

We consider an extension of the classical model of overall telecommunication system in which a queuing system is included in the switching stage. It is proposed and described in detail in [4]. The graphical representation of the model is shown in Figure 1. Two types of virtual devices are included in the model: base and comprising base devices. The graphic representations of the base virtual devices together with their names and types are also shown in Figure 1 (see [2]). Each base virtual device belongs to one of the following types: Generator, Terminator, Modifier, Server, Enter Switch, Switch, Queue and Graphic connector.

The names of the virtual devices are concatenations of the first letters of the branch exit, branch and stage, in that order (see Figure 1). For example, **ad** stands for the virtual device "abandoned dialling" while **rad** – for "repeated abandoned dialling".

For better understanding of the model and for a more convenient description of the intensity of the flow, a special notation including qualifiers (see [3]) is used. For example, $dem.F$ stands for demand flow; $inc.Y$ for incoming traffic; $ofr.Y$ for offered traffic; $rep.Y$ for repeated traffic.

The following comprising virtual devices denoted by **a, b, s** and **ab** are considered in the model.

- **a** comprises all calling terminals (A-terminals) in the system. It is not shown in Figure 1, but includes the four shown stages: dialing, switching, ringing and communication;
- **b** comprises all called terminals (B-terminals) in the system. It is shown in a bold line box in Figure 1;
- **ab** comprises all the terminals (calling and called) in the system. It is not shown in Figure 1;
- **s** virtual device corresponding to the switching system.

In our model, the queuing system in the switching stage of the telecommunication network in Kendall's notation (see [5]) is represented as $M|M|Ns|Ns + Nq|Nab|FIFO$, where M stands for exponential distribution, Ns is the capacity of the Switching system (number of equivalent internal switching lines), Nq is the buffer length and Nab is the total number of active terminals which can be calling and called. This is related to the derivation of the analytical model of the system.

The queuing system in the model differs from other well known and studied queuing systems [6]–[8] in that: it has more than one exit to the server; the duration of service of the requests in the server depends on the overall state of the telecommunication system; there is a feedback in terms of call attempts.

II. MAIN ASSUMPTIONS AND PREVIOUS RESULTS

We consider the conceptual model of overall telecommunication system with queue shown in Figure 1 and described briefly in the previous section. Parameters with known values

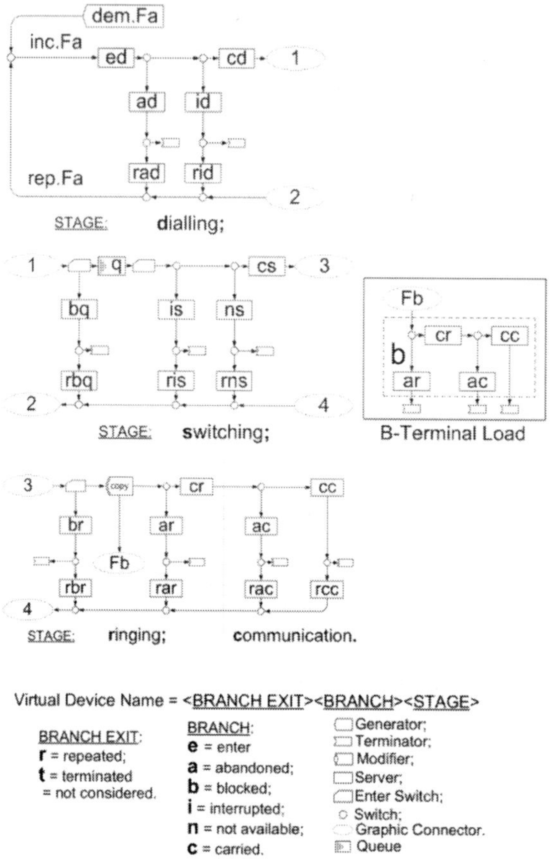

Figure 1. Conceptual model of an overall telecommunication system with a queue in the switching stage.

are all probabilites for directing the call to a device (the P–parameters), the holding time parameters of the base virtual devices (T – parameters) and the values of the intensity of the incoming calls flow – $inc.Fa = Fa$. The unknown parameters are the parameters of the comprising virtual devices except Fa and Nab.

To obtain simple analytical expressions in the process of solving different teletraffic tasks, as in [1], we need to state the following assumptions:

1) We consider a closed telecommunication system which is represented graphically and functionally in Figure 1.
2) All base virtual devices except the Queue device have unlimited capacity. The Queue has capacity Nq, which is the buffer size. The comprising virtual devices have limited capacity: the **ab** device contains all active terminals $Nab \in [2, \infty)$. The switching system (**s**) has capacity Ns. One internal switching line can carry only one call for both incoming and outgoing calls.
3) Every call from the incoming flow to the system ($inc.Fa$) occupies only a free terminal which becomes a busy A-terminal.
4) The system is in a stationary state and the Little's theorem [5] can be applied for every device.
5) Every call occupies one place in a base virtual device independently from the other devices.
6) Any calls in the telecommunication network's environment (outside the **a** and **b** devices) do not occupy any of the telecommunication system's devices.
7) The probabilities of directing the calls to the base virtual devices and the holding time in the devices are independent of each other and of the intensity of the incoming flows $inc.Fa$. Their values are determined by the users' behavior and the technical characteristics of the telecommunication system. Exception to this assumption are the devices of type Enter Switch corresponding to Pbq and Pbs, and Pbr (see Figure 1).
8) For the base virtual devices **ar, cr, ac** and **cc**, the probabilities of directing the calls to them and the duration of occupation of the device are the same for the **a** and the **b** comprise virtual devices.
9) The variables in the model are random with fixed distributions. The Little's theorem allows us to use their mean values.
10) Every call occupies simultaneously all base virtual devices through which it has passed, including the device where it is at the current moment of observation. When a call leaves the comprising devices **a** or **b**, the places occupied by it in all base virtual devices are released.

The following propositions proved for the classical conceptual model of overall telecommunication system in [1] can be used without proof due to analogy. They obviously hold for the conceptual model of overall telecommunication network with queue, considered in the present paper.

Proposition 1: The traffic intensity of all terminals (Yab) is a sum of the traffic intensities of the calling terminals (Ya) and the called terminals (Yb):

$$Yab = Ya + Yb\,. \tag{1}$$

Proposition 2: (Total terminal traffic (Yab) is restricted)

$$0 \leq Yab \leq Nab\,, \tag{2}$$

and here Nab is the total number of all active terminals.

Proposition 3: The calls flow intensity occupying all A and B terminals (Fab) is a sum of the intensities of the calls flow occupying the A-terminals (Fa) and the B-terminals (Fb):

$$Fab = Fa + Fb\,. \tag{3}$$

The Little's formula for the comprised virtual devices **a** and **b** gives dependences for the intensities of the calling (Ya) and called (Yb):

Proposition 4:

$$Ya = Fa Ta\,. \tag{4}$$

Proposition 5:

$$Yb = Fb Tb\,. \tag{5}$$

In [4], with the help of the above assumptions, analytical expressions for the parameters of the queuing system – expected length of the queue (Yq), mean time of service in the q device (Tq) and the probability of blocked queuing (Pbq) are derived. Here, we present them without proof, but using a more appropriate notation.

Proposition 6:

$$Yq = \frac{p_0 r^{Ns} \rho}{Ns!(1-\rho)^2}[(\rho-1)\rho^{Nq}(Nq+1)+1-\rho^{Nq+1}]\,. \tag{6}$$

Proposition 7:

$$Tq = \frac{p_0 r^{Ns} \rho}{Ns!(1-\rho)^2}\frac{[(\rho-1)\rho^{Nq}(Nq+1)+1-\rho^{Nq+1}]}{\lambda(1-Pbq)}\,. \tag{7}$$

Proposition 8:

$$Pbq = \frac{\lambda^{Ns+Nq}}{Ns^{Nq} Ns! \mu^{Ns+Nq}} p_0\,. \tag{8}$$

In the above three propositions, we have used the following notation:

$$p_0^{-1} = \begin{cases} \sum_{n=0}^{Ns-1} \frac{r^n}{n!} + \frac{r^{Ns}}{Ns!}\frac{1-\rho^{Nq+1}}{1-\rho} & \text{for } \rho \neq 1\,. \\ \sum_{n=0}^{Ns-1} \frac{r^n}{n!} + \frac{r^{Ns}}{Ns!}(Nq+1) & \text{for } \rho = 1\,, \end{cases} \tag{9}$$

$$\frac{1}{\mu} = Ys\left[\frac{Yis+Yns+Ycs}{Fis+Fns+Fcs} + \frac{Ybr+Yar+Ycc+Yac}{Fbr+Far+Fac+Fcc}\right],$$

$$\lambda = ofr.Fq\,, r = \frac{\lambda}{\mu}\,, \rho = \frac{r}{Ns}\,.$$

III. Derivation of Analytical Expressions for Some of the Parameters of Overall Telecommunication System with Queue

Here, we demonstrate how the conceptual model shown in Figure 1 can be used for derivation of analytical expressions for some of the parameters of the model. In particular, we shall derive expressions for the mean intensity of the **B**-terminals (Fb), the mean service time of the **A**-terminals (Ta) and the intensity of the repeated flow of the **A**-terminals ($rep.Fa$).

Theorem 1:

$$Fb = Fa(1-Pad)(1-Pid)(1-Pbq)(1-Pis)(1-Pns) \cdot(1-Pbr)\,. \tag{10}$$

Proof: Before occupying the intent **B**-terminals with mean intensity Fb, the **a**-calls have to avoid all six types of losses considered in the model in Figure 1 with probability 1 minus the corresponding probabilities for directing the calls to each of the devices **ad, id, bq, is, ns, br**. These probabilities are multiplied since we have independent events. Here, we use assumptions 1, 5, 6, 7, 8 and 9. ■

Theorem 2:

$$Ta = Ted + Pad Tad + (1-Pad)[Pid Tid + (1-Pid)[Tcd + Pbq Tbq + (1-Pbq)[Tq + Pis Tis + (1-Pis)[Pns Tns + (1-Pns)[Tcs + Pbr Tbr + (1-Pbr)Tb]]]]]\,. \tag{11}$$

Proof: From the conceptual model on Figure 1, the parameters' independence (Assumption 7) and the virtual channel switching (Assumption 10), we have that Ya is a sum of the traffics of all base virtual devices included in the comprising **a** device.

$$Ya = Yed + Yad + Ycd + Yid + Ybq + Yq + Yis + Ycs + Yns + Ybr + Yar + Ycr + Yac + Ycc\,. \tag{12}$$

Using Little's formula, we can express the traffic intensities in the following way:

$$Yed = Fa Ted\,, \tag{13}$$

$$Yad = Fad Tad = Fa\, Pad Tad\,, \tag{14}$$

$$Yid = Fid Tid = Fa(1-Pad) Pid Tid\,, \tag{15}$$

$$Ycd = Fcd Tcd = Fa(1-Pad)(1-Pid) Tcd\,, \tag{16}$$

$$Ybq = Fbq Tbq = Fa(1-Pad)(1-Pid) Pbq Tbq\,, \tag{17}$$

$$Yq = Fq Tq = Fa(1-Pad)(1-Pid)(1-Pbq) Tq\,, \tag{18}$$

$$Yis = Fis Tis = Fa(1-Pad)(1-Pid)(1-Pbq) Pis Tis\,, \tag{19}$$

$$Yns = Fns Tns = Fa(1-Pad)(1-Pid)(1-Pbq)$$

$$\cdot(1-Pis)Pns\,Tns\,, \tag{20}$$

$$Ycs = Fcs\,Tcs = Fa(1-Pad)(1-Pid)(1-Pbq) \cdot(1-Pis)(1-Pns)Tcs\,, \tag{21}$$

$$Ybr = Fbr\,Tbr = Fa(1-Pad)(1-Pid)(1-Pbq) \cdot(1-Pis)(1-Pns)Pbr\,Tbr\,. \tag{22}$$

From Assumption 8, we have that Yar, Ycr, Yac, and Ycc are the same for the **A** and **B** terminals. Therefore, using Theorem 1, we obtain

$$Yb = Yar + Ycr + Yac + Ycc = Fa(1-Pad)(1-Pid) \cdot(1-Pbq)(1-Pis)(1-Pns)(1-Pbr)Tb\,. \tag{23}$$

After substitution of (13)-(23) in (12) and using (4) we obtain (11). ■

Theorem 3:

$$\begin{aligned} rep.Fa = Fa\{&Pad\,Prad + (1-Pad)[Pid\,Prid + (1-Pid) \\ &\cdot[Pbq\,Prbq + (1-Pbq)[Pis\,Pris + (1-Pis) \\ &\cdot[Pns\,Prns + (1-Pns)[Pbr\,Prbr + (1-Pbr) \\ &\cdot[Par\,Prar + (1-Par)[Pac\,Prac+ \\ &+(1-Pac)Prcc]]]]]]]\}\,. \end{aligned} \tag{24}$$

Proof: Using Figure 1 and Assumption 1, $rep.Fa$ can be expressed as a sum of intensities of repeated attempts flows in all branches:

$$rep.Fa = Frad + Frid + Frbq + Fris + Frns + Frbr + Frar + Frac + Frcc\,. \tag{25}$$

Using the graphical representation in Figure 1, the intensities of the reapeated attempts flows in all branches can be expressed as a function of Fa in the following ways:

$$Frad = Fa\,Pad\,Prad\,, \tag{26}$$

$$Frid = Fa(1-Pad)Pid\,Prid\,, \tag{27}$$

$$Frbq = Fa(1-Pad)(1-Pid)Pbq\,Prbq\,, \tag{28}$$

$$Fris = Fa(1-Pad)(1-Pid)(1-Pbq)Pis\,Pris\,, \tag{29}$$

$$Frns = Fa(1-Pad)(1-Pid)(1-Pbq)(1-Pis) \cdot Pns\,Prns\,, \tag{30}$$

$$Frbr = Fa(1-Pad)(1-Pid)(1-Pbq)(1-Pis) \cdot(1-Pns)Pbr\,Prbr\,, \tag{31}$$

$$Frar = Fa(1-Pad)(1-Pid)(1-Pbq)(1-Pis) \cdot(1-Pns)(1-Pbr)\,Par\,Prar\,, \tag{32}$$

$$Frac = Fa(1-Pad)(1-Pid)(1-Pbq)(1-Pis) \cdot(1-Pns)(1-Pbr)(1-Par)Pac\,Prac\,, \tag{33}$$

$$Frcc = Fa(1-Pad)(1-Pid)(1-Pbq)(1-Pis)(1-Pns) \cdot(1-Pbr)(1-Par)(1-Pac)Prcc\,. \tag{34}$$

Adding equations (26)-(34) and performing elementary operations, we obtain the right-hand side of (24). This completes the proof. ■

Using Theorem 3, we can determine the intensity of the input flow to the telecommunication system ($Fa = inc.Fa$). From the graphical representation of the system shown in Figure 1, we have that the intensity of the incoming flow can be represented as a sum of the intensities of the demand calls ($dem.Fa$) and the repeated attempts ($rep.Fa$):

$$Fa = dem.Fa + rep.Fa\,. \tag{35}$$

As in the classical model of overall telecommunication system [1], we use the following equation for the intensity of the demand calls:

$$dem.Fa = Fo(Nab + M\,Yab)\,, \tag{36}$$

where Fo is the intensity of the input flow from one idle terminal, Nab is the number of active terminals and M is a parameter characterizing Bernoulli-Poisson-Pascal (BPP) flow of demand calls [1]. When $M = -1$, demand flow corresponds to Bernoulli (Engset) distribution. When $M = 0$ – to Poisson (Erlang) and when $M = 1$ – to Pascal (Negative binomial) distribution. In general, M can take every value in the interval $[-1, 1]$.

The following classification of the parameters is proposed in [4]:

- Static parameters: $M, Nab, Ns, Ted, Pad, Tad, Prad, Pid, Tid, Prid, Ted, Pis, Tis, Pris, Pns, Tns, Tes, Prns, Tbr, Prbr, Par, Tar, Prar, Tcr, Pac, Tac, Prac, Tcc, Prcc, Nq, Tbq, Trbq, Prbq$. Their values are considered independent of the system state Yab (see [9]) but may depend on other factors. For the model time interval, they are considered constants.
- Dynamic parameters: $Fo, Yab, Fa, dem.Fa, rep.Fa, Pbs, Pbr, ofr.Fq, crr.Fs, Tq, Pbq$. Their values are mutually dependent.

Using this classification, we can express $rep.Fa$ as a function of the dynamic parameters Fa, Pbr and Pbq.

Theorem 4: The intensity of the calls of repeated attempts $rep.Fa$ can be determined by

$$rep.Fa = Fa[R_1 + R_2(1-Pbq)Pbr + R_3Pbq]\,, \tag{37}$$

where

$$R_1 = PadPrad + (1 - Pad)[PidPrid + (1 - Pid)[PisPris + (1 - Pis)[PnsPrns + (1 - Pns)[ParPrar + (1 - Par)[PacPrac + (1 - Pac)Prcc]]]]] , \quad (38)$$

$$R_2 = (1 - Pad)(1 - Pid)(1 - Pis)(1 - Pns)[Prbr - ParPrar - (1 - Par)[PacPrac + (1 - Pac)Prcc]] , \quad (39)$$

$$R_3 = (1 - Pad)(1 - Pid)[Prbq - [PisPris + (1 - Pis)[PnsPrns + (1 - Pns)[ParPrar + (1 - Par)[PacPrac + (1 - Pac)Prcc]]]]] . \quad (40)$$

Proof: Adding equations (26)-(34), taking into account (25) and separating static from dynamic parameters, we obtain

$$rep.Fa = Fa\{PadPrad + (1 - Pad)[PidPrid + (1 - Pid)[PisPris + (1 - Pis)[PnsPrns + (1 - Pns) \cdot [ParPrar + (1 - Par)[PacPrac + (1 - Pac)Prcc]]]]] + (1 - Pbq)Pbr(1 - Pad)(1 - Pid)(1 - Pis)(1 - Pns)[Prbr - ParPrar - (1 - Par)[PacPrac + (1 - Pac)Prcc]] + Pbq(1 - Pad)(1 - Pid)[Prbq - [PisPris + (1 - Pis)[PnsPrns + (1 - Pns)[ParPrar + (1 - Par)[PacPrac + (1 - Pac)Prcc]]]]]\} . \quad (41)$$

Now, we denote the expression in (41) which does not contain dynamic parameters by R_1, the coefficient of $(1 - Pbq)Pbr$ by R_2 and the coefficient of Pbq by R_3 and we obtain (37). This proves the theorem. ■

Similarly, after separating static from dynamic parameters in (11) and using the Little's formula for the A-terminals' traffic intensity (Ya), we obtain the following representation:

Theorem 5:

$$Ya = Fa[Sa_1 + Sa_2(1 - Pbq)Tq + Sa_3(1 - Pbq)Pbr + Sa_4Pbq] , \quad (42)$$

where

$$Sa_1 = Ted + PadTad + (1 - Pad)[PidTid + (1 - Pid)[Tcd + PisTis + (1 - Pis)[PnsTns + (1 - Pns)[Tcs + Tb]]]] , \quad (43)$$

$$Sa_2 = (1 - Pad)(1 - Pid) , \quad (44)$$

$$Sa_3 = (1 - Pad)(1 - Pid)(1 - Pis)(1 - Pns)(Tbr - Tb) . \quad (45)$$

$$Sa_4 = (1 - Pad)(1 - Pid)[Tbq - PisTis - (1 - Pis)[PnsTns + (1 - Pns)[Tcs + Tb]]] . \quad (46)$$

Proof: We denote by Sa_1 the sum of all expressions in (11) that do not include dynamic parameters:

$$Sa_1 = Ted + PadTad + (1 - Pad)[PidTid + (1 - Pid)[Tcd + PisTis + (1 - Pis)[PnsTns + (1 - Pns)[Tcs + Tb]]]] . \quad (47)$$

We denote by Sa_2 the coefficient of $(1 - Pbq)Tq$ in (11):

$$Sa_2 = (1 - Pad)(1 - Pid) . \quad (48)$$

We denote by Sa_3 the coefficient of the expression $(1 - Pbq)Pbr$ in (11) :

$$Sa_3 = (1 - Pad)(1 - Pid)(1 - Pis)(1 - Pns)(Tbr - Tb) . \quad (49)$$

We denote by Sa_4 the coefficient of Pbq in (11):

$$Sa_4 = (1 - Pad)(1 - Pid)[Tbq - PisTis - (1 - Pis)[PnsTns + (1 - Pns)[Tcs + Tb]]] . \quad (50)$$

In this way, for Ta we obtain the representation:

$$Ta = Sa_1 + Sa_2(1 - Pbq)Tq + Sa_3(1 - Pbq)Pbr + Sa_4Pbq . \quad (51)$$

After substitution of (51) in (4), we confirm the validity of (42). ■

Theorem 6: The traffic of all simultaneously busy terminals Yab as a function of Fa and other parameters is given by

$$Yab = Fa[S_1 + S_2(1 - Pbq)Tq + S_3(1 - Pbq)Pbr + S_4Pbq] , \quad (52)$$

where

$$S_1 = Ted + PadTad + (1 - Pad)[PidTid + (1 - Pid)[Tcd + PisTis + (1 - Pis)[PnsTns + (1 - Pns)[Tcs + 2Tb]]]] , \quad (53)$$

$$S_2 = (1 - Pad)(1 - Pid) , \quad (54)$$

$$S_3 = (1 - Pad)(1 - Pid)(1 - Pis)(1 - Pns)(Tbr - 2Tb) , \quad (55)$$

$$S_4 = (1 - Pad)(1 - Pid)[Tbq - PisTis - (1 - Pis)[Pns + (1 - Pns)[Tcs + 2Tb]]] . \quad (56)$$

Proof: From (1), (4), (5) and Theorem 1 we have

$$Yab = Ya + Yb = FaTa + FbTb = Fa\{Ta + (1 - Pad)(1 - Pid)(1 - Pbq)(1 - Pis)(1 - Pns)(1 - Pbr)Tb\} . \quad (57)$$

After substitution of Ta in the above equation with its equal expression from (51), we obtain:

$$Yab = Fa\{Sa_1 + Sa_2(1 - Pbq)Pbr + Sa_3(1 - Pbq)Pbr + Sa_4Pbq - (1 - Pad)(1 - Pid)(1 - Pis)(1 - Pns) \cdot (1 - Pbq)PbrTb + (1 - Pad)(1 - Pid)(1 - Pis) \cdot (1 - Pns)(1 - Pbq)Tb\} . \quad (58)$$

In the above expression, we denote by S_1 the part which does not contain T_q, Pbq and Pbr:

$$S_1 = Sa_1 + (1 - Pad)(1 - Pid)(1 - Pis)(1 - Pns)Tb =$$
$$Ted + PadTad + (1 - Pad)[PidTid + (1 - Pid)[Tcd + PisTis$$
$$+(1 - Pis)[PnsTns + (1 - Pns)[Tcs + 2Tb]]]] . \quad (59)$$

By S_2 we denote the coefficient of $(1 - Pbq)Tq$ and it is equal to Sa_2:

$$S_2 = Sa_2 = (1 - Pad)(1 - Pid) . \quad (60)$$

By S_3 we denote the coefficient of $(1 - Pbq)Pbr$:

$$S_3 = Sa_3 - (1 - Pad)(1 - Pid)(1 - Pis)(1 - Pns)Tb$$
$$= (1 - Pad)(1 - Pid)(1 - Pis)(1 - Pns)(Tbr - 2Tb) . \quad (61)$$

Finally,we denote the coefficient of Pbq in (58) by S_4:

$$S_4 = Sa_4 - (1 - Pad)(1 - Pid)(1 - Pis)(1 - Pns)Tb =$$
$$(1 - Pad)(1 - Pid)[Tbq - PisTis - (1 - Pis)[PnsTns$$
$$+(1 - Pns)[Tcs + 2Tb]]] . \quad (62)$$

This proves Theorem 6. ∎

Now, we can express Fa as a function of the intensity of the input flow of one idle terminal (Fo), Pbr, Pbq and Tq.

Theorem 7:

$$Fa[1 - Fo\,M[S_1 + S_2(1 - Pbq)Tq + S_3(1 - Pbq)Pbr$$
$$+S_4 Pbq] - R_1 - R_2(1 - Pbq)Pbr - R_3] = Fo\,Nab . \quad (63)$$

Proof: From (35) and (36), we have

$$Fa = Fo\,Nab + Fo\,M\,Yab + rep.Fa . \quad (64)$$

After substitution of Yab and $rep.Fa$ with their equal expressions from (52) and (37), respectively, and regrouping we obtain (63). ∎

IV. Conlusions and Future Work

The analytical expressions derived here are the first step towards the construction of a complete analytical model of the overall telecommunication system with queue. The analytical model can be used for solving different teletraffic tasks such as Quality of Service (QoS) prediction task, technical characteristics task (e.g., network dimensioning / re-dimensioning for guaranteeing the target QoS), human behavior task (investigate possible effects of users' behavior and prepare recommendations and administrative limitations, e.g., of the maximal duration of ringing and busy tone), etc. For the purpose of constructing an analytical model that is easier to work with, in the expression for Ta derived here, the static and dynamic parameters are separated. The presented results allow definitions of new overall telecommunication system performance indicators, including human users' characteristics, following the approach described in [10]. A problem will be the numerical solution of the derived system of equations, because it is non-linear due to comprising Erlang-type queuing blocking formula. The current investigations confirm our belief in a successful numerical solution of the system, using the methods discussed in [1] and [11].

Acknowledgment

The work of Velin Andonov was partially funded by the Bulgarian NSF under grant DM 12/2 – "New Models of Overall Telecommunication Networks with Quality of Service Guarantees".

The work of Emiliya Saranova was supported by the National Scientific Program "Information and Communication Technologies for a Single Digital Market in Science, Education and Security (ICT in SES)" financed by the Bulgarian Ministry of Education and Science.

References

[1] S. Poryazov and E. Saranova, "Some general terminal and network teletraffic equations for virtual circuit switching systems," in Modeling and Simulation Tools for Emerging Telecommunication Networks, N. I. A. and T. E., Eds. Boston, MA: Springer, 2006, pp. 471–505.

[2] ——, Models of Telecommunication Networks with Virtual Channel Switching and Applications. Sofia, Bulgaria: Academic Publishing House "Prof. M. Drinov", 2012.

[3] ITU-T Recommendation E.600: Terms and Definitions of Traffic Engineering, Helsinki, 1993.

[4] V. Andonov, S. Poryazov, A. Otsetova, and E. Saranova, "A queue in overall telecommunication system with quality of service guarantees," in Proc. of the 4th EAI International Conference on Future Access Enablers of Ubiquitous and Intelligent Infrastructures - FABULOUS 2019, Sofia, Bulgaria, March 2019 (in press).

[5] B. R. Haverkort, Performance of Computer Communication Systems: A Model-Based Approach. New York, NY, USA: John Wiley & Sons, 1998.

[6] M. Schneps-Schneppe, Systems for Distribution of Information. Moscow, USSR: Svyaz Publishing House, 1979, (in Russian).

[7] L. Lakatos, L. Szeidl, and M. Telek, Introduction to Queueing Systems with Telecommunication Applications. New York, NY: Springer, 2013.

[8] A. Alfa, Queueing Theory for Telecommunications. Discrete Time Modelling of a Single Node System. New York, NY: Springer US, 2010.

[9] S. Poryazov, I. Ganchev, and E. Saranova, "Conceptual and analytical models for predicting the quality of service of overall telecommunication systems," in Autonomous Control for a Reliable Internet of Services, ser. Lecture Notes in Computer Science, v. d. B. H. Ganchev I., van der Mei R., Ed. Cham: Springer, 2018, vol. 10768, pp. 471–505.

[10] ——, "Scalable traffic quality and system efficiency indicators towards overall telecommunication system's qoe management," in Autonomous Control for a Reliable Internet of Services, ser. Lecture Notes in Computer Science, v. d. B. H. Ganchev I., van der Mei R., Ed. Cham: Springer, 2018, vol. 10768, pp. 81–103.

[11] S. Poryazov, E. Saranova, and M. Spiridonova, "Modeling of telecommunication processes in an overall complex system," Physics of Particles and Nuclei Letters, vol. 12, no. 3, May 2015, pp. 416–419.

A Knowledge-centric Computation Architecture and the Case of Knowledge Mining

Claus-Peter Rückemann
Westfälische Wilhelms-Universität Münster (WWU), Germany;
Knowledge in Motion, DIMF, Germany;
Leibniz Universität Hannover, Germany
Email: ruckema@uni-muenster.de

***Abstract*—This paper presents a new architecture framework, which is the research result of a series of practical problem solving implementations and further developments of the common knowledge base and integrated application components. The framework is considered knowledge-centric, based on the fundamental knowledge resources, which constitute the fundamental base and imply the core of key assets. Besides the further knowledge development, the knowledge-centric architecture flexibly allows implementations of computation components for many scenarios and the employment of available computation infrastructures. An important quality of the architecture framework is the intrinsic value to assign different roles for the professional tasks in creation and development cycles. These roles regards the major complements of knowledge, including factual, conceptual, and procedural components as well as documentation. This paper refers to a base excerpt of previous implementations and illustrates the framework for an advanced implementation case of knowledge mining. The main goal of this research is to outline the new knowledge-centric architecture and to provide a base for further long-term multi-disciplinary implementations and realisations.**

Keywords–Knowledge Mining and Mapping; Computation Architecture; Context Creation; Universal Decimal Classification; Knowledge-centric Computing.

I. INTRODUCTION

All implementations of mathematical machines, which we call 'computer systems' today, can strictly only deal with formal systems. Knowledge is a capability of a living organism and can itself not be incorporated by formal systems. Neither can intrinsic meaning, which is an essential characteristics of real knowledge and a unique stronghold of knowledge be a matter of formal systems nor can mathematical relations, the theory of sets, exlusiveness or creating completeness be applied to knowledge.

Solutions requiring a wide range of knowledge content as well as implementations of algorithms and components are often difficult to handle, the more when it comes to operating the resulting solutions for decades or even further developing content and implementations for long-term. Over time, the further developments and services are becoming more complicated without a common, holistic frame for content and implementation. When gathering a large number of independent implementations, we experienced an increasing heterogeneity in content development but also in implementations of computing components.

This background is the major motivation for the development of an advanced framework based on long-term Knowledge Resources and integrated application components providing a valuable means of tackling the challenges. Nevertheless, in complex cases even such major component groups cannot protect long-term challenges, if there is no basic framework architecture caring for knowledge and computational implementation. The practice of creating solutions, which have to deal with the complements of knowledge suggests that flexible but nevertheless methodological, systematical approaches are required. The goal of this research is to create such knowledge-centric architecture, based on a wide range of multi-disciplinary implementations and practical case studies in different disciplines and dealing with different foci, for many years. While further developing and updating the knowledge related attributes, data, implementations, and solutions, all of them had to be revisited over time, improving and where necessary recreating implementation and content.

Knowledge Resources and originary resources cover the complements of factual, conceptual, procedural, and metacognitive complements, e.g., from collections and references resources. The architecture presented here aims to seamlessly integrating separate roles of contributing parties, e.g., scientific staff creating research data, professional classification by experienced research library specialists, and developers of application components as well as services. The guideline was enabling to retain the knowledge required to resemble the intrinsic complexity of realia situations, real and material instead of abstract situations, while allowing lex parsimoniae principles of William of Ockham for problem solving. The overall outcome gained from the development of practical solutions led to the creation of a knowledge-centric architecture, which essentials are presented in the following sections.

This paper is organised as follows. Section II introduces to fundaments and previous work, Section III presents the architecture being result of this research. Sections IV and V deliver an implementation case of two major use-cases, including a discussion. Section VI summarises the results and lessons learned, conclusions, and future work.

II. FUNDAMENTS AND PREVIOUS WORK

With one of the best and most solid works, Aristotle outlined the fundaments of terminology and of understanding knowledge [1] being an essential part of 'Ethics' [2]. Information sciences can very much benefit from Aristotle's fundaments and a knowledge-centric approach, e.g., by Anderson and Krathwohl [3], but for building holistic and sustainable solutions they need to go beyond the available technology-based approaches and hypothesis [4] as analysed in Platons' Phaidon. So far, there is no other practical advanced knowledge-centric architectural specification known, which implements these fundaments. Making a distinction and creating interfaces between methods and applications [5], the principles are based on the methodology of knowledge mapping [6]. The implementation can make use of objects and conceptual knowledge [7] and shows being able to build a base for applications scenarios like associative processing [8] and advanced knowledge discovery [9]. Based on this background, during the last decades, a number of different case solutions were created, implemented, and realised on this fundament, including: Dynamical visualisation, knowledge mining, knowledge mapping, Content Factor, phonetic algorithms, Geoscientific Information Systems (GIS), Environmental Information Systems (EIS), cartographic mapping, service design, service management, and High End Computation. All such implementations include extensive use of Knowledge Resources and computation algorithms. This paper, presenting the new architecture, does not allow to illustrate the details of any implementation. Therefore, an excerpt of practical solutions is cited, which have been reimplemented by the collaboration of the participated research groups and published, creating a base for this architecture. Representative examples are a) integrated systems and supercomputing resources used with phonetic algorithms and pattern matching [10] for knowledge mining [11], b) multi-dimensional context creation based on the methodology of Knowledge Mapping [12], and c) an exemplary resulting, widely used conceptual knowledge subset for geo-spatial scenarios [13]. The Knowledge Resources cover the factual, conceptual, procedural, and metacognitive complements in all cases, e.g., from collections and references resources.

An understanding of the essence and complexity of universal, multi-disciplinary knowledge can be achieved by taking a closer look on classification. The state-of-the-art of classifying 'universal knowledge' is the Universal Decimal Classification (UDC) [14] and its solid background, flexibility, and long history. The LX Knowledge Resources' structure and the classification references [15] based on UDC [16] are essential means for the processing workflows and evaluation. Both provide strong multi-disciplinary and multi-lingual support. For the research, all small unsorted excerpts of the Knowledge Resources objects only refer to main UDC-based classes, which for this publication are taken from the Multilingual Universal Decimal Classification Summary (UDCC Publication No. 088) [17] released by the UDC Consortium under the Creative Commons Attribution Share Alike 3.0 license [18] (first release 2009, subsequent update 2012). These components and their qualities are integrated in the resulting architecture with the methodologies and systematic use.

III. Resulting Knowledge-centric Architecture

As discussed above, the presented architecture is the result based on a series of previously implemented problem solutions and Knowledge Resources developments over the last years.

A. *General Computation Architecture*

The complements diagram of the implementation architecture [19][20][21] is shown in Figure 1. The major components

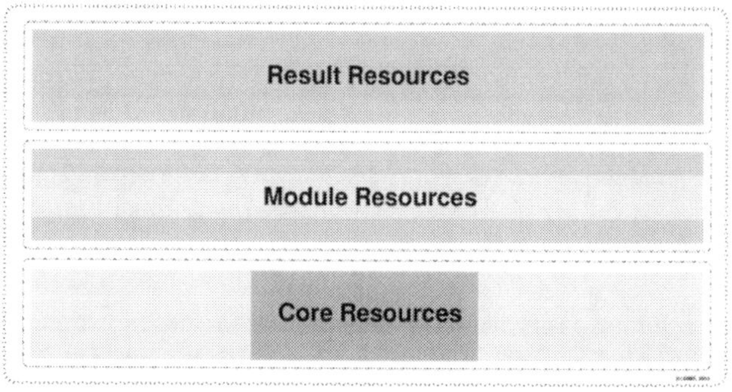

Figure 1. Complements diagram of the resources components architecture, including the three main complements of core, module, and result resources.

are core resources and module resources. The result resources include objects collections, which result from the application of core and module resources in arbitrary scenarios. The sizes of this figure and the associated complements diagrams correspond, the following figures show complementary details from this context. The core resources in this architecture comprise required resources. The complements diagram (Figure 2) shows the essential detail.

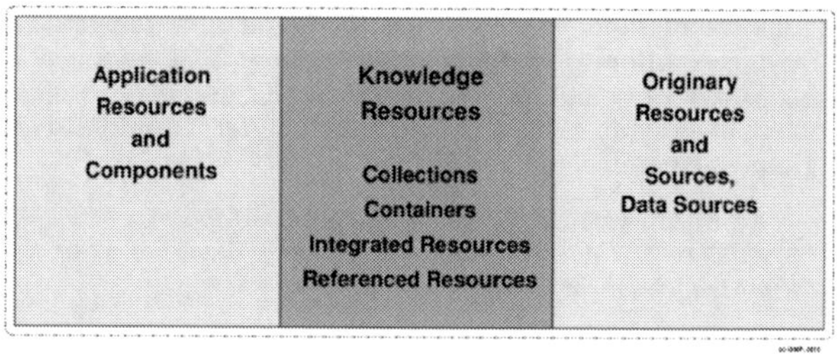

Figure 2. Computation architecture: Complements diagram of general core resources, from originary to knowledge and application resources.

The core resources can be divided into three categories: The central Knowledge Resources, originary resources, and application resources and components. The first, the Knowledge Resources, can include collections and containers as well as integrated resources and references to resources. The second, the originary resources, can include realia and original sources, which in many cases may have instances in the Knowledge Resources. The third, the application resources, can include implementations of algorithms, workflows, and procedures, which form applications and components. Instances of these components can also be employable in solutions due to their procedural nature, e.g., in module resources.

The complements diagram of general module resources is shown in Figure 3. A general set of module resources consists of input resources, modules, and output resources. The central workflow module entities are accompanied by interface module entities for input and output resources. For many architecture

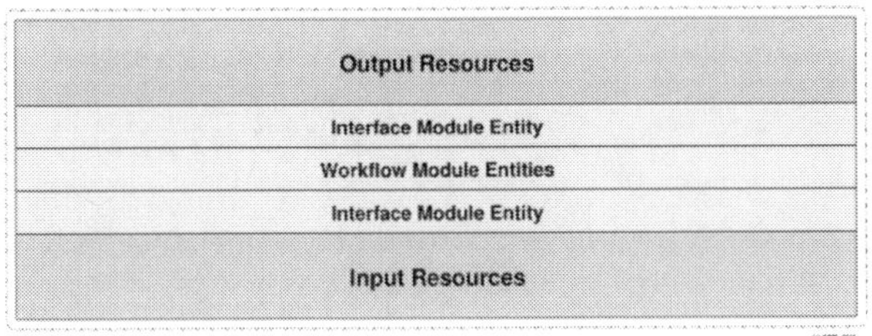

Figure 3. Computation architecture: Complements diagram of module resources, from input, interfaces and workflow entities to output.

implementations, chains of module resources can be created, which can, for example, be used in pipeline and in parallel.

B. Architecture Complements for Knowledge Mining

For the case of knowledge mining, the complements diagram of the core resources is shown in Figure 4. Application re-

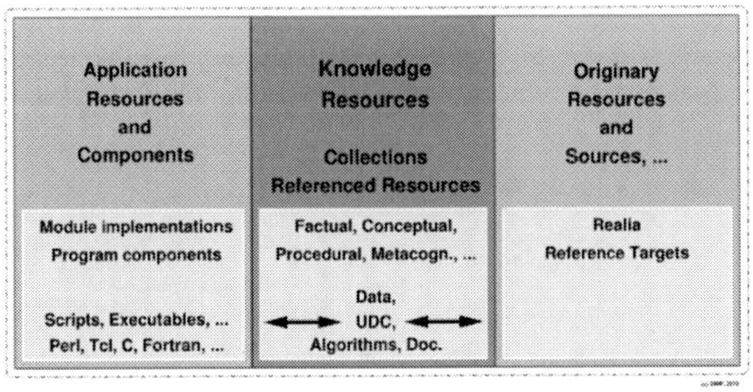

Figure 4. Knowledge Mining: Complements diagram of the core resources and examples of their contribution implementations.

sources and components are based on module implementations and program components for the knowledge mining realisation. Implementations employ scripting, high level languages, and third party components. Knowledge Resources and originary resources cover the complements of factual, conceptual, procedural, and metacognitive complements, e.g., from collections and references resources.

The respective complements diagram of a module resource for a text based knowledge mining implementation consists of several features (Figure 5). The input and output resources

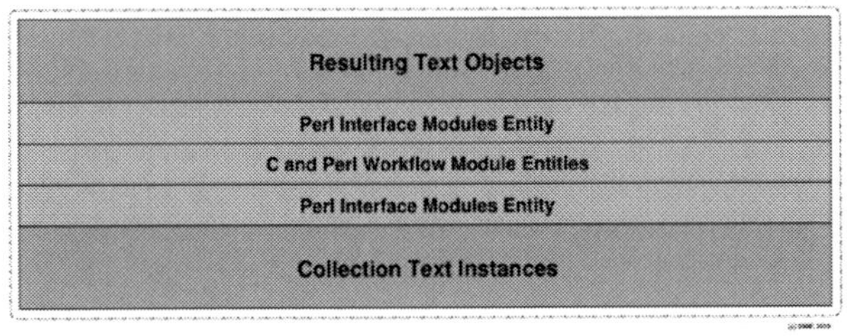

Figure 5. Knowledge Mining: Complements diagram of a module resource used for creating module chains for text based knowledge mining.

consist of text object instances in text based cases of knowledge mining. Here, the module entity implementations were implemented in C and Perl [22] for the respective implementations. The interface module entities are implemented in Perl, with the option to be on-the-fly generated within a workflow.

The knowledge-centric architecture does focus on resources and application scenarios, one of the most important is computation cases. Large computation workflow chains can be built with the architecture as was demonstrated with the reimplemented solutions for different cases, which were above referred to. An implementation sequence of module resources can be considered an intermediate step in building a workflow. Results within an implementation sequence can be considered intermediate results and instances, e.g., from the integrated mining of collection and container resources.

IV. Implementation Case and Discussion

The goal was to create a knowledge-centric computation architecture, which allows a close integration of Knowledge Resources with wide spectra of complementary knowledge and flexible, efficient computational solutions, while being able to specify practically required roles for creation and long-term development. The knowledge-centric architecture can provide a base for an arbitrary range of use-cases and associated components. Two major groups of use-cases are

- resources creation and development and
- knowledge mining and selected associated methods.

A. Major use-case groups

Figure 6 shows an use-case diagram of the knowledge-centric computation architecture. The excerpt illustrates an

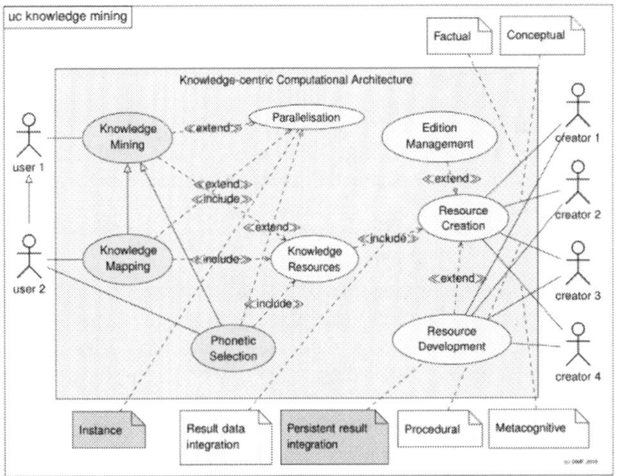

Figure 6. Use-case diagram of the knowledge-centric computation architecture: Two major use-case groups with four creator roles.

integrated view on the two groups of knowledge mining (blueish), which was implemented spanning knowledge mining use-cases and knowledge creation and development use-cases (greenish). In this widely deployed scenario, the implementation does have two main types of actors, namely creators and users. The use-cases have different actors, two 'user' roles and four 'creator' roles.

The selected system context is given by the grey box. The selected use-cases (ellipses) can be distinguished in use-cases for creators (greenish: resource creation, resource development, edition management, parallelisation) and use-cases for users (bluish: knowledge mining, knowledge mapping, phonetic selection).

Knowledge mining is supported by and using the cases of knowledge mapping and phonetic selection, which inherit to the knowledge mining instance the implemented methods and algorithms contributed by other user groups. For clearness, the creator and other roles for these two cases are not included in this diagram. Knowledge mining, mapping, and phonetic selection include the use-case of Knowledge Resources. The cases of this group are extended by parallelisation, respective computation, here instance based workflow parallelisation, which enables the computation-relevant optimisation for individual implementations and infrastructures.

The Knowledge Resources include the use-case of resource creation, which allows to integrate persistently added results. The use-case of resource creation itself is extended by the use-cases of resource development and edition management, which allows to define editions of resources for consistency in advanced complex application scenarios.

The use-case scenario reflects the professional practice of having separate roles for creating and developing factual, conceptual, procedural, and documentation, respective metacognitive knowledge. In most cases, different specialists are employed for creating and developing

- factual knowledge, e.g., research data and its documentation,
- conceptual knowledge, e.g., classification of knowledge objects,
- procedural knowledge, e.g., procedures, workflows, programs, and their respective documentation,
- metacognitive knowledge, e.g., documentation of experiences.

In practice, the creators are commonly represented by different groups of experts, e.g., scientists, classification experts in scientific libraries, and designers of scientific algorithms and workflows.

B. Main Components

The core components of a basic knowledge mining implementation with the Knowledge Resources, based on the knowledge-centric computation architecture, can be summarised with a block diagram (Figure 7). The block diagram shows the Knowledge Resources and two types of knowledge object groups, namely object collections and containers. Each type and implementation can have individual and specialised interfaces. Knowledge mining is provided by an interface with the Knowledge Resources. The diagram also contains the interface block, due to the importance of the resource creation use-case. The individual groups have ports, interaction points, which can be used via interfaces, e.g., Knowledge Resources Creation (KRC) port and Knowledge Resources Mining (KRM) port. Components can have further interfaces, with and without delegating ports. It is common that independent resources are in many cases not necessarily orchestrated.

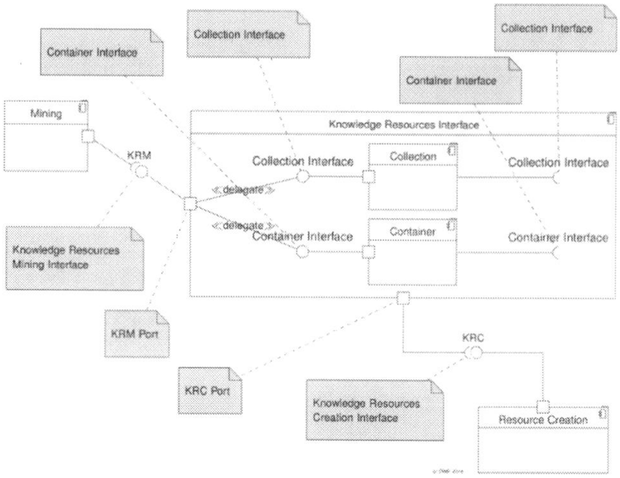

Figure 7. Block diagram of respective knowledge-centric computation architecture components: Excerpt of Knowledge Resources and interfaces.

C. Activity groups

A number of activities are associated with different components. An important activity regarding the resource creation is the creation-update (Figure 8). The resource creation component has to provide creation and update activities for the different creator groups. A simple but important example for resource creation and development is the creation of an object instance and respective updating an existing object with a new instance.

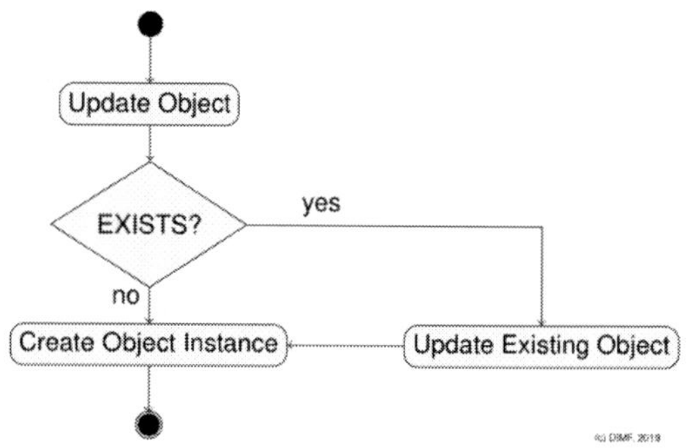

Figure 8. Activity diagram illustrating the essential object creation-update activities in the knowledge-centric computation architecture.

Start state is any state of the Knowledge Resources. End state is a new state of the Knowledge Resources. Regarding resource creation and development use-cases the start and end states should be considered intermediate states. As shown in the use-case diagram, professional practice affords the implementation of according activities for all required, specialised creator roles. A fundamental mining activity with Knowledge Resources is a resource request targeting to create an intermediate result (Figure 9). Start state is any state in a knowledge mining workflow chain. End state is a new state in a knowledge mining workflow chain. Regarding knowledge mining use-cases the start and end states should be considered intermediate states. If a resource is not available then an

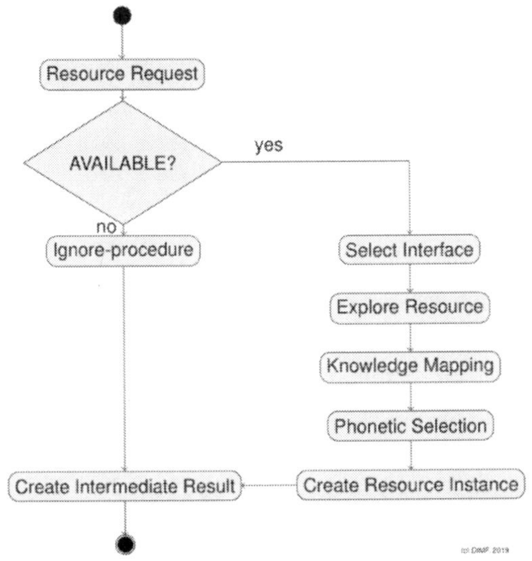

Figure 9. Activity diagram of a basic resource request for creating an intermediate knowledge mining result.

ignore-procedure continues for creating an intermediate result. The ignore-procedure can contribute its status to the workflow chain. If the resource is available then an interface is selected for the resource exploration. The exploration can use available activities, e.g., knowledge mapping and phonetic selection, in order to create a resource instance, which contributed to creating an intermediate result for the workflow chain. Examples of activities are multi-dimensional context creation by knowledge mapping [6] and phonetic association, e.g., using Soundex [23][24][25]. Sample Soundex codes developed [11] are used for names in various textual, contextual, and linguistical situations, implemented in order to be integrated in a large number of situations.

V. Discussion

The computation architecture provides the flexibility that workflow chain modules and whole workflow chains can be employed sequential or parallel. The components in general are not limited by the architecture to be implemented for synchronous or asynchronous accesses if required for arbitrary algorithms and workflows.

The implementations for practical case studies built upon this architecture span different disciplines and deal with different foci. The excerpted cases include general, simplified cases of knowledge mining and practical knowledge development scenarios from realisations, which were implemented for large practical solutions. These cases are relevant because of the professional background and practice required to deal with development of resources and application components for long-term tasks.

In complex scenarios, different disciplines contribute fulfilling different tasks. In case of knowledge creation and development and its valorisation different specialised expertise is required. In general, content and applications are created by different disciplines. Even different aspects of content may require different specialists groups, different roles, e.g., natural sciences research data and conceptual valorisation are often done by scientists from a respective discipline and information scientists. Many components have to be revisited and improved over time as the results and facilities should be continued and preserved and be available for long-term. In the implementation cases, factual, conceptual, procedural, and metacognitive knowledge is cared for by different experts. The architecture allows flexible and efficient separation of roles. For example, research data can be created by a role and can at any time be amended with classification and procedural documentation by experienced research library specialist and researcher roles.

The Knowledge Resources are containing a lot more content and references than can be used at present time in most cases. The architecture allowed to support retaining the associated knowledge required to resemble the intrinsic complexity of realia situations while implementing selected solutions for isolated as well as complex situations. The development of knowledge mining and the provisioning of services based on these tasks can continuously be done by application developers, accessing the continuously extendable Knowledge Resources.

VI. Conclusion

The paper presented the research results of creating a knowledge-centric computation architecture. The resulting architecture was developed in continuous cross development of multi-disciplinary, multi-lingual Knowledge Resources and practical knowledge-centric solutions. This paper presented the major qualities of the computation architecture. The practical employment of the architecture was illustrated for advanced knowledge mining and practical development uses-cases.

The contributing research collaboration achieved to create a practical approach for a knowledge-centric computation architecture, which allows the methodological and systematical development and employment of components, including Knowledge Resources. The architecture covers the creation of flexible solutions, which allow to most widely employ the complements of knowledge.

Computation architecture and use-cases proved in practice to support both the seamless separation and integration of roles for different disciplines and tasks while implementing and realising solutions. In addition to the implemented and referred case studies, we showed that major use-cases can be efficiently be managed. Especially, on the one hand, knowledge creation and development can be professionally dealt with by groups from responsible disciplines. On the other hand, knowledge mining relying on the resources can be based on the work of these disciplines while service based use and implementation can be given different roles.

Future research will concentrate on further extending and developing Knowledge Resources in order to provide long-term capacities and creating new advanced algorithms and mining workflows for enabling fundaments for new insight, participating different institutions and roles, based on the knowledge-centric computation architecture.

Acknowledgements

We are grateful to the "Knowledge in Motion" (KiM) long-term project, Unabhängiges Deutsches Institut für Multidisziplinäre Forschung (DIMF), for partially funding implementations, case studies, and publications under grants D2016F5P04648, D2017F1P04812, and D2018F6P04938 and to its senior scientific members and members of the permanent commission of the science council and the board of trustees, especially to Dr. Friedrich Hülsmann, Gottfried Wilhelm Leibniz Bibliothek (GWLB) Hannover, to Dipl.-Biol. Birgit Gersbeck-Schierholz, Leibniz Universität Hannover, to Dipl.-Ing. Martin Hofmeister, Hannover, and to Olaf Lau, Hannover, Germany, for collaboration, practical multi-disciplinary case studies, and the analysis and implementation of advanced concepts. We are grateful to Dipl.-Ing. Hans-Günther Müller, Cray, Germany, for his excellent contributions and assistance, providing practical private cloud and storage solutions. We are grateful to all national and international partners in the Geo Exploration and Information cooperations for their constructive and trans-disciplinary support. We are grateful to the Science and High Performance Supercomputing Centre (SHPSC) for long-term support and The International ARS Science and History Network for providing multi-disciplinary application scenarios and assistance. / DIMF-PIID-DF98_007.

References

[1] Aristotle, Nicomachean Ethics, 2008, (Written 350 B.C.E.), Translated by W. D. Ross, Provided by The Internet Classics Archive, URL: http://classics.mit.edu/Aristotle/nicomachaen.html [accessed: 2019-03-24].

[2] Aristotle, The Ethics of Aristotle, 2005, Project Gutenberg, eBook, EBook-No.: 8438, Release Date: July, 2005, Digitised Version of the Original Publication, Produced by Ted Garvin, David Widger, and the DP Team, Edition 10, URL: http://www.gutenberg.org/ebooks/8438 [accessed: 2018-01-01].

[3] L. W. Anderson and D. R. Krathwohl, Eds., A Taxonomy for Learning, Teaching, and Assessing: A Revision of Bloom's Taxonomy of Educational Objectives. Allyn & Bacon, Boston, MA (Pearson Education Group), USA, 2001, ISBN-13: 978-0801319037.

[4] Plato, Phaedo, 2008, (Written 360 B.C.E.), Translated by Benjamin Jowett, Provided by The Internet Classics Archive, URL: http://classics.mit.edu/Plato/phaedo.html [accessed: 2019-03-24].

[5] C.-P. Rückemann and F. Hülsmann, "Significant Differences: Methodologies and Applications," KiMrise, Knowledge in Motion Meeting, November 27, 2017, Knowledge in Motion, Hannover, Germany, 2017.

[6] C.-P. Rückemann, "Methodology of Knowledge Mapping for Arbitrary Objects and Entities: Knowledge Mining and Spatial Representations – Objects in Multi-dimensional Context," in Proceedings of The Tenth International Conference on Advanced Geographic Information Systems, Applications, and Services (GEOProcessing 2018), March 25 – 29, 2018, Rome, Italy. XPS Press, Wilmington, Delaware, USA, 2018, pp. 40–45, ISSN: 2308-393X, ISBN-13: 978-1-61208-617-0, URL: http://www.thinkmind.org/index.php?view=article&articleid=geoprocessing_2018_3_20_30078 [accessed: 2019-03-24].

[7] C.-P. Rückemann, "Creation of Objects and Concordances for Knowledge Processing and Advanced Computing," in Proceedings of The Fifth International Conference on Advanced Communications and Computation (INFOCOMP 2015), June 21–26, 2015, Brussels, Belgium. XPS Press, 2015, ISSN: 2308-3484, ISBN-13: 978-1-61208-416-9, URL: http://www.thinkmind.org/index.php?view=article&articleid=infocomp_2015_4_30_60038 [accessed: 2019-03-24].

[8] C.-P. Rückemann, "Advanced Association Processing and Computation Facilities for Geoscientific and Archaeological Knowledge Resources Components," in Proceedings of The Eighth International Conference on Advanced Geographic Information Systems, Applications, and Services (GEOProcessing 2016), April 24 – 28, 2016, Venice, Italy. XPS Press, 2016, pages 69–75, ISSN: 2308-393X, ISBN-13: 978-1-61208-469-5.

[9] C.-P. Rückemann, "Advanced Knowledge Discovery and Computing based on Knowledge Resources, Concordances, and Classification," International Journal On Advances in Intelligent Systems, vol. 9, no. 1&2, 2016, pp. 27–40, ISSN: 1942-2679.

[10] "Perl Compatible Regular Expressions (PCRE)," 2019, URL: https://www.pcre.org/ [accessed: 2019-03-24].

[11] C.-P. Rückemann, "Archaeological and Geoscientific Objects used with Integrated Systems and Scientific Supercomputing Resources," International Journal on Advances in Systems and Measurements, vol. 6, no. 1&2, 2013, pp. 200–213, ISSN: 1942-261x, URL: http://www.iariajournals.org/systems_and_measurements/sysmea_v6_n12_2013_paged.pdf [accessed: 2019-03-24].

[12] C.-P. Rückemann, "Multi-dimensional Context Creation Based on the Methodology of Knowledge Mapping," International Journal on Advances in Software, vol. 11, no. 3&4, 2018, pp. 286–298, ISSN: 1942-2628, URL: http://www.iariajournals.org/software/soft_v11_n34_2018_paged.pdf [accessed: 2019-03-24].

[13] C.-P. Rückemann, "Superordinate Knowledge Based Comprehensive Subset of Conceptual Knowledge for Practical Geo-spatial Application Scenarios," in Proceedings of The Eleventh International Conference on Advanced Geographic Information Systems, Applications, and Services (GEOProcessing 2019), February 24 – 28, 2019, Athens, Greece. XPS Press, Wilmington, Delaware, USA, 2019, pp. 52–58, ISSN: 2308-393X, ISBN: 978-1-61208-687-3, URL: http://www.thinkmind.org/index.php?view=article&articleid=geoprocessing_2019_3_30_30039 [accessed: 2019-03-24].

[14] UDC, Universal Decimal Classification. British Standards Institute (BSI), 2005, complete Edition, ISBN: 0-580-45482-7, Vol. 1 and 2.

[15] C.-P. Rückemann, "Enabling Dynamical Use of Integrated Systems and Scientific Supercomputing Resources for Archaeological Information Systems," in Proc. INFOCOMP 2012, Oct. 21–26, 2012, Venice, Italy, 2012, pp. 36–41, ISBN: 978-1-61208-226-4.

[16] "UDC Online," 2018, URL: http://www.udc-hub.com [ac.: 2019-03-24].

[17] "Multilingual Universal Decimal Classification Summary," 2012, UDC Consortium, 2012, Web resource, v. 1.1. The Hague: UDC Consortium (UDCC Publication No. 088), URL: http://www.udcc.org/udcsummary/php/index.php [accessed: 2019-03-24].

[18] "Creative Commons Attribution Share Alike 3.0 license," 2012, URL: http://creativecommons.org/licenses/by-sa/3.0/ [accessed: 2019-03-24].

[19] B. Oestereich and A. Scheithauer, Analyse und Design mit der UML 2.5: Objektorientierte Softwareentwicklung, 11th ed. De Gruyter Oldenbourg, 2013, ISBN: 978-3486721409.

[20] "Unified Modeling Language (UML)," 2019, URL: http://uml.org/ [accessed: 2019-03-24].

[21] "About the Unified Modeling Language Specification 2.5.1," Dec. 2017, OMG – Object Management Group, URL: https://www.omg.org/spec/UML/ [accessed: 2019-03-24].

[22] "The Perl Programming Language," 2019, URL: https://www.perl.org/ [accessed: 2019-03-24].

[23] R. C. Russel and M. K. Odell, "U.S. patent 1261167," 1918, (Soundex algorithm), patent issued 1918-04-02.

[24] D. E. Knuth, The Art of Computer Programming: Sorting and Searching. Addison-Wesley, 1973, vol. 3, ISBN: 978-0-201-03803-3, OCLC: 39472999.

[25] National Archives and Records Administration (NARA), "The Soundex Indexing System," 2007, 2007-05-30, URL: http://www.archives.gov/research/census/soundex.html [accessed: 2019-03-24].

Automatic Generation of Adjoint Operators for the Lattice Boltzmann Method

Stephan Seitz, Andreas Maier

Pattern Recognition Lab
Friedrich-Alexander-University Erlangen-Nürnberg
Erlangen, Germany
email: {stephan.seitz, andreas.maier}@fau.de

Martin Bauer, Negar Mirshahzadeh, Harald Köstler

Chair for System Simulation
Friedrich-Alexander-University Erlangen-Nürnberg
Erlangen, Germany
email: {martin.bauer, negar.mirshahzadeh, harald.koestler}@fau.de

Abstract—**Gradient-based optimization techniques for Computational Fluid Dynamics have been an emerging field of research in the past years. With important applications in industrial product design, science and medicine, there has been an increasing interest to use the growing computational resources in order to improve realism of simulations by maximizing their coherence with measurement data or to refine simulation setups to fulfill imposed design goals. However, the derivation of the gradients with respect to certain simulation parameters can be complex and requires manual changes to the used algorithms. In the case of the popular Lattice Boltzmann Method, various models exists that regard the effects of different physical quantities and control parameters. In this paper, we propose a generalized framework that enables the automatic generation of efficient code for the optimization on general purpose computers and graphics processing units using symbolic descriptions of arbitrary Lattice Boltzmann Methods. The required derivation of corresponding adjoint models and necessary boundary conditions are handled transparently for the user. We greatly simplify the process of fluid-simulation-based optimization for a broader audience by providing Lattice Boltzmann simulations as automatic differentiable building blocks for the widely used machine learning frameworks Tensorflow and Torch.**

Keywords–Lattice Boltzmann method; Computational Fluid Dynamics; Adjoint Methods; Gradient-based Optimization; Tensorflow.

I. Introduction

Applications for optimization using Computational Fluid Dynamics (CFD) range from numerical weather prediction [1], medicine [2], computer graphics [3], scientific exploration in physics to mechanical [4] and chemical engineering [5]. The Lattice Boltzmann Method (LBM) is a promising alternative to established finite element or finite volume flow solvers due to its suitability for modern, parallel computing hardware and its simple treatment of complex and changing geometries [6]. These properties make it also well suited for gradient-based optimization schemes. The gradient calculation for LBMs is based on a backward-in-time sensitivity analysis called Adjoint Lattice Boltzmann Method (ALBM) [7][8]. Manually deriving the adjoint method is a tedious and time-consuming process. It has to be done for each concrete setup because the adjoint method is highly dependent on the chosen LBM, its boundary conditions, the set of free parameters, and the objective function. This effortful workflow currently impedes the usage of LBM-based optimization by a greater audience with no experience in the implementation of this CFD algorithm, despite the wide range of possible applications. Also for experts, it might be tedious to efficiently implement ALBM for a specific Lattice Boltzmann (LB) model and instance of a problem, especially if MPI-parallel (message passing interface) execution or Graphics Processing Unit (GPU) acceleration is desired.

A great simplification for the efficient implementation of optimization algorithms by non-experts has been achieved recently in the field of machine learning. Array-based frameworks like *Tensorflow* [9] and *Torch* [10] have dramatically accelerated the pace of discovery and led to a democratization of research in this discipline. Commonly needed building blocks are exposed to scripting languages like Python or Lua while preserving a relatively high single-node performance through their implementation in C++ or CUDA. Most of the available operators provide an implementation for the calculation of their gradient which enables the automatic differentiation and optimization of user-defined objective functions. We are convinced that providing automatically generated implementations for arbitrary LBMs as building blocks for optimization frameworks could greatly simplify their usage and increase the efficiency of their implementation. In this paper, we thus present a code generation framework for a wide range of LBMs with automatic derivation of forward and adjoint methods. Our tool generates highly optimized, MPI-parallel implementations for Central Processing Units (CPUs) and GPUs, including boundary treatment. We automatically account for optimizable, constant and time-constant variables. The integration of our tool in the automatic differentiation frameworks *Tensorflow* and *Torch* allows for rapid prototyping of optimization schemes while preserving the flexibility of switching between various LB models without making trade-offs in terms of execution performance.

While many stencils code generation tools have been proposed before, ours is the first to our knowledge which facilitates automatic optimization using ALBM, given only a specification of the LB model, the geometry and boundary conditions. Another strength of our approach is that no new domain-specific language is introduced. Instead, we rely on an extension of the widespread computer algebra system *SymPy* [11] which allows code generation in the familiar programming environment of Python. The novel generation of custom operations from symbolic mathematical representation for both major machine learning frameworks might also be useful for other applications.

Our framework [12] is available as open-source software without the LBM abstraction layer [13]. The results of this paper providing automatically derived operators and integration for PyTorch and Tensorflow are about to be published in the same place.

The remainder of this paper is organized as follows: Section II presents related work regarding LBM, ALBM and frameworks for automatic differentiation. Section III explains the architecture of our framework, while Section IV evaluates and Section V discusses its application on an example problem.

II. Related Work

A. Lattice Boltzmann Method

The Lattice Boltzmann Method is a mesoscopic method that has been established as an alternative to classical Navier-Stokes solvers for Computational Fluid Dynamics (CFD) simulations [6]. It is a so-called kinetic method, using particle distribution functions (PDFs) $f_i(\boldsymbol{x}, t)$ to discretize phase space. The PDFs thus represent the probability density of particles at location $\boldsymbol{x}$ at time t traveling with the discrete velocity $\boldsymbol{c}_i$. Macroscopic quantities like density and velocity are obtained as moments of the distribution function. Space is usually discretized into a uniform Lattice of cells which can be addressed using Cartesian coordinates. An explicit time stepping scheme allows for extensive parallelization even on extreme scales due to its high locality. The Lattice Boltzmann equation is derived by discretizing the Boltzmann equation in physical space, velocity space and time:

$$f_i(\boldsymbol{x} + \boldsymbol{c}_i \Delta t, t + \Delta t) = f_i(\boldsymbol{x}, t) + \Omega_i(f). \tag{1}$$

Ω_i denotes the collision operator that models particle collisions by relaxing the PDFs towards an equilibrium distribution. Depending on the concrete collision operator, various different LB models exist [6]: From single-relaxation-time (SRT) models using the Bhatnagar–Gross–Krook approximation over two-relaxation-time (TRT) models proposed by Ginzburg et al. [14] up to generic multi-relaxation-time schemes [15][16]. Recent contributions aim to increase the accuracy and stability of the method by relaxing in cumulant-space instead of moment space [17] or by choosing relaxation rates subject to an entropy condition [18]. Several LBM frameworks exist that aid the user with setting up a full LB simulation, e.g., Palabos [19][20], OpenLB [21] and waLBerla [22][23]. However, none of these frameworks support both LB code generation as well as automatic differentiation for adjoint problems.

B. Adjoint Methods

Adjoint methods provide efficient means to evaluate gradients of potentially complex time-dependent problems. Given a mathematical model to simulate forward in time, the method of Lagrangian multipliers can be used to derive a complementary backward model [24]. The adjoint can either be determined from a mathematical description of the direct problem (analytical derivation) or by an algorithmic analysis of the code used for forward calculation (automatic differentiation). Examples for automatic derivation of forward and backward code from a high-level symbolic description of partial differential equations (PDEs) are the *Devito* [25][26] and the *Dolfin Adjoint* framework [27][28]. *Devito* generates code for finite-differences whereas *Dolfin* uses the finite element method. Frameworks implementing the adjoint method using automatic differentiation are usually not bound to a specific method.

For LBM, manual derivations of the adjoint dominate, either by an analytical gradient of the discrete time stepping step [7] (discretize-then-optimize approach) or by re-discretizing the gradient of a continuous formulation of the Lattice-Boltzmann equation [8] (optimize-then-discretize). Despite most authors recommend the usage of a computer algebra system for the derivation and Laniewski et al. [4] even use a source-to-source auto-differentiation tool on a forward LBM implementation to obtain backward code, a fully-automated derivation of an ALBM scheme is still missing. ALBMs have been applied to a wide range of problems, e.g., parameter identification [7], data assimilation to measurement data [8], or topology optimization [4][29]–[31]. Also, comparisons with finite-element-based optimization have been made, giving comparable results [30].

C. Automatic Differentiation

As alternative to analytical derivation, adjoint models can also be obtained using automatic differentiation (AD). Sequential chaining of elementary differentiable operations often helps to avoid typical problems of numerical and analytical differentiation arising in highly complex expressions, like numerical instabilities [24]

AD is based on the multi-dimensional chain rule where the gradient ∇f of $f = f_1 \circ f_2 \circ \cdots \circ f_N$ with respect to the inputs of f_1 can be calculated as

$$\nabla f = J_N \cdot J_{N-1} \cdot \dots \cdot J_2 \cdot J_1 \tag{2}$$

where J_1 to J_N are the respective Jacobians of f_1 to f_N.

The evaluation of this expression can be performed in different ways [32]: **forward-mode** automatic differentiation corresponds to a direct evaluation of Equation 2. This corresponds to a direct tracing of the computation paths of the input variables, such that the computation order and memory access pattern is conserved.

In optimization applications, the last Jacobian J_N usually correspond to a scalar objective function. In this case, the **backward-mode** evaluation order becomes favorable, that is obtained by taking the transpose or adjoint of above expression.

$$\nabla f = \left(J_1^T \cdot J_2^T \cdot \dots \cdot J_{N-1}^T \cdot J_N^T\right)^T. \tag{3}$$

Now, with J_N^T being a vector, only matrix-vector multiplications have to be performed. This approach is more memory-efficient and also facilitates the incremental calculation of partial gradients. However, this comes with a disadvantage: the paths in the calculation graph are inverted and the evaluation can only begin after the forward pass has completed. All the intermediate results of the forward pass need to be stored and all memory accesses have to be transformed by turning write operations into read operations and vice versa. Changing the memory access pattern can critically harm execution performance, since efficient "pull" kernels that read multiple neighbors and write only locally are transformed into "push" kernels that read local values and write to neighboring cells. This change also affects the parallelization strategy i.e. the halo layer exchange for MPI execution.

For this reason, Hückelheim et al. proposed a scheme called transposed forward-mode automatic differentiation (**TF-MAD**) for stencil codes that mimics memory access patterns of the forward pass [32]. In this scheme, the summations that evaluate the gradients are re-ordered inside a single time step in similar ways as in the forward differentiation. This preserves the memory access structure while keeping the desired backward-in-time evaluation order.

III. Methods

In this section we first present a code generation tool for forward LBMs that automates the derivation, performance optimization, and implementation of LBMs for CPUs and GPUs.

Then an extension of this tool for adjoint LBMs is described. Finally, we show how the integration into popular automatic differentiation frameworks enables the user to flexibly describe a wide range of optimization problems.

A. Automatic LBM Code Generation

The main contribution of this work is a code generation tool for Adjoint Lattice Boltzmann Methods that can be fully integrated into popular automatic differentiation frameworks. Our code generation approach aims to overcome the following flexibility-performance trade-off: On the one hand, the application scientist needs a flexible toolkit to set up the physical model, boundary conditions and objective function. On the other hand, a careful performance engineering process is required, to get optimal runtime performance. This process includes a reformulation of the model to save floating point operations, loop transformations for optimal cache usage and manual vectorization with single-instruction-multiple-data (SIMD) intrinsics. While previously, this had to be done manually, our tool fully automates this process.

On the highest abstraction layer, the Lattice Boltzmann collision operator is symbolically formulated using the formalism of multi relaxation time methods. A set of independent moments or cumulants has to be provided, together with their equilibrium values and relaxation times. This formalism includes the widely used single relaxation time (SRT) and two relaxation time (TRT) methods as a special case. Relaxation times can be chosen either constant or subject to an entropy condition [18]. This layer allows for flexible modification of the model, e.g., by introducing custom force terms or by locally adapting relaxation times for turbulence modeling or simulation of non-Newtonian fluids. One important aspect that increases the complexity of LB implementations significantly is the handling of boundary conditions. Our code generation framework can create special boundary kernels for all standard LB boundary conditions including no-slip, velocity and pressure boundaries.

This high-level LBM description is then automatically transformed into a stencil formulation. The stencil formulation consists of an ordered assignment list, containing accesses to abstract arrays using relative indexing. These assignments have to be independent of each other, such that they can all be executed in parallel.

Both representations are implemented using the *SymPy* computer algebra system [11]. The advantages of using a Python package for symbolic mathematics are evident: a high number of users are familiar with this framework and problems can be formulated intuitively in terms of abstract formulas. Mathematical transformations like discretization, simplifications and solving for certain variables can be concisely formulated in a computer algebra system. To reduce the number of operations in the stencil description, we first simplify the stencil description by custom transformations that make use of LBM domain knowledge, then use *SymPy*'s generic common subexpression elimination to further reduce the number of operations.

Next, the stencil description is transformed into an algorithmic description, explicitly encoding the loop structure. Loop transformations like cache-blocking, loop fusion and loop splitting are conducted at this stage. The algorithmic description is then finally passed to the C or CUDA backend. For CPUs, an OpenMP parallel implementation is generated that is also explicitly vectorized using SIMD intrinsics. We support the

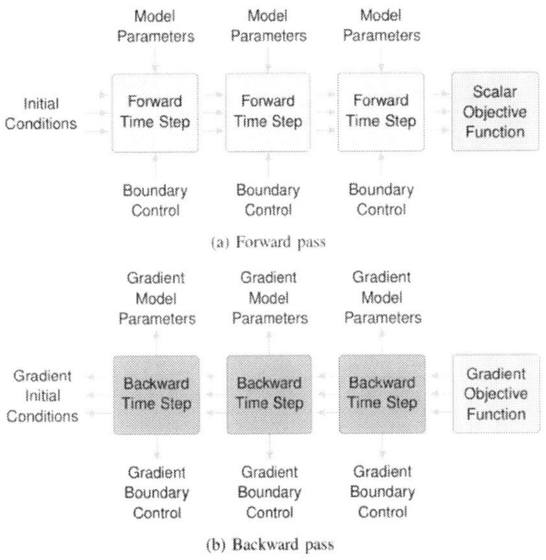

Figure 1. Auto-differentiation-based optimization with automatically generated kernels for forward and backward pass.

Intel SSE, AVX and AVX512 instruction sets. Vectorization can be done without any additional analysis steps since our pipeline guarantees that loop iterations are independent. Conditionals are mapped to efficient blend instructions. To run large scale, distributed-memory simulations, the generated compute kernels can be integrated in the *waLBerla* [22][23] framework that provides a block-structured domain decomposition and MPI-based synchronization functions for halo layers.

Feasibility and performance results for this framework have been shown already in the context of large-scale phase-field simulations using the finite element method [12].

B. Automatic Stencil Code Differentation

In the following, we take advantage of the symbolic representation of the forward stencils as *SymPy* assignments and use the capabilities of this computer algebra system to implement a set of rules to automatically generate the assignments defining the corresponding adjoint. This distinguishes our method from automatic derivation of adjoint finite difference in the *Devito* framework [25] which uses *SymPy* to derive the adjoint directly from the symbolic representation of the partial differential equation and its discretization for finite differences. Our approach is not bound to a specific discretization scheme and can therefore also be applied for LBM.

1) Backward Automatic Differentiation: As aforementioned, we can automatically generate CPU or GPU code for one time step of the targeted method if we are able to express the necessary calculations as a set of symbolic assignments operating on relative read and write accesses. We consider therefore one time step as an elementary operation for our automatic backward differentiation procedure (see Figure 1). This means we determine the gradients of an arbitrary objective function by successively applying the chain rule for each time step and propagate the partial gradients backward in time.

We will represent the forward kernel mathematically as a vector-valued function $f(.) = (f_1(.), f_2(.), \ldots, f_M(.))$ which depends on argument symbols $r_0, r_1, \ldots, r_N$ for N read accesses. The result of each component will be assigned to one of the symbols $w_0, w_1, \ldots, w_M$ representing M write accesses. Both w_i and r_j operate on two sets of fields that may not be disjunctive.

$$w_i \longleftarrow f_i(r_0, r_1, \dots, r_N) \qquad i \in \{1, \dots, M\} \tag{4}$$

Symbolic differentiation as provided by *SymPy* is used to determine and simplify corresponding assignments for the calculation of the discrete adjoint and also for common subexpression elimination. For automatic backward differentiation, an additional buffer for each intermediate result in the calculation graph is required. We denominate relative write and read accesses to adjoint variables corresponding to w_i and r_j with $\hat{w}_i$ and $\hat{r}_j$. In other words, our adjoint kernel calculates the Jacobian of the outputs w_i of one time step of the forward pass with respect to its inputs r_j in order to apply the multidimensional chain rule and to backpropagate the accumulated gradients $\hat{w}$ to $\hat{r}$.

$$\hat{r}_j \longleftarrow \sum_{i=1}^{M} \frac{\partial f_i}{\partial r_j}(r_0, r_1, \dots, r_N) \cdot \hat{w}_i \qquad j \in \{1, \dots, N\} \tag{5}$$

Equation 5 is represented, symbolically evaluated, and simplified directly in *SymPy*. Note that store accesses are transformed into loads and load accesses into stores, while the relative offsets remain unchanged. As long as the stencils defined by r_j do not overlap, stores to $\hat{r}_j$ can be performed in parallel. Otherwise, the stores have to be realized by atomic additions, accumulating the contributions of each grid cell. This can critically harm execution performance.

In the case of a two-buffer LBM scheme, there are no overlapping read and write accesses. Hence, automatic backward differentiation can safely be applied for parallel execution.

2) Backward Automatic Differentation with Forward Memory Access Patterns: A change in the memory access patterns by transforming forward kernels into backward kernels may not be an issue if the parallel execution can still be guaranteed. However, this is not the case for most stencil operations and one must be aware of the fact that a change in the memory access pattern also affects the implementation of boundary handling. As previously proven by Hückelheim et al. [32], the derivations in the sum of equation 5 can be reordered to mimic the access patterns of the forward pass if certain conditions are met. This is based on the observation that in most cases the forward assignments are written in a form that the write operations can be performed collision-free and in parallel on each output cell. If the perspective is changed and indexing based on the read buffers, Equation 5 can be reformulated in order to yield equivalent operations with collision-free writes in the backward pass: For the sake of simplicity of notation, we assume that all read accesses $r_0, r_1, \dots, r_N$ operate on the same scalar field r. In this case, we can state that each cell of r will have exactly once the role of each $r_0, r_1, \dots, r_N$. Therefore, we can simply sum over all the read accesses in the forward kernel in order to obtain the gradient $\hat{r}$ for each cell of the read field r:

$$\hat{r} \longleftarrow \sum_{j=1}^{N} \sum_{i=1}^{M} \frac{\partial f_i}{\partial r_j}(r_0, r_1, \dots, r_N) \cdot \overline{w}_j \tag{6}$$

Since in TF-MAD, the indexing is based on the read accesses in the forward pass, the sign of the relative indexes of $\hat{w}$ has to be switched, which is indicated by $\overline{w}$, e.g., the south-east neighbor of the forward write is the north-west neighbor of the forward read.

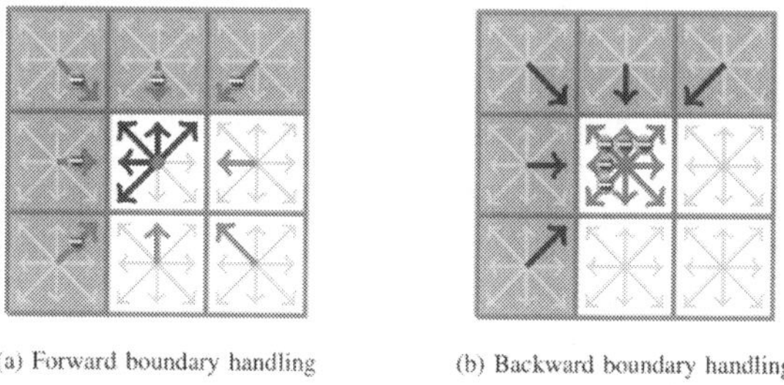

(a) Forward boundary handling (b) Backward boundary handling

Figure 2. Adjoint bounce-back boundary: invalid red memory locations and have to be swapped with facing violet locations.

C. Automatic Generation of Adjoint Lattice Boltzmann Methods

To calculate the correct adjoint, not only the method itself but also the boundary handling has to be adapted. Using backward-mode automatic differentiation, a LB scheme with pull-reads from neighboring cells is transformed into a push-kernel that writes to neighboring cells. This transformation also changes the memory access pattern of all boundaries as shown for a bounce-back boundary in Figure 2. Similar to compute kernels, the boundary treatment is also generated from a symbolic representation. This allows us to re-use the same auto-differentiation techniques that we applied earlier to compute kernels and generate backward boundary kernels from their respective forward implementations. The only difference of boundary kernels is their iteration pattern. While compute kernels are executed for each cell, a boundary kernel is executed only in previously marked boundary cells. Boundary values like density or velocity can either be set to a constant or marked for optimization. In the latter case, the gradient with respect to the boundary parameters is automatically derived and calculated as well. All boundary options are accessible to the user through a simple, high-level user interface.

D. Interface to Machine Learning Frameworks

Next, the automatically generated, efficient CPU/GPU implementations of a LB time step with boundary treatment are integrated into the *Tensorflow* and *Torch* packages. We provide building blocks for the LB time step itself and for initialization and evaluation steps that compute LB distribution functions from macroscopic quantities and vice versa. For performance reasons, it is beneficial to combine multiple LB time steps into a single *Tensorflow/Torch* block.

This allows the user to easily specify an optimization problem by constructing a computation graph in *Tensorflow* or *Torch*. The user can choose which quantities should be optimizable, constant or constant over time. The system then automatically derives the necessary gradient calculations. Both machine learning frameworks offer test routines that check whether gradients are calculated correctly by comparing them to results obtained via a time-intensive but generic numerical differentiation method. We use these routines to ensure the correctness of our generated implementations. For simplicity, we do not use advanced checkpointing schemes, like *revolve* [33], and instead save all the intermediate results of the forward pass. Alternatively, the user can opt to checkpoint only each n-th time step and use interpolated values for determination of the Jacobian of the missing forward time steps.

IV. Evaluation

For evaluation of our framework, we chose a simple geometry optimization problem after verifying the correctness of our gradient calculations for standard LBM methods by numerical differentiation. Many LBM-based approaches were proposed to make cell-wise optimization stable and feasible, mainly differing in the way of defining the objective functions and their porousity models. The values of various parameters are crucial for the existence of non-trivial solutions and the stability of an optimization scheme.

Our code generation framework allows us to specify objective functions and porous media models in an abstract way that is very close to their mathematical description. Thus one can implement setups from literature without much development effort. As an example we present here a setup investigated by Nørgaard et al. [31]. They use the partial bounceback model of Zhu and Ma [34] and achieve better optimization stability by separating the design domain from the physical permeability. Physical permeability is obtained by applying a filter followed by a soft-thresholding step. The "hardness" of the thresholding is increased during the optimization procedure to enforce a zero/one solution.

We set up a similar problem as described in their work, by requiring a generated geometry in the design domain to have as close area as possible to a certain fraction θ of the total available domain space and enforcing minimal pressure drop in steady-state. We operate in a low Reynolds number regime with fixed velocity (0.01 lattice units per time step, inlets on left side) and fixed pressure conditions (1 in lattice units, outlets on right side) as shown in Figure 3. With the same objective function [31], that penalizes pressure drop, deviation from a given volume fraction and instationarity of the LB simulation, we obtain the results as shown in Figure 3.

V. Conclusion

Our work shows that adjoint LBMs can be automatically derived from a high-level description of the forward method. This makes optimization based on this method also tractable for non-CFD-experts in a wide range of problem domains, by hiding the inherent complexity caused by adjoint derivation, boundary handling, and model implementation.

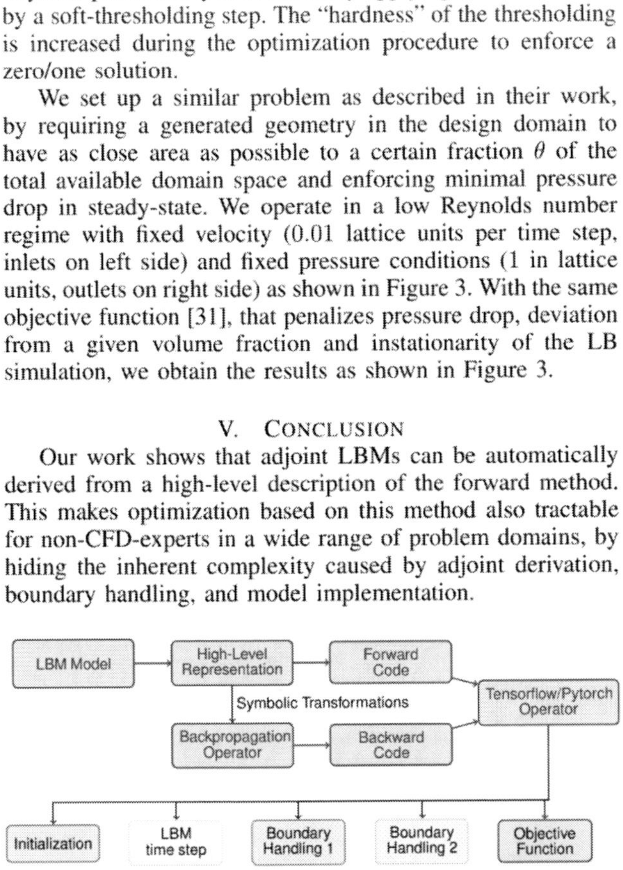

Figure 4. Proposed work flow for optimization with ALBM.

In our exemplary geometry optimization problem, we could successfully apply our suggested automated work flow (Figure 4): a high-level LB model layer is used to derive a porous media LB scheme, define the simulated geometry and generate corresponding *SymPy* expressions for all necessary operations including initialization, time stepping and boundary handling. Forward expressions are transformed into their respective adjoint and finally combined into *Tensorflow* and *Torch* operations. Note that we decided for performance reasons to fuse time steps and boundary operations to a single operation. Derived gradients are automatically assessed for correctness in concrete problem instances by numerical differentiation.

Code generation is well suited for adjoint-based optimization, especially ALBM. Our tool can be used to experiment with different LB models, boundary treatments, optimizers and objective functions without facing the burden of a manual implementation. The symbolic intermediate representation facilitates a simple automatic derivation of gradients for 2D and 3D models. This helps to maintain clean and re-usable code bases. Our code generation approach still guarantees good performance by delegating hardware-specific optimizations to different backends (CPU, GPU), which has been proven for large-scale phase-field simulations [12], though a performance evaluation for LBM and ALBM is still future work. Portability is provided since integration for new frameworks only requires minimal wrapper code to call our dependency-free C code. We hope that this approach could help to save time and money to bring future code from prototypical experiments to large-scale production.

Our initial work leaves room for a lot of open questions, which need to be evaluated in the future under more realistic conditions. Scientific computing applications need to proof optimum execution performance also on large scale MPI systems. Efficient CFD-based optimization needs to use dedicated optimization frameworks with support for MPI simulations and efficient step size control while machine learning frameworks might be sufficient only for prototyping. Also a more advanced checkpointing strategy, like *revolve* [33] is needed to reduce memory usage. Furthermore, more research is required to test which generated ALBM models are suited in practice by analyzing their performance in real world examples.

Acknowledgments: Stephan Seitz thanks the International Max Planck Research School Physics of Light for supporting his doctorate.

References

[1] I. M. Navon, "Data assimilation for numerical weather prediction: A review," Data Assimilation for Atmospheric, Oceanic and Hydrologic Applications, 2009, pp. 21–65.

[2] F. Klemens, S. Schuhmann, G. Guthausen, G. Thäter, and M. J. Krause, "CFD-MRI: A coupled measurement and simulation approach for accurate fluid flow characterisation and domain identification," Computers & Fluids, vol. 166, 2018, pp. 218–224.

[3] T. Kim, N. Thürey, D. James, and M. Gross, "Wavelet turbulence for fluid simulation," ACM Trans. Graph., vol. 27, no. 3, Aug. 2008, pp. 50:1–50:6.

[4] Ł. Łaniewski-Wołłk and J. Rokicki, "Adjoint lattice boltzmann for topology optimization on multi-gpu architecture," Computers & Mathematics with Applications, vol. 71, no. 3, 2016, pp. 833–848.

[5] S. Yang, S. Kiang, P. Farzan, and M. Ierapetritou, "Optimization of reaction selectivity using CFD-based compartmental modeling and surrogate-based optimization," Processes, vol. 7, no. 1, Dec 2018, p. 9.

[6] T. Krüger, H. Kusumaatmaja, A. Kuzmin, O. Shardt, G. Silva, and E. M. Viggen, The Lattice Boltzmann Method. Springer International Publishing, 2017.

[7] M. M. Tekitek, M. Bouzidi, F. Dubois, and P. Lallemand, "Adjoint lattice boltzmann equation for parameter identification," Computers & fluids, vol. 35, no. 8-9, 2006, pp. 805–813.

[8] M. J. Krause, G. Thäter, and V. Heuveline, "Adjoint-based fluid flow control and optimisation with lattice boltzmann methods," Computers & Mathematics with Applications, vol. 65, no. 6, Mar 2013, pp. 945–960.

[9] M. Abadi *et al.*, "TensorFlow: Large-scale machine learning on heterogeneous systems," 2015, http://arxiv.org/abs/1603.04467, Software available from tensorflow.org.

[10] R. Collobert, S. Bengio, and J. Marithoz, "Torch: A modular machine learning software library," 2002, technical report, infoscience.epfl.ch/record/82802/files/rr02-46.pdf.

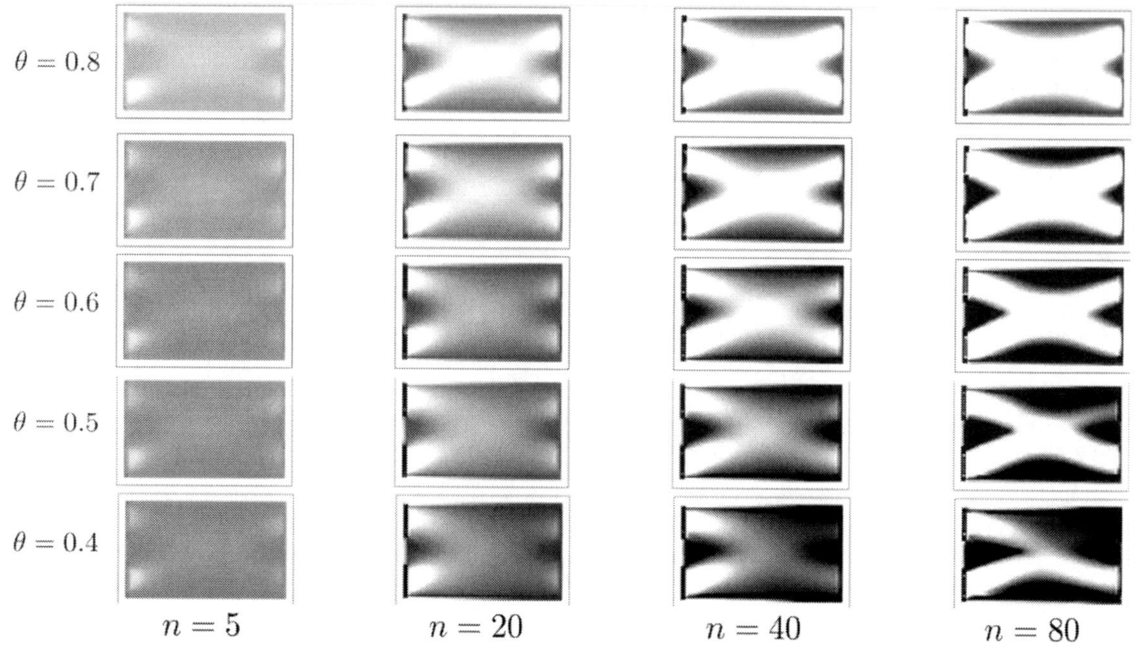

Figure 3. Optimization solution for a simple minimal-pressure-drop design after n optimization steps for given fraction θ of the design area targeted. Gray value intensity indicates permeability.

[11] A. Meurer *et al.*, "SymPy: symbolic computing in Python," PeerJ Computer Science, vol. 3, Jan. 2017, p. e103.

[12] M. Bauer *et al.*, "Code generation for massively parallel phase-field simulations," in Accepted at: Proceedings of the International Conference for High Performance Computing, Networking, Storage and Analysis. ACM, 2019, in press.

[13] M. Bauer *et al.*, "pystencils," software available at www.github.com/mabau/pystencils.

[14] I. Ginzburg, F. Verhaeghe, and D. d'Humieres, "Two-relaxation-time lattice boltzmann scheme: About parametrization, velocity, pressure and mixed boundary conditions," Communications in computational physics, vol. 3, no. 2, 2008, pp. 427–478.

[15] P. Lallemand and L. Luo, "Theory of the lattice boltzmann method: Dispersion, dissipation, isotropy,galilean invariance, and stability," Physical Review E, vol. 61, no. 6, 2000, pp. 6546–6562.

[16] D. D'Humières, I. Ginzburg, M. Krafczyk, P. Lallemand, and L.-S. Luo, "Multiple-relaxation-time lattice Boltzmann models in three dimensions." Philosophical transactions. Series A, Mathematical, physical, and engineering sciences, vol. 360, no. 1792, 2002, pp. 437–451.

[17] M. Geier, M. Schönherr, A. Pasquali, and M. Krafczyk, "The cumulant lattice Boltzmann equation in three dimensions: Theory and validation," Computers and Mathematics with Applications, vol. 70.4, 2015, pp. 507–547.

[18] F. Bösch, S. S. Chikatamarla, and I. V. Karlin, "Entropic multirelaxation lattice boltzmann models for turbulent flows," Physical Review E - Statistical, Nonlinear, and Soft Matter Physics, 2015, p. 043309.

[19] J. Latt and *et al.*, "Palabos, parallel lattice Boltzmann solver," 2009, software available at palabos.org.

[20] D. Lagrava, O. Malaspinas, J. Latt, and B. Chopard, "Advances in multi-domain lattice boltzmann grid refinement," Journal of Computational Physics, vol. 231, no. 14, 2012, pp. 4808–4822.

[21] M. Krause, A. Mink, R. Trunk, F. Klemens, M.-L. Maier, M. Mohrhard, A. Claro Barreto, H. M., M. Gaedtke, and J. Ross-Jones, "Openlb release 1.2: Open source lattice boltzmann code," 2019, online openlb.net, Accessed Jan. 2019.

[22] C. Godenschwager, F. Schornbaum, M. Bauer, H. Köstler, and U. Rüde, "A framework for hybrid parallel flow simulations with a trillion cells in complex geometries," in Proceedings of the International Conference on High Performance Computing, Networking, Storage and Analysis, ser. SC '13. New York, NY, USA: ACM, 2013, pp. 35:1–35:12.

[23] F. Schornbaum and U. Rüde, "Massively parallel algorithms for the lattice boltzmann method on nonuniform grids," SIAM Journal on Scientific Computing, vol. 38, no. 2, 2016, pp. C96–C126.

[24] M. Asch, Data assimilation. Methods, algorithms, and applications, ser. Fundamentals of algorithms. Philadelphia, PA: SIAM, Society for Industrial and Applied Mathematics, 2016, vol. 11.

[25] F. Luporini *et al.*, "Architecture and performance of devito, a system for automated stencil computation," Geosci. Model Dev., July 2018, preprint available at https://arxiv.org/abs/1807.03032.

[26] M. Louboutin *et al.*, "Devito: an embedded domain-specific language for finite differences," Geoscientific Model Development, vol. 12, Aug 2018, pp. 1165–1187.

[27] P. Farrell, D. Ham, S. Funke, and M. Rognes, "Automated derivation of the adjoint of high-level transient finite element programs," SIAM Journal on Scientific Computing, vol. 35, no. 4, 2013, pp. C369–C393.

[28] S. W. Funke and P. E. Farrell, "A framework for automated PDE-constrained optimisation," CoRR, vol. abs/1302.3894, 2013, preprint available at https://arxiv.org/pdf/1302.3894.pdf.

[29] G. Pingen, A. Evgrafov, and K. Maute, "Topology optimization of flow domains using the lattice boltzmann method," Structural and Multidisciplinary Optimization, vol. 34, no. 6, Dec 2007, pp. 507–524.

[30] K. Yaji, T. Yamada, M. Yoshino, T. Matsumoto, K. Izui, and S. Nishiwaki, "Topology optimization using the lattice boltzmann method incorporating level set boundary expressions," Journal of Computational Physics, vol. 274, 2014, pp. 158–181.

[31] S. Nørgaard, O. Sigmund, and B. Lazarov, "Topology optimization of unsteady flow problems using the lattice boltzmann method," Journal of Computational Physics, vol. 307, 2016, pp. 291–307.

[32] J. Hückelheim, P. Hovland, M. Strout, and J.-D. Müller, "Parallelizable adjoint stencil computations using transposed forward-mode algorithmic differentiation," Optimization Methods and Software, vol. 33, no. 4-6, 2018, pp. 672–693.

[33] A. Griewank and A. Walther, "Algorithm 799: Revolve: An implementation of checkpointing for the reverse or adjoint mode of computational differentiation," ACM Trans. Math. Softw., vol. 26, 03 2000, pp. 19–45.

[34] J. Zhu and J. Ma, "An improved gray lattice Boltzmann model for simulating fluid flow in multi-scale porous media," Advances in Water Resources, vol. 56, 2013, pp. 61–76.

Imperative Functional Programming

Software Engineering with I4

Lutz Schubert, Athanasios Tsitsipas
Institute of Information Resource Management
University of Ulm
Ulm, Germany
Email: {lutz.schubert, athanasios.tsitsipas}@uni-ulm.de

Keith Jeffery
Keith G. Jeffery Consultants
Shrivenham, UK
Email: keith.jeffery@keithgjefferyconsultants.co.uk

Abstract—**Applications need to be constantly re-developed for new devices and infrastructures, and to address new user needs. This leads to an increasing maintenance cost that only large-scale companies can afford. The problem with traditional Turing based programming models is that algorithms cannot be easily adjusted and thus bind the application to an environment. In this paper, we discuss how mathematical definitions can be used to not only describe algorithms, but specifically to allow their transformation and (re-)generation to principally address different infrastructures and requirements at considerably reduced effort.**

Keywords-software engineering; I4; abstraction; declarative programming; imperative programming.

I. Introduction

Modern infrastructures are defined by a degree of heterogeneity and complexity never encountered before. Myriads of new devices are connected to the internet and want to be used and controlled. Each infrastructure and resource have their own specific characteristics that are difficult to fully exploit without adjusting the application to it. Modern resources may not even be Industry Standard Architecture (ISA) compliant. Hence, such new devices demand significant changes in existing software and a large part of the software industry is already just occupied with ensuring that code runs on and with these new devices.

Traditional programming models based on Turing's concepts [1] are close to the hardware organization. In order to achieve best performance and meet the desired constraints best, every new ISA and hardware organization therefore necessitates a re-thinking and hence re-development of the algorithmic structure to meet the hardware specific characteristics. This leads to significant cost for code maintenance and portability, leading to more than 75% of the development cost [2][3]. Implicitly, smaller companies with new software ideas will not be able to stand the growing pressure to fix bugs, adapt the software to new devices, etc., whereas the pressure on big companies from small innovative, but un-sustainable ideas, grows constantly.

To overcome these constraints, software engineers have always been working on ways of abstracting from the hardware and thereby trying to get closer to the natural way of specifying tasks. However, in general all new models "just" build up on the existing constraints, thus incorporating and wrapping them, rather than addressing the problem directly. In the following we will investigate how developers think about software and how they go about addressing specific objectives. Based on these observations, we will try to derive more flexible software engineering principles that will allow for higher portability and adaptability to different platforms. We will demonstrate that by exploiting intrinsic mathematical properties of code and its properties, we can emulate the developer's behavior in code transformation and adaptation, whilst maintaining or addressing specific properties. The work presented here builds up on discussions in the European Commission's Cloud Computing Expert Group and documented in [4][5] which include any background and related work with respect to the approach.

This paper is structured as follows: in Section II, we will examine the typical software engineering principles and try to derive a generalized model from this. Our principles are based on the assumption of mathematical equivalence to code, which we will examine in Section III. Section IV will try to apply this assumption to the full software engineering principles. We discuss the approach in the concluding Section V.

II. The Software Development Process

Developers are guided by four main principles in their programming process, which we call the four "I"s [5][6]: (1) the *Intention* behind the application, i.e., what the developer actually wants to achieve with it; (2) the *Information* used, processed and generated by the application; (3) the *Incentive* defines the mode in which the functionalities are to be offered, i.e., fast, reliable, etc.; and finally (4) the *Infrastructure* on which the application is to be executed. Let us see how a developer makes use of these four parameters when programming a (new) software:

A. Intention

All software starts with an intention, i.e., with an idea of what the application is supposed to do, once finished. Most programmers already think in terms of steps and procedures at this point, but this is just because of their experience, as can be easily observed on programming beginners. In itself, the intention is not bound to any algorithm or process other than by logical constraints: to make a banana milkshake, it is sensible to switch on the blender after banana and milk have been added, but the order of banana and milk are independent, as is the amount, the type, flavours, etc..

In principle, Turing has already shown that any solvable problem can be solved in a near infinite number of ways, if the individual steps are small enough (think of *how* to add the banana). The process is not prescribed at this point, though the principle steps involved will be known to most humans, though everyone will execute it differently. The things relevant to know in this context, are only the *principle steps involved*, the *logical constraints* and *relationships*.

B. *Information*

Data is one specific form of representing information, and as any communication scientist will know, information is frequently lost by converting it into data. Vice versa, extracting information from data is not always possible and frequently requires human intervention (think of a book as data and the information you extract by reading from it).

For a software engineer, finding the right way of representing information is a challenge on multiple aspects, as it will (1) define the data structure, thereby (2) influencing the algorithmic behavior and (3) constrain the processing and reusability. In general, data is hardly ever the desired outcome of an application, but the information behind it. Even large scale, data-bound applications, such as fluid simulations actually just want to identify where and what kind of turbulences occur, not the pressure and velocity at any given point – we are just constrained in the way that we compute said information without breaking it down into (particle) data. This relationship is complex and requires considerable expertise by the developer.

C. *Incentive*

Incentive may seem the least intuitive at first, as it is something that most developers and users specify only indirectly. By nature, the incentive is closely related to the intention, yet changes the "flavor" of the latter ever so slightly, for example if the application is supposed to be fast versus reliable. Incentives can create the most contradiction and confusion, so that developers will have to find the best middle way between all requirements posed towards them.

The incentive is the main deciding factor for generation of the algorithm, as the developer will have to choose whether to generate a parallel code, a service-oriented or modular approach, whether an algorithm is reliable, fast, storage-consuming etc. Traditionally, software developers are trained in a specific direction and will make the choices intuitively, such as is the case for HPC programmers. Thus, to interpret and "enact" an incentive, we need to know the *properties of an algorithm*. This is a highly theoretical field and, as we shall see, poses many obstacles for automated code generation.

D. *Infrastructure*

Obviously, the final algorithmic choices are made when the target infrastructure is known. Obviously, the incentive already plays a large role in selecting the target infrastructure and vice versa – for example a complex code that needs to be executed as fast as possible will probably have to be parallelised and will have to run hence on a parallel infrastructure; whereas an application with multiple users will probably be destined for a cloud-like web infrastructure, etc.

In this final step, the final code details will be decided, leading to the final algorithm that can be compiled. To realise this, the developer has to know something about the *relationship between hardware properties* and *code behaviour*.

E. *Summary*

The four parameters (Intention, Information, Incentive, Infrastructure), are sufficient to describe all aspects that guide a developer from idea to code (see Figure 1).

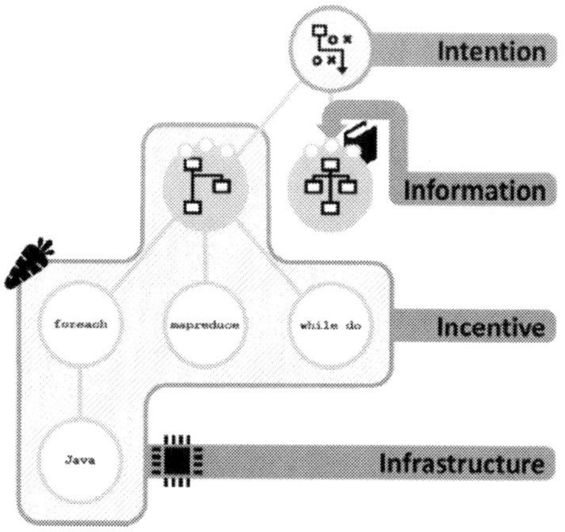

Figure 1. The Software Engineering process.

How can such parameters and the necessary background knowledge for transformation be encoded? We built up on Turing's main principle, namely that computer programs are *mathematically solvable problems* and hence are mathematically expressible. This means for us that they are hence also treatable as mathematical objects, including all according transformation rules. Based on this assumption, most computable problems and therefore applications should be transformable the same way as mathematical formulas. As an implication, if we can express the (human) software engineering process mathematically, we can also use according rules to perform the transformation steps.

III. PRINCIPLES OF I4

The idea here is based on the following main principles: (1) any mathematically expressible problem can be converted into an algorithmic structure; (2) mathematical expressions can be treated mathematically; (3) algorithmic structures can be distinguished by their structural properties, which in turn relate to the specific properties of the code.

As a simple example, let us assume we have a simple task (*Intention*) to count the number of elements in a set of objects. Mathematically, we can define count recursively:

$$count(P) \equiv |P| := \begin{cases} 1\ if\ \forall p \in P: P\backslash p = \emptyset \\ |Q| + |R|; Q \subset P; R = P\backslash Q\ else \end{cases}$$

We can resolve this function by counting the recursively generated leaves (see Figure 2).

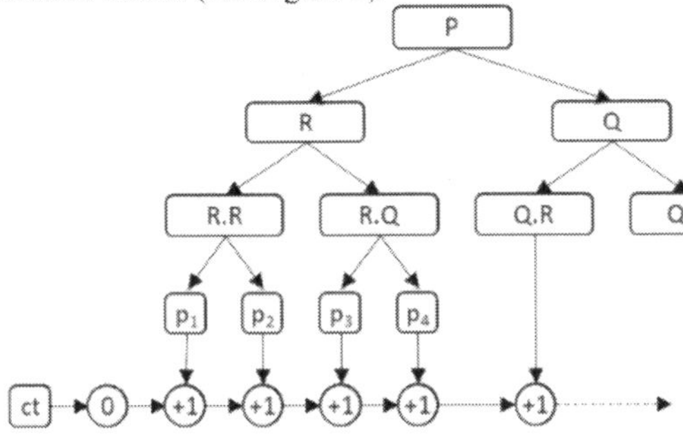

Figure 2. Recursive solution of "count(P)".

It is obvious from Figure 2 that the code can be distributed, serialized, etc. – in other words, we can associate different properties with the structures. What is more, the pattern can be easily described in a higher-order-function as:

```
count(P) ≡ foldl (+1) 0 P
```

which can be realized as a for loop over all elements in P – no matter how P is organized. With this definition, we can also apply simple transformations which in turn affect the code behavior again. For example, we know that

```
count(P) = count(Q)+count(R) for R∪Q=P
```

and thus implicitly

```
count(P) ≡ foldl (+1) 0 P ≡ foldl (foldl (+1)) 0
(R Q)
```

which represents two consecutive loops. This leads to an execution cost of $p = r+q$ operations ($|P|=|R|+|Q|$) and thus the same as without transformation. However, as evidenced by Figure 2, we can easily apply a further transformation

```
foldl (+1) 0 P ≡ foldl (+) 0 (map (foldl (+1) 0)
(R Q))
```

which is fully equivalent according to the base properties of *foldl* and *map*, but obviously can now be executed in parallel (see Figure 3) and thus leads to operational cost of *max(r,q)+1* which is considerably lower than *r+q*.

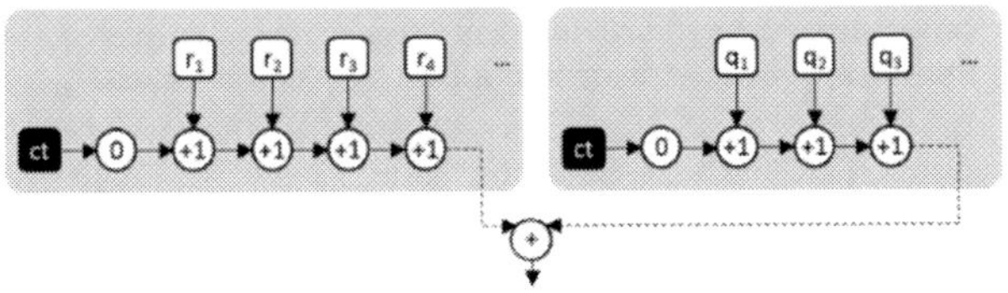

Figure 3. Recursive solution of "count(P)".

Though this is clearly a very simple example, it still shows how a descriptive task ("count") can be (1) converted into an algorithmic structure which (2) can be transformed on a mathematical basis so as to (3) change its properties, such as computational complexity and degree of parallelism.

IV. Application to Software Engineering

With this base principle in place, we can examine how the full software engineering process, as described in Section II, could look like based on mathematical principles. Building up on the "count" example, we can investigate how to count unique elements following the software engineering cycles above, for example to perform statistical evaluations:

A. Specifying the Intention

As a developer, we have immediately multiple ideas and algorithms in mind how to count unique elements in a given set (array, list) and thus this can serve as a full specification for an application. We can thus define:

Intention: count unique elements

To convert this into the form of mathematical specifications that can be reasoned over, we need to first of all specify the relationship between the "intentions", as "unique before count" with a place holder for the set, i.e.

```
count ∘ unique (P)
```

where *count* is defined as above and

$unique(P) := \{\forall p_i \in P: \nexists p_j \in P, i \neq j: p_i = p_j\}$

It is important to stress here that even though an equality operator (=) is used in the definition, this operation may differ completely between types of objects (i.e. Information, see below), just as we could override operators in C/C++. As long as we uphold all equality properties, this definition holds true, even if only partial aspects are used. This is important for the developer, as the code will change substantially with definition of the data structure.

Notably, again we can split P into subsets R and Q, so that P=R∪Q with R=P\Q, leading to

$unique(Q \cup R) :=$
$\{\forall p_i \in (Q' \cup R'): \nexists p_j \in (Q' \cup R'), i \neq j: p_i = p_j\}$
with $Q' = \{\forall q_i \in Q: \nexists p_j \in Q, i \neq j: q_i = p_j\}$
and $R' = \{\forall r_i \in R: \nexists p_j \in R, i \neq j: r_i = p_j\}$

This looks very similar to a direct split, yet it will be noticed that by default Q' and R' will be smaller than Q and R, respectively, thus reducing the workload for the final uniqueness test. Since we also know that *unique* must be executed before *count*, we can specify a general task-flow on basis of the knowledge so far, such as depicted in Figure 4.

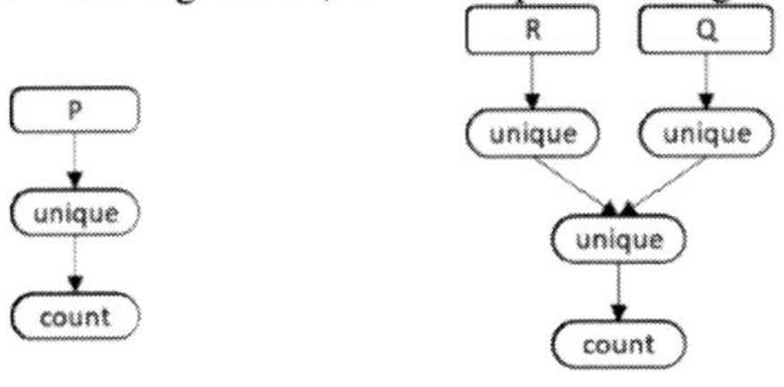

Figure 4. Simple task flow for "count unique members of P" (left), respectively the options for splitting P into R and Q (right).

Any reader with development skills will immediately get an idea for the code just from the specifications above – in particular given the capabilities of most higher order languages for operator overloading. From the specification, we can see that all elements need to be compared against each other (see below for optimization), and that the elements of the resulting set then needs to be counted. We can also already see that both operations can be combined and executed in different distributions, depending on context (*Incentive*). At this point, a pseudo-code could look like this:

```
Q=P
foreach (q in Q)
  foreach (p in (P\q))
    if (q==p) Q=Q\q
ct=0
foreach (q in Q)
  ct++
```

Note that the code would not execute for multiple reasons, among others because we manipulate the set during traversal. More correctly we would temporarily save the values and remove them in the end – the behavior is nonetheless sufficiently defined at this time.

B. *Influence of Information*

It has already been noted that information will greatly influence the code definition above – this is already obvious by the simple circumstance that "uniqueness" is a highly subjective and philosophical notion. We can for example specify that two people are identical if they have the same tax id, or that two objects are the same if they have the same shape and color, etc. As a developer, we would specify the object as a complex struct and overload the equality operation to allow for such behavior. However, as a High Performance Computing (HPC) or Embedded Systems developer, you would probably point out that this structure is not aligned to data access, consider:

```
struct molecule {double px, py, pz, w }
foreach (mol in molecules)
  mol.w = mol.w*c
```

As can be seen, this leads to a stride in memory usage and thus to an 75% underutilized memory, which in turn affects cache performance, leading to 4 times more cache misses than necessary (see Figure 5).

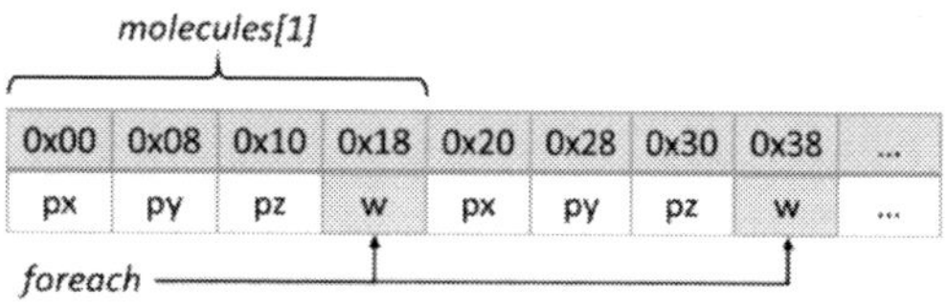

Figure 5. Memory organisation for an array of structs.

By converting this array of structs into a struct of arrays, we can easily improve memory utilization and thus cache performance (see Figure 6):

```
struct molecules {double px[], py[], pz[], w[] }
foreach (weight in molecules.w)
  weight = weight*c
```

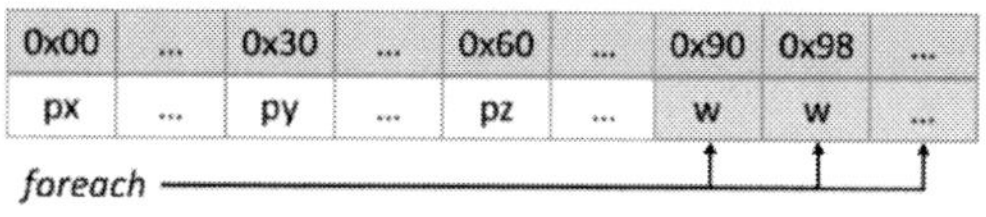

Figure 6. Memory organisation for a struct of arrays.

With the decision for a specific layout, the developer has constrained adaptability of the algorithm considerably at this point. Few compilers support the conversion from array of structs to structs of arrays and vice versa and will always need additional information by the developer to do so. By exploiting *Information*, we do not specify the layout yet – it is in fact often considered a weakness of functional programming that memory layouting cannot be influenced by the programmer [7]:

$P \subset People$

People have *name, location, ...*

By adding a specification that we consider two elements in people as identical if they have said the same names:

$\forall p1, p2 \in P: p1 = p2 \Leftrightarrow$

stringmatch(name of *p1, name* of *p2)*

We thus have a data structure without a concrete layout and we can easily see that both memory arrangements (see Figure 5 and Figure 6) are possible with this definition.

C. *Setting the Incentives*

Notably, the memory layout is directly related to the incentive behind it: a struct of arrays may be more sensible in situations with high performance requirements, whereas an array of struct is sensible if the work is distributed, i.e., when different operations may be performed on the array. Thus, with defining the incentive, we make a concrete instantiation choice for parts of the algorithm, which is closely related to the infrastructure impact, below:

The *incentive performance* can be seen as a projection function from the data access structure and the executional pattern to cost. We have already indicated above that the operational load can be roughly derived from the number of operations resulting from the size of the set. In algorithm theory, we generally assess the order of complexity based on the execution patterns [8] which gives us an indicator for workload and thus performance of an algorithm. Communication overhead can be assessed through data size, messaging frequency and network properties (see infrastructure). Notably, this provides only relative information, as the size of the data set will still affect distribution, degree of parallelism, etc., but it already allows to distinguish between different choices.

We can see that the parallel implementation of the count o unique function leads to a significant reduction of operational load (per processor). Since we also just access the *name* property, we can not only reduce the memory load through a struct of arrays, we can even completely discard all other properties associated with *People* (though this obviously depends on the intention in the first instance).

To realise this, we need to associate the data access cost to a complexity function similar to the algorithmic operation load. Obviously, this is directly related to communication modalities and can thus be assessed similarly, where the cost must be related to non-accessed areas. In other words, we can use indicators, such as ratio between accessed and non-accessed data size based equally on the access patterns (see Figure 3), as well as on the data structure decisions.

D. *Specifying the target Infrastructure*

Only when the task flow is mapped onto a system model can the Incentives be fully assessed and properly matched.

Traditionally, infrastructures are modelled as network graphs, where each node represents a resource and each edge a connection between resources. This allows distribution of deployment graph and thus analysis of the impact on performance, respectively on other Incentives. Given the scale and complexity of modern systems, this approach is not feasible for real world problems. Furthermore, it is as yet unclear, which resource characteristics impact on application properties how –simple properties, such as number of cores, are used, or the hardware is profiled for an application and said profile is then used instead of characteristics.

The I4 model combines these two aspects and relaxes the characteristics definition. We foresee that future machine learning methods building up on the profiling principles devised, e.g. in CACTOS [9], that will automatically categorize profiling information according to the resources used and thus generate more meaningful properties. For now, we assume a relationship graph similar to a network model with annotations meaningful in relation to the Incentives and Intentions, here such as: *multicore* or simply *number of cores*, and *bandwidth, latency*, etc. We can thus define, e.g.

```
User.Dev = {Smartphone}
DB1.Dev = {Virtual, MySQL, 4 cores, ...}}
DB2.Dev = {Virtual, MySQL, 4 cores, ...}}
G = ({User.Dev, Internet}, {(User.Dev, Internet)})
Gt = ({DB1.Dev, DB2.Dev}, {(DB1.Dev, DB2.Dev)})
Gp1 = ({DB1.Dev, Internet}, {(DB1.Dev, Internet)})
Gp2 = ({DB2.Dev, Internet}, {(DB2.Dev, Internet)})
```

This information allows us to generate a simple network graph such as depicted in Figure 7. Comparing this to the potential instantiations of our task graph (see Figure 4), we can immediately recognize the potential task distribution, respectively how the work could be split between resources. This is principally a "simple" graph matching task, bearing in mind that multiple solutions are valid, so greedy matching approaches will be sufficient [10].

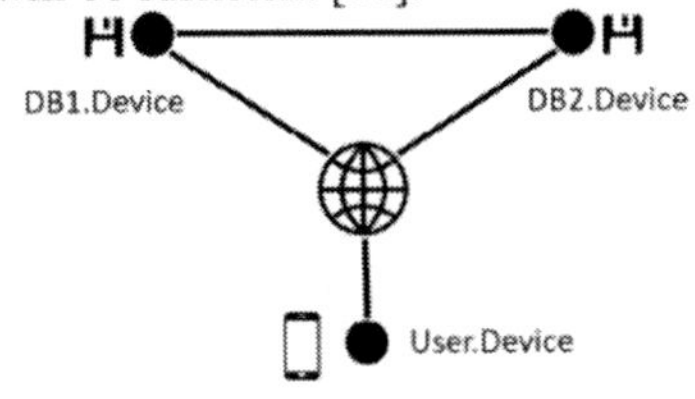

Figure 7. Target infrastructure network graph.

Based on the *performance* incentive, we would try to parallelise and reduce the communication between points, which gives us a general guide to the matching strategy.

E. Generating the Algorithm

We now have all the relevant information in place that would allow a developer to generate an algorithm that meets the specified requirements (the four "I" s). An experienced developer will also see that some of the choices made above will lead intuitively to sub-optimal solutions. Specifically, the separation of unique and count seems less than optimal, since the loops could be fused. Now, we should note at this point that the approach suggested here does aim at replacing existing compiler techniques and, e.g. loop fusion can also be performed by most compilers. Nonetheless, we will show in the following how such techniques can be respected and will influence the transformation choices and outcome.

Following the strict usage of all information, we can derive that if both database sources should be considered, the best approach treats the databases DB1 and DB2 as R and Q, respectively (see Figure 4 (right)). We can also see how mapping to the infrastructure allows different distribution of *count* to exploit task parallelism and communication delays (see Figure 8).

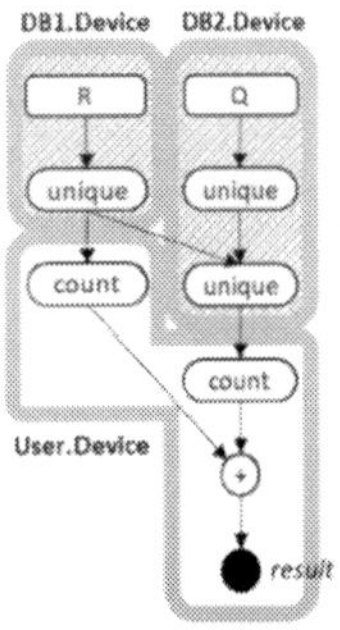

Figure 8. Task flow (see Figure 4) mapped to target infrastructure (see Figure 7).

This analysis is straight-forward and can be directly derived from the individual task-flow graphs that can be spanned by such simple transformations as (1).

We have already seen in Section IV.A, how algorithms can be generally derived from Higher Order Functions. In general, this relationship is more or less straight-forward, though we must bear in mind that different algorithmic presentations exist. For example,

```
foldl f a P
```

can be expressed as

```
z=a; for (i=0; i<P.length(); i++) z = f(z, P[i]);
```

or, since no order is given by foldl, also as

```
z=a; foreach (p in P) z = f(z, p);
```

Obviously, we could use while loops, serialise the execution, recurse it, etc. Similarly,

```
map f P
```

can be represented as

```
for (i=0; i<P.length(); i++) z = f( P[i]);
```

and so on. So, with the definitions for *count* and *unique* as discussed, we can derive algorithms for the individual target resources, e.g.

DB2.Device:

```
Q'=Q
foreach (q1 in Q)
  foreach (q2 in (Q\q1))
    if (q1==q2) Q'=Q\q1
Q''=Q'
foreach (r in R')
  foreach (q3 in Q')
    if (r==q3) Q''=Q'\q3
```

It will be noticed that due to the symmetry of equality, not all elements need to be checked with all others, but in fact that if $q1=q2$ then $q2=q1$ and hence the algorithm for *unique* can be changed to

```
if (q1==q2)
  Q'=Q\q1
  Q=Q\q2
```

It is important to note that *q2* is removed from the search set, due to equality and not from the result set. If we follow the whole process through for each resource, task and all relationships, we thus can generate a task-based execution pattern such as depicted in Figure 9.

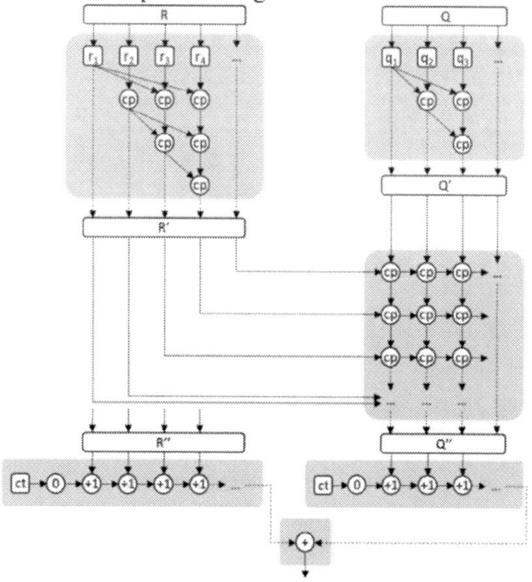

Figure 9. Full flow graph for *count ○ unique (R∪Q)*.

By investigating the dependencies between operations, we will also notice that, in principle, counting can be directly merged with testing for uniqueness (see Figure 10). Even though beneficial for cache access, the actual operational load does not change this way though and it is up to the service owners, which versions they prefer – in principle, the transformation processes described here can derive principally any viable distribution, leaving it up to the developer to make a final decision (or just choosing one).

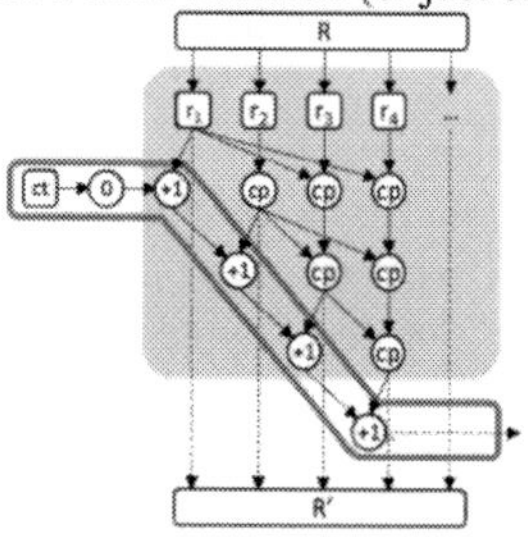

Figure 10. count and unique combined.

V. CONCLUSIONS

In this paper, we have presented an approach to generate *Incentive-* and *Infrastructure-* adapted code using a specification of the *Intention* of the application and the *Information* to be processed. The principles build up from the initial discussions under "Complete Computing" [5] and are still work in progress. For example, while the general principles are clear, the full assumptions and scope of applicability still need to be fully developed and analysed. Even though the same methods will apply for more complex application specifications, the computational complexity rises considerably, necessitating the introduction of metrics to guide the transformation process. Such metrics can be derived from executional properties and backpropagation over the decision tree – this is currently under investigation. Additionally, due to the status of the approach industrial applications cannot be addressed.

Another question obviously arises from problems that are not directly mathematically expressible. Many algorithms have been developed that are basically a set of tasks to be performed, much rather than solving a mathematical problem as such. It can be argued that any computational problem can still be expressed mathematically, though the question would be whether the additional effort is worth the gain. The principles laid out above however easily allow for incorporation of "black boxes" that expose an interface and adhere to well-defined mathematical properties, so that they can be reasoned over, but not changed. This concept will be developed further in the follow-up project to ProThOS.

ACKNOWLEDGMENT

This work was partially funded by the German Federal Ministry of Education and Research (BMBF) in the ProThOS project, Grant No. 01IH16011.

REFERENCES

[1] A. M. Turing, "On Computable Numbers, with an Application to the Entscheidungsproblem," *Proceedings of the London Mathematical Society*, vol. s2-42, no. 1, pp. 230–265, 1937.

[2] J. Hanby, "Software Maintenance: Understanding and Estimating Costs," 21-Oct-2016.

[3] Krugle Enterprise, "The Four Hidden Costs of Software Maintenance," 2014.

[4] K. Jeffery and L. Schubert, "Challenges in Software Engineering, H2020: Analysis and Summary of the Cloud Expert Group Reports," *European Commission*, 2014.

[5] L. Schubert and K. Jeffery, "Complete Computing: toward information, incentive and intention," *European Commission*, 2014.

[6] L. Schubert, A. Tsitsipas, and K. Jeffery, "Establishing a basis for new software engineering principles," *Internet of Things*, vol. 3–4, pp. 187–195, Oct. 2018.

[7] H. Nilsson and International Symposium on Trends in Functional Programming, Eds., *Trends in Functional Programming. Volume 7 Volume 7*. Bristol, UK; Chicago, IL: Intellect Books, 2007.

[8] I. Wegener, Complexity theory: exploring the limits of efficient algorithms. Berlin ; New York: Springer, 2005.

[9] P.-O. Ostberg *et al.*, "The CACTOS Vision of Context-Aware Cloud Topology Optimization and Simulation," 2014, pp. 26–31.

[10] B. O. Fagginger Auer and R. H. Bisseling, "A GPU Algorithm for Greedy Graph Matching," in *Facing the Multicore - Challenge II*, vol. 7174, R. Keller, D. Kramer, and J.-P. Weiss, Eds. Berlin, Heidelberg: Springer Berlin Heidelberg, 2012, pp. 108–119.

Non-Linear Mathematical Models based on Analytical Multiplicative-Additive Transformations Approximating Experimental Data

Rudolf A. Neydorf
Department of Software Computer Technology and Automated Systems
Don State Technical University
Rostov-on-Don, Russia
e-mail: rudolf.neydorf.44@mail.ru

Anna R. Neydorf
Department of Aquaculture technology
Don State Technical University
Rostov-on-Don, Russia
e-mail: neydan@yandex.ru

Dean Vučinić
Vesalius College (VeCo)
Vrije Universiteit Brussel (VUB)
Brussel, Belgium
e-mail: dean.vucinic@vub.be

Anatoly R. Gaiduk
Department of Control Systems
Southern Federal University
Taganrog, Rostov region, Russia
e-mail: gaiduk_2003@mail.ru

Nikita V. Kudinov
Department of Software Computer Technology and Automated Systems
Don State Technical University, Rostov-on-Don, Russia
e-mail: kudinov_nikita@mail.ru

Abstract—**The paper presents the creation of mathematical models from experimental data, which are nonlinear and multidimensional. Such approach is required in many computer-based simulations for a variety of technical objects. It is well known that modern mathematical methods are not able to define, at the same time, both the needed numerical accuracy and the analytical properties. The presented approximation method for non-linear experimental data is a highly accurate mathematical model which contains interesting analytical properties. The method correctness has been validated analytically and experimentally for 1-dimensional and 2-dimensional objects. The method accuracy is based on the data "piecewise" approximation, i.e. their local fragmentation. However, in contrast to the "piecewise" approximation, the numerical model fragments are combined by multiplicative-additive transformation, and not by fulfilling coordinate-logical conditions. Therefore, such numerical model has analytical properties, which are used in the mathematical transformations, as multiplicative transformation of the created analytic functions, called "cut out" functions. These functions are locally approximating the data fragments and have analytical properties, which enable them to be added, when the combined analytical model is defined. The method implementation consists of the following successive and relatively independent stages: (1) splitting the data array into fragments, (2) their polynomial approximation, (3) the multiplicative transformation of fragments and (4) their additive combination into only one analytical function. The proposed method is appropriate for the experimental mathematical modeling of complex non-linear objects, in particular, for their use in the physical and technical simulation processes. The authors envisage that this proposed method would be especially useful for the mathematical modeling of the physics occurring in turbulent flows.**

Keywords—nonlinear multidimensional mathematical models; experimental data approximation; multiplicative analytical transformations.

I. INTRODUCTION

The creation of Mathematical Models (MM) for various simulations, objects, systems, etc., involves acquiring their experimental raw-point data having a certain structure. Usually, the experimental input data is acquired on a regular basis, and often the principle of so-called variation by coordinates is used. The processed variables can have duplicate values, which allow the use of matrix algebra and matrix-vector data representation, as multidimensional tables and multidimensional matrices. Difficulties of formally presenting the data arise, but this can be overcome by applying the proposed mathematical methods. However, the complexity increases when the data do not have a smooth, but a fragmented structure. The term "fragmented structure" is related to the point data arrangement, when there are clearly separated fragments with significantly different slopes along the lines of their interfacing boundaries. The tabular or matrix representation does not always allow evaluating the fragments data structure nature. However, this property is clearly shown in Fig. 1.

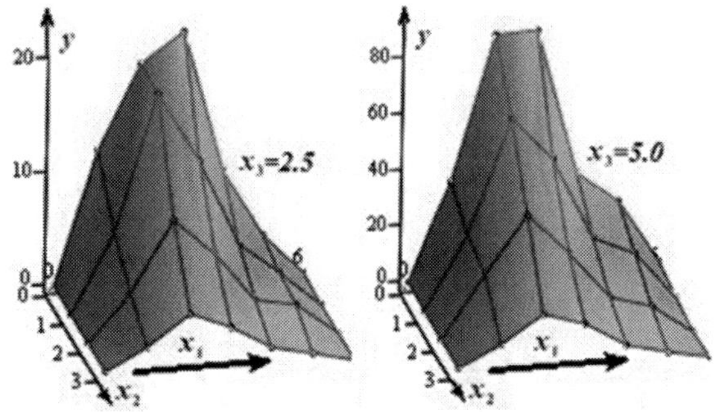

Figure 1. An example of 3-dimensional dependence $y = f^{(3)}(x_1, x_2, x_3)$ with fragment structure

The methods used can describe the "kink" with the desired accuracy. The most simple and effective approach is to apply the piecewise approximation [1] - [3] with any required accuracy. However, the resulting MM has discontinuities in its derivatives along the fragments interfacing boundary lines, and thus excludes analytical transformations. The fragments spline approximation [4] - [6] disables the use of analytical MM transformations. In addition to the "fragment-oriented" approaches, there are methods aimed to build a single analytical MM, such as regression analysis [7] - [10], polynomial expansions [11] [12], methods of radial basis functions [13] [14] and others. It is important to note that they do not provide accurate data approximation for "kinks", discontinuities and finding multiple extremes.

In order to eliminate the existing approximation methods drawbacks, as mentioned above, the Cut-Glue-Approximation (CGA) method was developed, having the first significant results published in [15] [16]. The CGA method combines the MM analytical properties and their quantitative accuracy. The MM approximation is based on processing the Experimental Data (ED) points arrays acquired for complex non-linear and multi-dimensional objects.

One important CGA method feature is the description of the nonlinear piecewise dependence by a single Analytical Function (AF), which has an additive structure consisting of multiplicative components. Multiplying the 2 CGA structure-forming functions: (1) the local approximating fragment (LAF) function of the ED array, and (2) a Multiplicative Isolating Function (MIF) applied to LAF, creates each component. The analytical multiplication of LAF by MIF "cuts out" the LAF section along the boundaries of the ED Fragment (EDF). This leads to a new AF, called Interval-Isolated Function (IIF), having the following unique properties:

1. The IIF fragment boundaries values coincide with LAF;
2. The IIF values beyond the EDF boundaries are almost zero;
3. IIF retains the analytical property [16].

These 3 enumerated IIF properties determine the fourth property: the possibility of IIF addition obtaining only one United AF (UAF), which approximates the whole piecewise dependences and fulfills the imposed accuracy for all IIF-s. The parametric tuning of the coefficients is enabled through the MIF arguments and they allow adjusting the overall approximation accuracy [15] [16].

In [15], the CGA method base was developed and applied in solving the 1-dimensional case. In [16], this method is generalized to the 2-dimensional case. However, it is often necessary to approximate multidimensional dependencies [1] [4] [9] [10]. For example, the strength properties of the composite materials depend on both the concentrations of the components and the technological parameters of their production [17]. For example, the positioning of the robot multilink working body is described by essentially non-linear and multidimensional dependencies [18] [19]. In some medical applications, the positions of detected organs, modeled as mathematical objects, may have discontinuous derivatives. Finally, the solution related to controlling nonlinear objects, by obtaining their MM in any form, is not enough to find practical solutions. What is required is that such MM, with their AFs, have the possibility to find an analytical solution by the synthesis of these objects control laws [20] - [23].

Thus, the follow up presented solution to such problem is applying the CGA method to essentially nonlinear problems of high dimensionality; this is an extremely relevant and promising approach [24] [25].

II. PROBLEM FORMULATION

The CGA method is applied to create MMs of arbitrary objects dimension, having nonlinear dependencies [15] [16] [24] [25] for the acquired experimental data sets. In addition, the paper addresses the generic CGA methodology, which is unique and does not have any similar analogs in the modern approximation theory, as MIF can be constructed for any dimension n of the model under consideration, which ensures that the construction of any n-dimensional IIF, as well as combining them into a single analytic differentiable UAF function, is made possible to describe any nonlinear dependence, which, in addition, might have discontinuous derivatives. It is also important to mention that EDFs have common boundaries taking into account any factor space dimension, which ensures the full coverage of the definition domain, for approximating dependence without affecting the approximation accuracy. Finally, the multidimensional IIFs are assembled into UAF (object's MM) by applying the algebraic summation to combine them.

III. THE CGA METHOD PROSPECTS

The ED object modeling, when applying CGA, is implemented in 4 stages, each applying various mathematical methods and using significantly different information technologies. Currently, the Russian Foundation for Basic Research supports the CGA method development. All its 4 development stages are carried out independently, and the future plan is to supplement the developed algorithms with feedback loops. The envisaged feedbacks are representing the corrective actions for the previously developed CGA stages. Such general approximation algorithm structure should improve their quality and the applicability to model MM for the experimental data. In this paper the applied CGA version has independent stages divided into 2 blocks. The first preparatory block contains the first and second stages of the ED preprocessing to approximate fragments. The second modeling block contains the third and fourth stage, which are responsible for assembling fragments into a single MM of an object modeling the acquired experimental data.

The first CGA preparatory stage is pre-partitioning the experimental data into EDF. The second CGA preparatory stage is the applying the EDF created in the first stage. The processing result of the preparatory block is a set of LAF, fragments of the ED array. The third stage, which is part of the CGA modeling block, performs the conversion of LAF into their local fragments - IIF. In the fourth stage, all IIF are combined in UAF, which is the MM of the object.

The fragmentation process divides the ED into areas which can be well approximated. For each variable, its multidimensional dependencies are divided into intervals. This is already difficult for 2-dimensional problems, since the dependency curvature of any coordinate can vary significantly when other coordinates change. This property is well illustrated by in Fig.1. For 3 -dimensional dependencies, it is practically impossible to show the fragmentation graphically. In addition, the CGA method uses the regular ED coordinate grid with the rectangular EDF faces structure. Their curvature is approximated as nonlinear hyper-surfaces, in general, arbitrary oriented. Therefore, it is extremely difficult to define an effective distribution of hyper-parallelepipeds. With an increase in the modeled dependence dimension, the complexity is related to the distribution of its properties in the factor space, and, accordingly, the fragments complexity increases the manifold dimension. From above mentioned, it can be concluded that the automation of the ED fragmentation procedure of any number of dimensions, and not only for $n \geq 3$, is challenging. The software supporting the CGA method is needed, especially to process the dependencies of 3 or more arguments. It should be noted that in the CGA methodology, the fragmentation of the ED multidimensional arrays differs significantly from the remaining CGA stages, which mostly perform mathematical analysis. Therefore, the CGA fragmentation can be considered as a separate task and it is not discussed in this paper.

In accordance with the CGA method paradigm [14] [15] [23] [24], its second stage performs the approximation of each k-th fragment, selected within the n-th dimension experimental data array. The fragments are approximated by explicit analytical LAFs defined with n-independent arguments, and forming the vector

$$\boldsymbol{x} = (x_1, \dots x_n)^T, \tag{3}$$

which for each k-th is

$$\boldsymbol{x_k} = (x_{1k}, \dots x_{nk})^T. \tag{4}$$

The functions of the vector argument x_k approximates the k-th fragment, which is denoted by n-LAF, and mathematically described by the expression

$$y_{jk} = \varphi_{jk}(\boldsymbol{x_k}), \tag{5}$$

The analysis of the results from [4-9] shows that constructing analytical functions to approximate experimental data having fairly smooth fragments of nonlinear objects should be carried out with a well-developed Classical Regression Analysis (CRA) [12] – [16]. When CRA is applied to the polynomial functions, the regression coefficients obtained from the Least Squares Method (LSM) can effectively optimized their parametric structure variation. In addition, Power Polynomials (PP) are extremely convenient to order the variation of their structure by including/excluding their respective polynomial members. This allows finding the appropriate accuracy by describing the MM for each EDF, with an effective parametric (in accuracy) and structural (MM complexity) optimization of the EDF approximation. The related implementation has structural regularity, which enables creating the Complete PP (CPP) with an arbitrary dimension n for the function y_{jk}, and approximation degree m, applying the following convenient recursive scheme:

$$y(\boldsymbol{x}) = b_0 + \Sigma_i b_i \cdot x_i + \Sigma_{ij} b_{ij} \cdot x_i \cdot x_j + \Sigma_{ijk} b_{ijk} \cdot x_i \cdot x_j \cdot x_k + \dots \tag{6}$$

where $b_{ijk...}$ are multiplicative compositions coefficients defining variants of polynomial members (containing 1 to m multiplied members), while the composition form «$x_i \cdot x_j \cdot x_k \dots$» may also include the power functions of independent variables, up to one variable in the degree, which corresponds to the PP member order (for example, b222 · (x2) 3); the number of forms that define such polynomial structure is n.

To simplify and generalize the algorithm for calculating the optimal accuracy of the EDF approximation, by using such PP, a pseudo-extension of the polynomial dimension in accordance to the number of pseudo-independent variables x_p is done. In this case, the nonlinear expression (6) turns into a pseudo-linear polynomial of the following form:

$$y(\boldsymbol{x}) = b_0 + \Sigma_n b_i \cdot x_i + \Sigma_{(n+1),N} b_p \cdot x_p \tag{7}$$

where $p=n+1$, N; $N-n$ is the number of possible multiplicative combinations x_i, $i=\epsilon(1, n)$ from 2 to n combination members; x_p - pseudo-arguments.

In the case of non-degeneracy of the matrix (X^TX), the vector $\boldsymbol{b}$ coefficients of the pseudo-linear polynomial (7) are optimized by the LSM criteria using the following universal matrix formula:

$$\boldsymbol{b} = (\boldsymbol{X}^T\boldsymbol{X})^{-1}\boldsymbol{X}^T\boldsymbol{Y}, \tag{8}$$

where $\boldsymbol{Y}$ is the output vector, and $\boldsymbol{X}$ is the input matrix under study, consisting of columns of independent variables $\boldsymbol{x_j}$, the rows are the values of these variables $\boldsymbol{x_{ij}}$ in the i-th tries when acquiring the experimental data modeled to support the related MM object.

Since formula (8) is obtained from the Fermat's theorem conditions for the quadratic error function approximating the point data by a power polynomial (7) of any structure, the parametric optimum of the vector $\boldsymbol{b}$ is guaranteed. However, in the general case, each JV structure is characterized by its optimum value. As a result, the discrete structural and optimized approximation polynomial for the set of all possible structures (6) arises. Thus, the EDF approximation, based on the universal polynomial MM, is a convenient tool for its structural-parametric optimization.

The polynomial MM structural optimization and the need to search for its structural and parametrical optimal approximation variant is found interesting to simplify the model. Studies of the authors have shown that, often, having defined the complete polynomial is not the guarantee to have the best approximation accuracy. This effect is due to the fact that the properties of some nonlinear terms contradict the nature of the approximated dependence. However, it is difficult to predict in advance, what are these polynomial terms, due to the peculiarities of the hyper surfaces curvature, which approximate the experimental data of each individual fragment.

The solution to such structural optimization problem requires separate explanation. 3 points require attention: 1) the methodology for solving a discrete optimization problem on a finite set of PP structures; 2) the technology for the formation and variation of these structures, which is associated with symbolic transformations, 3) the formalization and quantitative representation of the criteria for the PP complexity, which is heuristic in nature.

The first problem has two solutions. With a small number of dimensions for modeling the object input space and with a small order of the approximation EDF polynomial, these 2 factors together give a multitude of structures that can be considered in the foreseeable time, and the problem can be solved by the full enumeration method, i.e. being combinatorial. When the cumulative properties of the same factors make a similar NP-complete problem impossible to solve in a reasonable time, it is necessary to apply heuristic search engine optimization, and the best is to apply the modified evolutionary-genetic algorithm for this problem. Its de research and development is discussed in a separate publication.

The solution of the second problem is necessary both for the combinatorial and the search optimization approaches. For coding of the nonlinear members of the PP with the dimension of the ED array $n <= 9$, it is convenient to use structure (6) for PP. The index of the independent variable x indicates the presence of this variable in the multiplicative term of PP, and the degree to which this variable is raised is indicated by the number of repetitions of this index in the code in the PP term. Thus, the free term b, in the polynomial code description, is denoted by "0", the first order term $b_i x_i$ is denoted by "i" (for example, $b_3 x_3$ is "3"), the second order term $b_{ij} x_i x_j$ is denoted by "ij", the third order term $b_{ijj} x_i (x_j)^2$ is denoted by "ijj", etc. The variant itself of the coded structure CPP of the polynomial P to be evaluated is indicated by a sequence of numeric codes separated by spaces.

For example, a 4-order incomplete 3-dimensional incomplete PP is encoded as follows:

$$P = b + b_1 x_1 + b_3 x_3 + b_{22}(x_2)^2 + b_{112}(x_1)^2 x_2 + b_{233} x_2 (x_3)^2 +$$
$$+ b_{1222} x_1 (x_2)^3 + b_{2233}(x_2)^2 (x_3)^2 + b_{3333}(x_3)^4 \sim$$
$$\sim K_P = 0\ 1\ 3\ 22\ 112\ 233\ 1222\ 2233\ 3333 \qquad (9)$$

Their correspondence is shown in (9) by the equivalence sign "~".

Due to the fact that there is not yet a universal and reliable theory for estimating the complexity of such mathematical expressions, the structure of PP has 2 heuristically formulated criteria, which have been proposed and tested when creating the CGA method. The first one is based on the expert evaluation, in the hierarchy of which the difficulty of using a first-order term (see Table 1, column 2) is taken as a unit, while the rest are estimated as shares of it (see Table 1, column 3). The second criterion, although heuristic, has physical justification, since its scale is based on experimental estimates of the time resources spent on the calculation of each PP term (see Table 1, column 2) on the PC used by the authors of the configuration (see Table 1, column 4). Table 2 is a fragment of a general table that can be constructed for any dimension and order of the PP. The fragment is limited to the fourth order of the 3-dimensional PP. The heuristic approach to estimate the complexity applies an average hybrid complexity estimate by scaling the dimensional resource time estimate with a factor of 0.01 (Table 1, column 5).

TABLE I. QUANTITATIVE ESTIMATES OF THE POLYNOMIAL STRUCTURES COMPLEXITY

№№	The structure of a polynomial term	Expert evaluation	Resource evaluation	Hybrid evaluation
1	0	0.5	~150	2.0
2-4	1,2,3	1	~275	3.75
5-10	11,12,13,22,23,33	2	~315	5.15
11-20	111,112,... 233,333	3	~375	6.75
21-35	1111,1112,... 3333	4	~450	8.5
...	...	...	...	...

The use of all 3 criteria showed their consistency, but the actual adequacy of any of them is difficult to prove. The research in this direction is ongoing.

The structuring of ED in the form of the EDF boundary set and building the LAF for all EDF allows moving from the CGA preparatory stages to the experimental MM construction stages.

IV. MODELING OF NONLINEAR OBJECTS FOR EXPERIMENTAL DATA USING CGA METHOD

The final stage of the CGA method is implemented in 2 operations: 1) obtaining an IIF from LAF, and 2) obtaining an UAF from IIF. The first operation is named "Cut the Fragments of LAF" (CF), and the second - "Glue the Fragments of LAF" (GF) [12] - [14] [17]. These 2 operations for one EDF describe LAF of the form (1), and can be represented by the following expressions:

$$\text{CF}: \quad f_k(\boldsymbol{x}) = \varphi_k(\boldsymbol{x})\, \Pi_{ik=1...nk} E^I(\boldsymbol{x}, x_{Lik}, x_{Rik}, \varepsilon_{Lik}, \varepsilon_{Rik}), \qquad (10)$$

$$\text{GF}: \quad F(\boldsymbol{x}) = \Sigma_{k=1...K} f_k(\boldsymbol{x}), \qquad (11)$$

where $f_k(\boldsymbol{x})$ is the k-th IIF; $\varphi_k(\boldsymbol{x})$ is the k-th LAF; n is the co-ordinate dimensionality of the object; $E^I(*)$ is the i-th one-dimensional MIF for the k-th LAF with approximation tuning arguments: x_{Lik}, x_{Rik} –the margin values of the approximation ranges of the k-th EDF in the i-th variables; ε_{Lik}, ε_{Rik} - parameters of the steepness of the fronts of the k-th IIF with respect to the i-th variables; K is the number of EDF and their IIF, respectively; x is an independent vector argument of the modeling object.

In other words, to create IIF of AF that locally approximates EDF, it is required that this function is multiplicative isolated along each independent variable coordinate xi with 1-dimensional MIF, denoted as 1-MIF. Their multiplication output forms n-MIF and supports their multidimensional LAF isolation. Thus, in expression (10) this multidimensional MIF is formulated as:

$$\boldsymbol{E}^n(\boldsymbol{x}, \boldsymbol{x}_L, \boldsymbol{x}_R, \boldsymbol{\varepsilon}_L, \boldsymbol{\varepsilon}_R) = \prod_{i=1\dots n} E^1(\boldsymbol{x}, x_{Li}, x_{Ri}, \varepsilon_{Li}, \varepsilon_{Ri}), \qquad (12)$$

where $\boldsymbol{E}^n(*)$ is n-MIF; $\boldsymbol{x}_L$, $\boldsymbol{x}_R$, $\boldsymbol{\varepsilon}_L$, $\boldsymbol{\varepsilon}_R$ – its n–vectors settings. The multiplicatively forming $\boldsymbol{E}^n(*)$ 1-dimensional MIF $E^1(*)$ is the main system-forming artifact of the CGA method. In this regard, it is necessary to study the properties of 1-MIF, which determine the result of the CF operation.

The developed 1-MIF functions in the first stages, when creating the CGA method had the following structure:

$$E^1(\boldsymbol{x}, \boldsymbol{x}_B, \boldsymbol{\varepsilon}_B) = L(\boldsymbol{x}, x_L, \varepsilon_L)\, R(\boldsymbol{x}, x_R, \varepsilon_R)/B(\boldsymbol{x}, \boldsymbol{x}_B, \boldsymbol{\varepsilon}_B) = \qquad (13)$$

where $L(\boldsymbol{x}, x_L, \varepsilon_L) = x - x_L + [(x - x_L)^2 + (\varepsilon_L)^2]^{1/2}$;
$L(\boldsymbol{x}, x_R, \varepsilon_R) = x_R - x + [(x_R - x)^2 + (\varepsilon_R)^2]^{1/2}$;
$B(\boldsymbol{x}, \boldsymbol{x}_B, \boldsymbol{\varepsilon}_B) = 4\{[(x-x_L)^2+(\varepsilon_L)^2][(x_R-x)^2+(\varepsilon_R)^2]\}^{1/2}$.

Expression (13) contains 2 pairs of $\boldsymbol{x}_B = (x_L, x_R)^T$ and $\boldsymbol{\varepsilon}_B = (\varepsilon_L, \varepsilon_R)^T$ settings to implement the conditions of additional LAF approximation, when transforming it into an IIF using 1-MIF:

- Values of the left and right EDF interval boundaries x_L and x_R along the x_i axis;
- Coefficients ε_L and ε_R of the steepness of the left and right edges of a one-dimensional pulse, which is the 1-MIF, which cuts out the IIF fragment from LAF.

The interval parameters x_L and x_R of the function $E^1(*)$ in (13) are determined by the results of the execution of the ED fragmentation stage and strictly fulfill the conditions of boundaries identity of the neighboring EDFs:

$$\varepsilon_{Li} \equiv x_{R(i-1)}; \quad (L) \quad x_{Ri} \equiv x_{L(i+1)}, \quad (R) \qquad (14)$$

which is due to the continuity requirement of the constructed MM.

More difficult is the problem of choosing the adequate values of the coefficients ε_L and ε_R. When moving from zero to a level equal to unity, on the left border of the x_L fragment, the slope of the pulse front and the smoothness of the transition to an asymptote parallel to the x_i axis are affected by the ε_L value. During the transition from the unit to the zero level on the right border of the x_R fragment, the same characteristics of the 1-dimensional pulse are affected by the setting ε_R.. Moreover, the smaller ε is, the closer is the function front to the threshold transition, and the narrower is the transition region between the vertical and horizontal asymptotes. For clarity, Fig. 2 shows a family of 1-MIF graphs for 3 values $\varepsilon_L = \varepsilon_R = \in \{0.01;\ 0.1;\ 0.3\}$, decoding the curves belonging.

The effect of ε on the accuracy of rectangular pulse reproduction is clearly distinguishable. It can be seen that already at $\varepsilon <= 0{,}01$ in the range between x_L and x_R multiplication by 1-MIF of fragmentary LAF $\varphi_k(\boldsymbol{x})$ practically does not affects its values, fulfilling the accuracy sufficient for the engineering calculations. For $\varepsilon <= 0{,}001$, the analytical "cutting out" of the LAF fragment does not practically differ from the conventionally logical one. In this case, also, all LAF values outside the boundaries x_L and x_R become little distinguishable from zero, which allows additive combining of the independent fragments without having noticeable distortion of their eigenvalues.

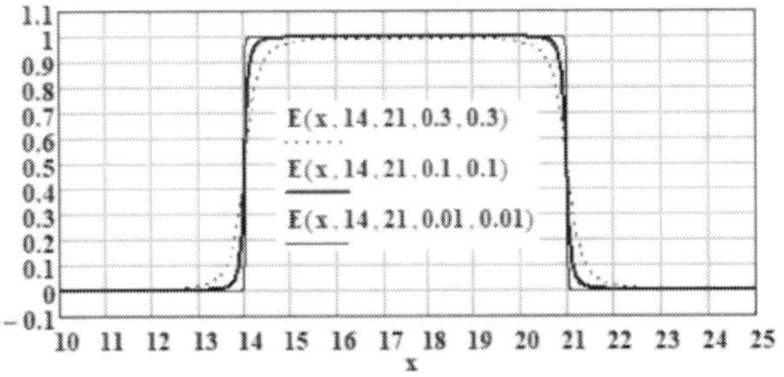

Fig. 2. Illustration of the approximation of the 1-MIF of the form (13) to an ideal rectangular pulse with a decrease in ε

An analytical study of the 1-MIF was carried out in [12]-[14]. These results showed that 1-MIF in the form of (13) have a number of properties that are useful for performing the analytical isolation of approximating functions sections. These properties are compactly summarized in Table II.

TABLE II. MAIN PROPERTIES OF 1-MIF, SUPPORTING THE MULTIPLICATIVE PROCESSING OF LAF

№	*Property Description*	*Values*
1	Function (13) is analytic, since decomposable in a Taylor series at any point in its domain of definition:	x∈]-∞, ∞[
2	Function (13) has a continuous range of values from zero to one:	E1(x)∈]0,1[
3	Function (13) has a single maximum x_{max}<1 at the point x_0, depending on $\boldsymbol{x}_B$, $\boldsymbol{\varepsilon}_B$:	E1extr=E1(x0)
4	The supremum $E^1_{supr}(\varepsilon)=1$ for ε→0 and for any range $[x_L, x_R]$: $x_L<x_R$.	∀xL,xR&ε→0 → E1(ε)→1
5	Function (13) has zero infimum on the set x: $\lvert x\rvert\to\infty$	E1inf=0
6	The function (13) at small ε_B even near the boundary of the interval (for example, at a distance in 0.05 of the scale division) deviates very little from zero outside the interval and from the unit inside it.	ε=0.01→ ΔE1<0.01; ε=0.001→ ΔE1<0.0001
7	The function (13) with $\varepsilon_L=\varepsilon_R$ is symmetric about the midpoint of the x_0 range of the approximated region, i.e. x_0 $E^1(x_0-\Delta x)= E^1(x_0+\Delta x)$	x0=(xL+xR)/2
8	At $\varepsilon_L\neq\varepsilon_R$, function (13) becomes asymmetric, which makes it possible to adapt the shape of the front of the IIF pulse to the boundary properties of neighboring EDF.	$E^1(x_0-\Delta x) \neq E^1(x_0+\Delta x)$
9	The values of function (13) at the pulse boundaries are within 0.25÷0.5 and depend only on the pulse width and on ε_B: $E^1{}_B(\Delta x,\varepsilon) = 0.25\cdot[\Delta x + (\Delta x^2 + \varepsilon_B)^{0.5}]/(\Delta x^2 + \varepsilon_B)^{0.5}$	E1B∈[0.25,0.5]

Analysis of the identified 1-MIF properties showed that all the formulated multiplicative paradigm tasks of the CGA method are performed.

First, the multiplicative processing preserves the analyticity property of the approximating function. That is,

IIF like LAF, a continuous analytic function (properties 1 and 2).

Second, 1-MIF has range values limits (infimum and supremum) 0 and 1. Multiplication of LAF and 1-MIF represents the cutouts of the LAF fragment, i.e. storing its values within the interval (with possible slight distortion - properties 3, 4). The same multiplicative operation isolates a fragment within its interval, making the LAF values outside the interval practically zero (property 5) for the entire ED definition domain.

Third, 1-MIF has the range limits (infimum and supremum) 0 and 1. When LAF and 1-MIF are multiplied, this provides a solution to the problem of cutting out the LAF fragment, i.e. storing its values within the interval (with possible slight distortion - properties 3, 4). The same multiplicative operation provides a solution to the problem of isolating a fragment within its interval, making the LAF values in the entire ED definition domain outside the interval practically zero (property 5).

Fourth, the magnitude of the distortion of the LAF values arising from its multiplicative processing manifests itself only near the fragment boundary, and is effectively regulated by the tuning arguments 1-MIF - εB = (εL, εR) T. In this case, the error can be made arbitrarily small (property 6). This property is illustrated in Fig. 3.

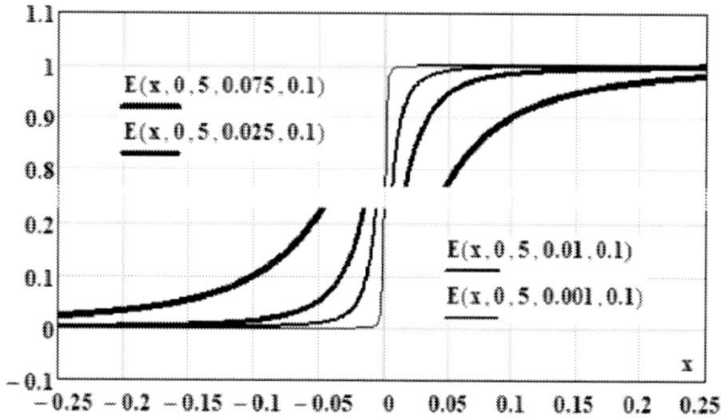

Fig. 3. Deviation dependence of 1-MIF values from 1 within the interval and from 0 beyond its boundaries

Five, the properties of symmetry and asymmetry, declared in clauses 7 and 8, offer ample opportunities for varying the 1-MIF settings to improve the quality of approximation of ED by the experimental MM as a whole. This is due to the fact that varying the value of εB can change the edge configuration of the IIF, reducing the error in joining the neighboring fragments. This factor is complemented by the special properties of the boundaries of 1-MIF, which are shown in paragraph 9.

The last of the 1-MIF properties considered is the variability property of the boundary settings. It plays a crucial role when used as the main tool of the CGA method. It makes it possible to formulate two important points. First, all the EDFs bordering on each other, formed at the first preparatory stage of the CGA method from the initial ED array, should have common borders (necessarily common, but not adjacent). Secondly, the tuning arguments of 1-MIF can be used for search optimization of the final error of the experimental MM obtained at the last stage of the CGA method.

The requirement postulated above for the fragmentation of ED at the EDF with an obligatory commonality of boundaries needs to be clarified in particular. Analysis of expression (13) for 1-MIF shows that the ordinate of crossing the border xB by its graph depends only on the pulse width $\Delta x = x_R - x_L$ and on ε_B, here ($B \in \{L, R\}$ depending on the boundary under study) . The formula for this dependence is given in the condition line 9. In Fig. 4, several curve graphics are plotted for several ε for this dependence. It is clearly seen that even with a sufficiently large ε = 0.2 ordinate, the intersection of the boundary abscissa is almost 0.5 already for Δx=2. When ε = 0.01, this is true in almost the entire range Δx=1. The value 0.5 is a supremum for $E^1(x_B, x_B, \varepsilon_B)$. Therefore, only additively combined boundaries of the EDF can reconstruct the values of the boundary experimental points with averaged accuracy of their description of LAF for neighboring fragments.

The considered rule is valid when implementing the GF-operation of the additive "gluing" IIF into a single UAF function, which is the experimental MM of the object under study. This is true not only for 1-dimensional ED. Studies have shown that $\boldsymbol{E}^n(\boldsymbol{x}, \boldsymbol{x}_L, \boldsymbol{x}_R, \boldsymbol{\varepsilon}_L, \boldsymbol{\varepsilon}_R)$, is formed by the product of n 1-MIF for all coordinates, according to (12). When multiplying by n-dimensional LAF, this n-dimensional MIF also forms n-dimensional IIF, which has common borders with neighboring IIF of various types. This is reflected in their boundary values.

In the 1-dimensional version, as shown above, 1-MIF has only 2 boundary points — the edges is a curve fragment, which gives a coefficient of ~0.5 for multiplicative processing.

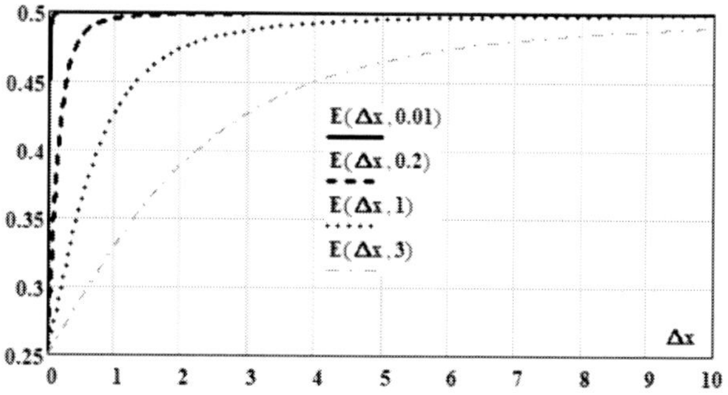

Fig. 4. Dependence of the 1-MIF borders properties on the pulse width and ε

This leads to the fact that the addition of two neighboring IIF $f_k(x)$ and $f_{k+1}(x)$, provided that $x_{Rk}=x_{Lk+1}$ and $E^1(x_{Rk}, x_{Rk}, \varepsilon_{Rk}) = E^1(x_{Lk+1}, x_{Lk+1}, \varepsilon_{Lk+1}) = 0.5$, is determined by the expression

$$f_k(x_{Rk}) + f_k(x_{Lk+1}) =$$

$$= \varphi_\kappa(x_{Rk}) \cdot E^1(x_{Rk}, x_{Rk}, \varepsilon_{Rk}) + \varphi_{\kappa+1}(x_{Lk+1}) \cdot E^1(x_{Lk+1}, x_{Lk+1}, \varepsilon_{Lk+1}) =$$

$$= 0.5 \cdot (\varphi_\kappa(x_{Rk}) + \varphi_{\kappa+1}(x_{Lk+1})) \qquad (15)$$

those will be equal to the average value of the output variable in LAF of these fragments in their common coordinate point.

As the dimension of the modeled dependencies increases, the number of different types of boundary sets increases linearly. So with $n = 2$ and the regular construction of the ED, which was declared at the beginning, its fragment will be a rectangle that is connected not with two segments along the x axis, but with 8 adjacent rectangles on the x_1-x_2 plane. At the same time, he forms 2 types of boundaries: straight line segments - 4 sides, and points - 4 vertices. At experimental points located on adjacent sides and common to 2 EDF, $E^2(x_{Bk},x_{Bk},\varepsilon_{Bk})$ will have a value of ~ 0.5, and at points that are vertices common to 4 EDF, the value 2-MIF will be equals ~ 0.25. This is easily verified by performing a mathematical analysis (13). At each such point four values are averaged to approximate this point for different EDF.

Table III shows the values of the MIF edge coefficients at the boundaries of various types for the dimensions of the objects being modeled up to and including 4. Very characteristic and useful for solving problems by the CGA method is the fact that the decreased coefficient of n-MIF for any of its boundary (boundary) point is always equal to the value close to the result of dividing one by the number of n-EDF bordering at that point.

The revealed phenomenon of MIF properties in the form of (12) allows, along with the main function of CF - the isolation of LAF values $\varphi_k(x_{Bk})$ along the fragment boundaries, to use CF to filter experimental errors and local approximation.

This allows to some extent reduce the overall methodological error of the ED approximation when performing a GF operation: the additive formation of the final UAF. The possibility of minimizing the error arises from the alternative trends in the dependence of the boundary values of 1-MIF on ε_{ij}. When ε_{ijL} and ε_{ijR} approach zero, the steepness of the isolated fragments fronts increases, i.e. improves the fragment isolation accuracy. The optimal values of the MIF settings - ε_{ij} can vary over a wide range of values, sometimes quite far from zero [12].

TABLE III. BOUNDARY VALUES *N*-MIF FOR EDF - PARALLELEPIPEDES UP TO 4 DIMENSIONS

n	1	2		3			4			
Border	Border point	Polygon side	Polygon vertex	Polyhedron face	Polyhedron edge	Polyhedron vertex	Polyhedron hyper surface	Polyhedron face	Polyhedron edge	Polyhedron vertex
Coefficient MIF	0.5	0.5	0.25	0.5	0.25	0.125	0.5	0.25	0.125	0.0625

However, the discussion on how the CGA method could be improved is too voluminous to be considered in this paper. Its follow up developments are envisaged in the coming future as extensions to the achieved results in this work.

V. CONCLUSION

The following 2 conclusions summarize the results achieved in this paper:

1. The presented CGA has a completely logical and has largely original structure, as follows:
   - Collection of experimental data (ED);
   - Fragmentation of ED to multiple EDFs;
   - Approximation of each EDF by a unique LAF;
   - Multiplicative transformation of each LAF using its unique function MIF with related IIF isolated in the argument space;
   - Algebraic summation of all IIFs forming UAF, which is MM of the studied object, created according to non-linear ED, but being, in this case, AF.
2. It was found that the CGA method characteristics are promising and motivate its application in solving the variety of engineering problems. The method has no analogues within the existing mathematical tools. It has practically unlimited application areas, especially adopted for modeling the non-linear n-dimensions dependencies. So far, the development and testing of the CGA method is validated for objects of the first and second order, which has been revealed and partially described in this paper, together with many of its promising developments aspects, to be undertaken in the future.

ACKNOWLEDGMENT

The research supporter by the Russian Foundation of Fundamental Research, project No. 18-08-01178/19 A.

REFERENCES

[1] P.-J. Loran "Approximation and optimization," Trans. with Engl. Publ. "World", M.: 1975.- 496 p.

[2] I. Insung and B. Naylor, "Piecewise Linear Approximations of Digitized Space Curves with Applications," (1990). Computer Science Technical Reports. Report Number: 90-1036. Paper 37. http://docs.lib.purdue.edu/cstech/37, [accessed: 2019-07-03].

[3] A. M. G. Pinheiro and M. Ghanbari, "Piecewise Approximation of Contours Through Scale-Space Selection of Dominant Points," IEEE Transactions on Image Processing, Vol. 19, No. 6, June, 2010.

[4] J. H. Ahlberg, E. N. Nilson and J. L. Walsh, The Theory of Splines and Their Applications, Academic Press, New York, 1967.

[5] C. De Boor, A practical guide to splines, Springer (1978)

[6] G. Micula and Sanda Micula, Handbook of Splines, Kluwer Academic Publishers, Dordrecht-Boston-London, 1999.

[7] J. O. Rawlings, G. Sastry, G. Pantula, D. A. Dickey, Applied Regression Analysis: A Research Tool, Second Edition. 1998.

[8] D. M. Bates and D. G. Watts, Nonlinear regression analysis and its applications, John Wiley & Sons, New York, 1988.

[9] N.R. Drapper and H. Smith, Applied regression analysis, vol. 1, John Wiley & Sons, New York, 1981.

[10] N.R. Drapper and H. Smith, Applied regression analysis, vol. 2, John Wiley & Sons, New York, 1981.

[11] V. Totik, Orthogonal Polynomials. Surveys in Approximation Theory, Volume 1, pp. 70–125, 2005.

[12] S. Khrushchev, Orthogonal Polynomials and Continued Fractions From Euler's Point of View, Atilim University, Turkey: Cambridge University Press 2008, www.cambridge.org/9780521854191, [accessed: 2019-07-03].

[13] M. J. D. Powell, "The theory of radial basis function approximation," in Adv. Num. Anal., Vol.II (ed. W. Light), OUP, Oxford, 1992.

[14] M.D., Buhmann, "Radial Basis Functions: Theory and Implementations," Cambridge University Press, 2003. http://catdir.loc.gov/catdir/samples/cam033/2002034983, [accessed: 2019-07-03].

[15] R.A., Neydorf, "Cut-Glue Approximation in Problems on Static and Dynamic Mathematical Model Development," proceedings of the ASME-IMECE 2014-37236. November 14-20, 2014, Montreal, Quebec, Canada.

[16] R. Neydorf, "Bivariate Cut-Glue Approximation of Strongly Nonlinear Mathematical Models Based on Experimental Data," SAE Int. J. Aerosp. 8(1), 2015, doi:10.4271/2015-01-2394. http://papers.sae.org/2015-01-2394/, [accessed: 2019-07-03].

[17] O.G. Osiaev, "Empirical Strength Criterion of Composite Materials," Vestnik Donskogo gosudarstvennogo tehničeskogo universiteta, Том 10, No. 3 (2010), ISSN 1992-6006 (Online). https://vestnik.donstu.ru/jour/article/view/983/0, [accessed: 2019-07-03].

[18] V. Pshikhopov, M. Medvedev, A. Gaiduk, R. Neydorf, R. Fedorenko, and V. Krukhmalev, "Mathematical Model of Robot on Base of Airship," proceedings of the IEEE Conference on Decision and Control, 2013.

[19] A.R. Gaiduk, S.G. Kapustyan, I.O. Shapovalov, "Self-Organization in Groups of Intelligent Robots," Advances in Intelligent Systems and Computing. vol. 345. p.p. 171-181, 2015.

[20] A.R. Gayduk, E.A. Plaksiyenko, K.V. Kolokolova, "Synthesis of control algorithms of nonlinear multidimensional objects on the basis of UFZh," the Scientific bulletin of NGTU. Novosibirsk, No. 2(59), pages 59-72. 2015.

[21] A.R. Gayduk, K.V. Kolokolova, E.A. Plaksiyenko, A.R. Neydorf, "Synthesis of system of off-line control by a nonlinear multidimensional object on the basis of UFZh," News of SFU. Technical science. No. 2(163), pages 50-60, 2015.

[22] Gayduk A.R., Gurenko B.V., Plaksiyenko E.A., Shapovalov I. O. Development of control algorithms of the unmanned boat, as multidimensional nonlinear object//News of SFU. Technical science. No. 1(162). 2015. Page 250-261. (RINTs).

[23] A.R. Gayduk, E.A. Plaksiyenko, I.O. Shapovalov, K.V. Kolokolova, "A synthesis algorithm on the computer of nonlinear managements of technical objects taking into account uncertainty of their models," Science and education at a turn of the millennia, research works. Release 1. Kislovodsk. KGTI publishing house, pages 21-32, 2015.

[24] R. Neydorf and A. Neydorf, "Technology of Cut-Glue Approximation Method for Modeling Strongly Nonlinear Multivariable Objects, Theoretical Bases and Prospects of Practical Application," SAE Technical Paper 2016-01-2035, 2016, doi:10.4271/2016-01-2035.

[25] R. Neydorf, A. Neydorf, D. Vučinić, "Approximation Method for Strongly Nonlinear and Multidimensional Object Dependencies Modeling," Improved Performance of Materials. Design and Experimental Approaches, Springer, pp. 155-173, 2017. URL: https://link.springer.com/chapter/10.1007/978-3-319-59590-0_13, [accessed: 2019-07-03].

Spatial Visibility Trajectory Planning Using Inverse Reinforcement Learning

Oren Gal and Yerach Doytsher
Mapping and Geo-information Engineering
Technion - Israel Institute of Technology
Haifa, Israel
e-mails: {orengal, doytsher}@technion.ac.il

Abstract—**In this paper, we present a conceptual Spatial Trajectory Planning (STP) method using Rapid Random Trees (RRT) planner, generating visibility motion primitives in urban environments using Inverse Reinforcement Learning (IRL) approach. Visibility motion primitives are set by using Spatial Visibility Clustering (SVC) analysis. Based on the STP planning method, we introduce IRL formulation and analysis which learns the value function of the planner from demonstrated trajectories and generates spatial visibility trajectory planning.**

Keywords-Visibility; 3D; Spatial analysis; Motion Planning.

I. INTRODUCTION

Spatial clustering in urban environments is a new spatial field from trajectory planning aspects [1]. The motion and trajectory planning fields have been extensively studied over the last two decades [2][4][6]. The main effort has focused on finding a collision-free path in static or dynamic environments, i.e., in moving or static obstacles, using roadmap, cell decomposition, and potential field methods [11].

The path-planning problem becomes an NP-hard one, even for simple cases such as time-optimal trajectories for a system with point-mass dynamics and bounded velocity and acceleration with polyhedral obstacles [7].

Path planning algorithms can be distinguished as local and global planners. The local planner generates one, or a few, steps at every time step, whereas the global planner uses a global search to the goal over a time-spanned tree. Examples of local (reactive) planners are [9][14]. These planners are too slow, do not guarantee safety and neglect spatial aspects.

Efficient solutions for an approximated problem were investigated by LaValle and Kuffner, addressing non-holonomic constraints by using the Rapidly Random Trees (RRT) method [15][16]. Over the years, many other semi-randomized methods were proposed, using evolutionary programming [5][18].

The randomized sampling algorithms planner, such as RRT, explores the action space stochastically. The RRT algorithm is probabilistically complete, but not asymptotically optimal [13]. The RRT* planner challenges optimality by a rewiring process each time a node is added to the tree. However, in cluttered environments, RRT* may behave poorly since it spends too much time deciding whether to rewire or not.

Overall, only a few works have focused on spatial analysis characters integrated into trajectory planning methods such as visibility analysis or spatial clustering methods [11].

Our research contributes to the spatial data clustering field, where, as far as we know, visibility analysis has become a leading factor for the first time. The SVC method, while mining the real pedestrians' mobility datasets, enables by a visibility analysis to set the number of clusters.

Analyzing pedestrian's mobility from a spatial point of view mainly focused on route choice [3], simulation model [19] and agent-based modeling [12].

The efficient computation of visible surfaces and volumes in 3D environments is not a trivial task. The visibility problem has been extensively studied over the last twenty years, due to the importance of visibility in GIS and Geomatics, computer graphics and computer vision, and robotics. Accurate visibility computation in 3D environments is a very complicated task demanding a high computational effort, which could hardly have been done in a very short time using traditional well-known visibility methods.

The exact visibility methods are highly complex, and cannot be used for fast applications due to their long computation time. Previous research in visibility computation has been devoted to open environments using Digital Elevation Model (DEM), representing raster data in 2.5D (Polyhedral model), and do not address, or suggest solutions for, dense built-up areas.

Most of these works have focused on approximate visibility computation, enabling fast results using interpolations of visibility values between points, calculating point visibility with the Line of Sight (LOS) method [7]. Lately, fast and accurate visibility analysis computation in 3D environments has been presented [10].

In this paper, we present, for the first time as far as we know, a unique conceptual Spatial Trajectory Planning

(STP) method based on RRT planner. The generated trajectories are based on visibility motion primitives set by SVC Optimal Control Points (OCP) as part of the planned trajectory, which takes into account exact 3D visible volumes analysis clustering in urban environments.

The proposed planner includes obstacle avoidance capabilities, satisfying dynamics' and kinematics' agent model constraints in 3D environments, guaranteeing probabilistic completeness. The generated trajectories are dynamic ones and are regularly updated during daylight hours due to SVC OCP during daylight hours. STP trajectories can be used for tourism and entertainment applications or for homeland security needs.

In the following sections, in Section II, we introduce the RRT planner and our extension for a spatial analysis case, such as 3D visibility. In Section III, we present the STP planner, using RRT and SVC capabilities. In the last section of the paper, we present the Inverse Reinforcement Learning (IRL) approach and algorithm based on the proposed STP planning method, learning the value function of the planner from demonstrated trajectories.

II. Spatial Rapid Random Trees

In this section, the RRT path planning technique is briefly introduced with spatial extension. RRT can also deal with high-dimensional spaces by taking into account dynamic and static obstacles including dynamic and non-holonomic robots' constraints.

The main idea is to explore a portion of the space using sampling points in space, by incrementally adding new randomly selected nodes to the current tree's nodes.

RRTs have an (implicit) Voronoi bias that steers them towards yet unexplored regions of the space. However, in case of kinodynamic systems, the imperfection of the underlying metric can compromise such behavior. Typically, the metric relies on the Euclidean distance between points, which does not necessarily reflect the true cost-to-go between states. Finding a good metric is known to be a difficult problem. Simple heuristics can be designed to improve the choice of the tree state to be expanded and to improve the input selection mechanism without redefining a specific metric.

A. RRT Stages

The RRT method is a randomized one, typically growing a tree search from the initial configuration to the goal, exploring the search space. These kinds of algorithms consist of three major steps:

1. **Node Selection:** An existing node on the tree is chosen as a location from which to extend a new branch. Selection of the existing node is based on probabilistic criteria such as metric distance.
2. **Node Expansion:** Local planning applied a generating feasible motion primitive from the current node to the next selected local goal node, which can be defined by a variety of characters.
3. **Evaluation:** The possible new branch is evaluated based on cost function criteria and feasible connectivity to existing branches.

These steps are iteratively repeated, commonly until the planner finds feasible trajectory from start to goal configurations, or other convergence criteria.

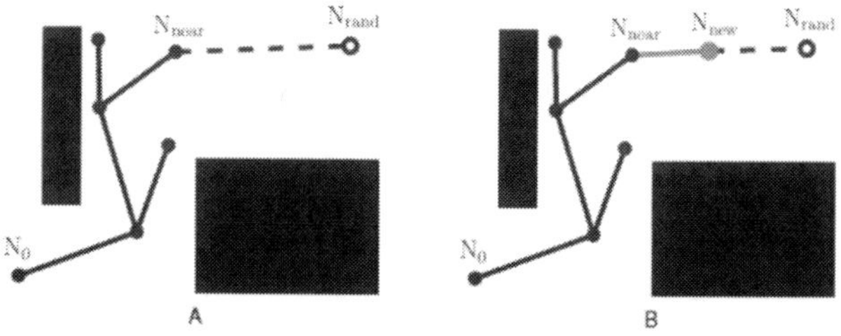

Figure 1. The RRT algorithm: (A) Sampling and node selection steps; (B) Expansion step.

A simple case demonstrating the RRT process is shown in Figure 1. The sampling step selects N_{rand}, and the node selection step chooses the closest node, N_{near}, as shown in Figure 1.A. The expansion step, creating a new branch to a new configuration, N_{new}, is shown in Figure 1.B. An example for growing RRT algorithm is shown in Figure 2.

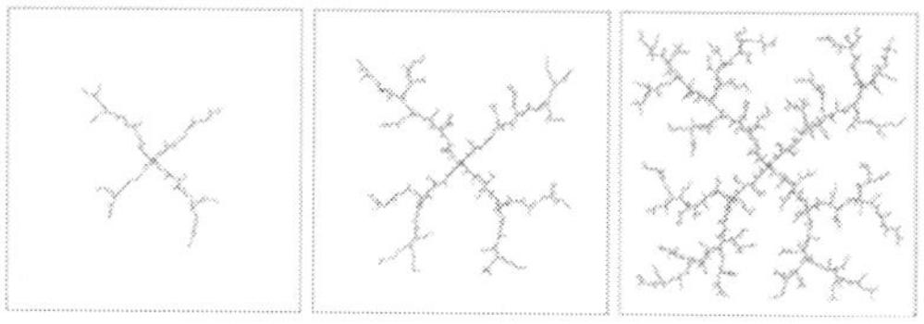

Figure 2. Example for growing RRT algorithm.

B. Spatial RRT Formulation

We formulate the RRT planner and revise the basic RRT planner for a 3D spatial analysis case for a continuous path from initial state x_{init} to goal state x_{goal}:

1. **State Space:** A topological space, X.
2. **Boundary Values:** $x_{init} \subset X$ and $x_{goal} \subset X$.
3. **Free Space:** A function $D: X \rightarrow \{true, false\}$ that determines whether $x(t) \subset X_{free}$ where X_{free} consist of the attainable states outside the obstacles in a 3D environment.
4. **Inputs:** A set, U, contains the complete set of attainable control efforts u_i, that can affect the state.
5. **Incremental Simulator:** Given a current state, $x(t)$, and input over time interval Δt, compute $x(t+\Delta t)$.
6. **3D Spatial Analysis:** A real value function, $f(x; u, OCP_i)$ which specifies the cost to the center of 3D visibility volumes cluster points (OCP) between a pair of points in X.

C. Spatial RRT Formulation

We present a revised RRT pseudo code described in Table I, for spatial case generating trajectory T, applying K steps from initial state x_{init}. The f function defines the dynamic model and kinematic constraints, $\dot{x} = f(x; u, OCPi)$, where u is the input and OCP_i sets the next new state and the feasibility of following the next spatial visibility clustering point.

TABLE I. SPATIAL RRT PSEUDO CODE

```
Generate Spatial RRT (x_init; K; Δt)
T.init (x_init);
For k = 1 to K do
        x_rand ← random.state();
        x_near ← nearest.neighbor (x_rand; T );
        u ← select.input (x_rand; x_near);
        x_new ← new.state (x_near; u; Δt; f);
        T.add.vertex (x_new);
        T.add.edge (x_near; x_new; u);
End
Return T
```

III. SPATIAL TRAJECTORY PLANNING (STP)

Next, we present a conceptual STP method based on RRT planner. The method generates visibility motion primitives in urban environments. The STP method is based on a RRT planner extending the stochastic search to specific *OCP*. These primitives connecting between nodes through OCP are defined as visibility primitives.

A common RRT planner is based on greedy approximation to a minimum spanning tree, without considering either path lengths from the initial state or following or getting close to specific OCP. Our STP planner consist of a tree's extension for the next time step with probability to goal and probability to waypoint, where trajectories can be set to follow adjacent points or through OCP. The planner includes obstacle avoidance capabilities, satisfying dynamics' and kinematics' agent model constraints in 3D environments. As we demonstrated in the previous section, the OCP are dynamic during daylight hours. Due to *OCP's* dynamic character, the generated trajectory is also a dynamic one during daylight hours.

We present our concept addressing the STP method formulating planner for a UGV model, integrating *OCP's* as part of the generated trajectories along with obstacle avoidance capability.

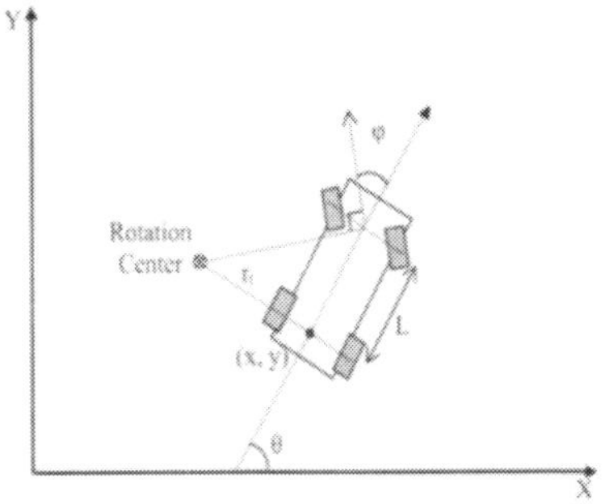

Figure 3. Four-Wheeled Car Model with Front-Wheel Steering [17]

A. Dynamic Model

In this section, we suggest an Unmanned Ground Vehicle (UGV) dynamic model based on the four-wheeled car system with rear-wheel drive and front-wheel steering [17]. This model assumes that only the front wheels are capable of turning and the back wheels must roll without slipping, and all the wheels turn around the same point (rotation center) which is co-linear with the rear axle of the car, as can be seen in Figure 3, where L is the length of the car between the front and rear axles. r_t is the instantaneous turning radius.

Thus, the UGV dynamic model can be described as:

$$\dot{x} = f(x, u) = \begin{Bmatrix} \dot{x} \\ \dot{y} \\ \dot{\theta} \end{Bmatrix} = \begin{Bmatrix} v\cos(\theta) \\ v\sin(\theta) \\ \frac{v}{L}\tan(\phi) \end{Bmatrix} \quad (1)$$

The state vector, x, is composed of two position variables (x, y) and an orientation variable, θ. The x-y position of the car is measured at the center point of the rear axle. The control vector, u, consists of the vehicle's velocity, v, and the angle of the front wheels, ϕ, with respect to the car's heading.

B. Search Method

Our search is guided by following spatial clustering points based on 3D visible volumes analysis in 3D urban environments, i.e., Optimal Control. The cost function for each next possible node (as the target node) consists of probability to closest *OCP*, P_{OCPi}, and probability to random point, P_{rand}.

In case of overlap between a selected node and obstacle in the environment, the selected node is discarded, and a new node is selected based on P_{OCPi} and P_{rand}. Setting the probabilities as P_{OCPi} =0.9 and P_{rand}=0.1, yield to the exploration behavior presented in Figure 4.

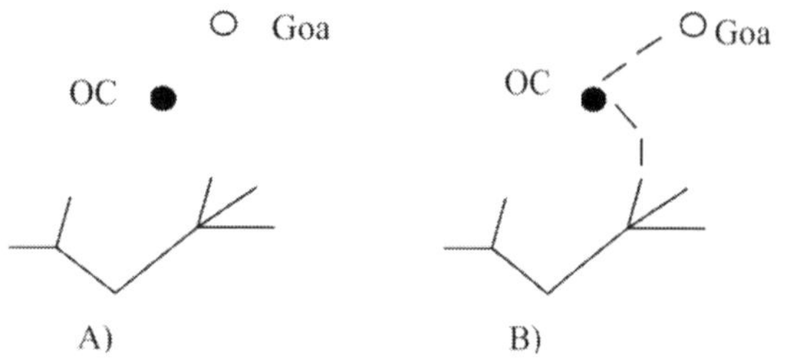

Figure 4. STP Search Method: (A) Start and Goal Points; (B) Explored Space to the Goal Through OCP

C. *STP Planner Pseudo-Code*

We present our STP planner pseudo code described in Table II, for spatial case generating trajectory T with the search space method presented in the Section V.B. The search space is based on P_{OCPi} and P_{rand}. We apply K steps from initial state x_{init}. The f function defines the dynamic model and kinematic constraints, $\dot{x} = f(x; u)$, where u is the input and $OCPi$ are local target points between start and goal states.

TABLE II. STP PLANNER PSEUDO CODE

```
STP Planner (x_init; x_Goal ;K; Δt; OCP)
T.init (x_init);
x_rand ← random.state();
x_near ← nearest.neighbor(x_rand; T );
u ← select.input(x_rand; x_near);
x_new ← new.state.OCP (OCP_i; u; Δt; f);
While x_new ≠ x_Goal do
    x_rand ← random.state();
    x_near ← nearest.neighbor(x_rand; T );
    u ← select.input(x_rand; x_near);
    x_new ← new.state.OCP (OCP_i; u; Δt; f);
    T.add.vertex(x_new);
    T.add.edge(x_near; x_new; u);
end
return T;
```

```
Function new.state.OCP (OCP_i;u; Δt; f)
Set P_OCPi , Set P_rand
p←uniform_rand[0..1]
  if  0 < p < P_OCPi
    return x_new = f(OCP_i,u,Δt);
else
  if P_OCPi < p < P_rand+ P_OCPi
then
    return RandomState();
    end.
```

D. *Completeness*

Motion-planning and search algorithms commonly describe 'complete planner' as an algorithm that always provides a path planning from start to goal in bounded time. For random sampling algorithms, 'probabilistic complete planner' is defined as: if a solution exists, the planner will eventually find it by using random sampling. In the same manner, the deterministic sampling method (for example, grid-based search) defines completeness as resolution completeness.

Sampling-based planners, such as the STP planner, do not explicitly construct search space and the space's boundaries, but exploit tests with preventing collision with obstacles and, in our case, taking spatial considerations into account. Similarly, to other common RRT planners, which share similar properties with the STP planner, our planner can be classified as a probabilistic complete one.

IV. STP-IRL ALGORITHM

In most Reinforcement Learning (RL) systems, the state is basically agent's observation of the environment. At any given state the agent chooses its action according to a policy. Hence, a policy is a road map for the agent, which determines the action to take at each state. Once the agent takes an action, the environment returns the new state and the immediate reward. Then, the agent uses this information, together with the discount factor to update its internal understanding of the environment, which, in our case, is accomplished by updating a value function. Most methods are using the use well-known simple and efficient greedy exploration method maximizing Q-value.

In case of velocity planning space as part of spatial analysis planning, each possible action is a possible velocity in the next time step, that also represents a viewpoint. The Q-value function is based on greedy search velocity, with greedy local search method. Based on that, the Temporal-Difference (TD) [10] and the State-Action-Reward-Action (SARSA) [21] methods for Reinforcement Learning (RL) can be used, generating a visible trajectory in 3D urban environment.

A. *Markov Decision Processes (MDP)*

The standard Reinforcement Learning set-up can be described as an MDP, consisting of:

- **A finite set of states** S, comprising all possible representations of the environment.
- **A finite set of actions** A, containing all possible actions available to the agent at any given time.
- **A reward function** $R = \psi(s_t, a_t, s_{t+1})$, determining the immediate reward of performing an action at from a state s_t, resulting in s_{t+1}.
- **A transition model** $T(s_t, a_t, s_{t+1}) = p(s_{t+1} | s_t, a_t)$, describing the probability of transition between states s_t and s_{t+1} when performing an action a_t.

B. *Temporal Difference Learning*

TD learning interpolates ideas from Dynamic Programming (DP) and from Monte Carlo methods. TD algorithms are able to learn directly from raw experiences without any particular model of the environment.

While in Monte Carlo methods an episode needs to reach completion to update a value function, Temporal-Difference learning is able to learn (update) the value function within each experience (or step). The price paid for being able to regularly change the value function is the need to update estimations based on other learnt estimations (recalling DP ideas). While in DP a model of the environment's dynamic is needed, both Monte Carlo and TD approaches are more suitable for uncertain and unpredictable tasks.

Since TD learns from every transition (state, reward, action, next state, next reward) there is no need to ignore/discount some episodes as in Monte Carlo algorithms.

C. STP Using Inverse Reinforcement Learning

In this section, we present the Inverse Reinforcement Learning (IRL) approach based on the proposed Spatial RRT planning method. It considers that the value function f is related to each point x. The Spatial RRT planner seeks to obtain the trajectory T^* that is based on visibility motion primitives set by SVC Optimal Control Points (OCP) as part of the planned trajectory, which takes into account exact 3D visible volumes analysis clustering in urban environments, based on optimizing the value function f along T.

The generated trajectories are then represented by a set of discrete configuration points $T = \{x_1, x_2, \cdots, x_N\}$. Without loss of generality, we can assume that the value function for each point can be expressed as a linear combination of a set of sub-value functions, that will be called features $c(x) = \sum c_j f_j(x)$. The cost of path T is then the sum of the cost for all points in the path. Particularly, in the RRT, the value is the sum of the sub-values of moving between pairs of states in the path:

$$c(\zeta) = \sum_{i=1}^{N-1} c(x_i, x_{i+1}) = \sum_{i=1}^{N-1} \frac{c(x_i) + c(x_{i+1})}{2} \|x_{i+1} - x_i\|$$
$$= \omega^T \sum_{i=1}^{N-1} \frac{f(x_i) + f(x_{i+1})}{2} \|x_{i+1} - x_i\| = \omega^T f(\zeta) \quad (2)$$

Based on the number of demonstration trajectories D, $D = \{\zeta_1, \zeta_2, \cdots, \zeta_D\}$, by using IRL, weights ω can be set for learning from demonstrations and setting similar planning behavior. As was shown by [10][21], this similarity is achieved when the expected value of the features for the trajectories generated by the planner is the same as the expected value of the features for the given demonstrated trajectories:

$$\mathbb{E}(f(\zeta)) = \frac{1}{D} \sum_{i=1}^{D} f(\zeta_i) \quad (3)$$

Applying the Maximum Entropy Principle [22] to the IRL problem leads to the following form for the probability density for the trajectories returned by the demonstrator:

$$p(\zeta|\omega) = \frac{1}{Z(\omega)} e^{-\omega^T f(\zeta)} \quad (4)$$

where $Z(\omega)$ is a normalization function that does not depend on ζ. One way to determine ω is maximizing the (log-) likelihood of the demonstrated trajectories under the previous model:

$$L(D|\omega) = -D\log(Z(\omega)) \quad + \sum_{i=1}^{D} (-w^T f(\zeta_i)) \quad (5)$$

The gradient of the previous log-likelihood with respect to ω is given by:

$$\nabla\mathcal{L} = \frac{\partial \mathcal{L}(\mathcal{D}|\omega)}{\partial \omega} = \mathbb{E}(f(\zeta)) - \frac{1}{D} \sum_{i=1}^{D} f(\zeta_i) \quad (6)$$

As mentioned in [22], this gradient can be intuitively explained. If the value of one of the features for the trajectories returned by the planner is higher than the value in the demonstrated trajectories, the corresponding weight should be increased to increase the value of those trajectories. The main problem with the computation of the previous gradient is that it requires to compute the expected value of the features $E(f(\zeta))$ for the generative distribution (4). We suggest setting large amount of D cased, with relative w values for our planner characters, as seen in Table III.

TABLE III. STP-IRL PLANNER PSEUDO CODE

```
STP - IRL Planner
Setting Trajectory S Examples D, D= T*.init (x_init);
Calculate function features Weight, w
f_D ← AverageFeatureCount(D);
w ← random_init();
Repeat
        for each T* do
            for rrt_repetitions do
                ζ_i ← getRRTstarPath(T*,ω)
                f(ζ_i) ← calculeFeatureCounts(ζ_i)
        end for
        f_RRT (T*) ← Σ_{i=1}^{rrt_repetitions} f( ζ_i))/rrt_repetitions
    end for
    f_RRT ←( Σ_{i=1}^{S} f_RRT)/s
    ∇L ← f_RRT - f_D
    w ←UpdatedWeigths (∇L)
Until convergence, Return w
```

V. CONCLUSIONS

In this paper, we have presented a unique planner concept, STP, generating trajectory in 3D urban environments based on the UGV model. The planner takes into account obstacle avoidance capabilities and passes through optimal control points calculated from spatial analysis. The spatial analysis defines the number of clusters in a dataset based on an analytic visibility analysis, named SVC.

Based on SVC and STP analysis, we presented an Inverse Reinforcement Learning (IRL) approach based on the proposed STP planning method, learning the value function of the planner from the demonstrated trajectories.

Future research will also include performances and algorithm complexity analysis for STP and SVC methods.

REFERENCES

[1] O. Gal and Y. Doytsher, "Spatial Visibility Clustering Analysis In Urban Environments Based on Pedestrians' Mobility Datasets," The Sixth International Conference on Advanced Geographic Information Systems, Applications, and Services, pp. 38-44, 2014.

[2] J. Bellingham, A. Richards, and J. How, "Receding Horizon Control of Autonomous Aerial Vehicles," in Proceedings ofthe IEEE American Control Conference, Anchorage, AK, USA, pp. 3741–3746, 2002.

[3] A. Borgers and H. Timmermans, "A model of pedestrian route choice and demand for retail facilities within inner-city shopping areas," Geographical Analysis, vol. 18, No. 2, pp. 115-128, 1996.

[4] S. A. Bortoff, "Path planning for UAVs," In Proc. of the American Control Conference, Chicago, IL, USA, pp. 364–368, 2000.

[5] B. J. Capozzi and J. Vagners, "Navigating Annoying Environments Through Evolution," Proceedings of the 40th IEEE Conference on Decision and Control, University of Washington, Orlando, FL, USA, 2001.

[6] H. Chitsaz and S. M. LaValle, "Time-optimal paths for a Dubins airplane," in Proc. IEEE Conf. Decision. and Control., USA, pp. 2379–2384, 2007.

[7] B. Donald, P. Xavier, J. Canny, and J. Reif, "Kinodynamic Motion Planning," Journal of the Association for Computing Machinery, pp. 1048–1066, 1993.

[8] Y. Doytsher and B. Shmutter, "Digital Elevation Model of Dead Ground," Symposium on Mapping and Geographic Information Systems (Commission IV of the International Society for Photogrammetry and Remote Sensing), Athens, Georgia, USA, 1994.

[9] W. Fox, D. Burgard, and S. Thrun, "The dynamic window approach to collision avoidance," IEEE Robotics and Automation Magazine, vol. 4, pp. 23–33, 1997.

[10] O. Gal and Y. Doytsher, "Fast and Accurate Visibility Computation in a 3D Urban Environment," in Proc. of the Fourth International Conference on Advanced Geographic Information Systems, Applications, and Services, Valencia, Spain, pp. 105-110, 2012.

[11] O. Gal and Y. Doytsher, "Fast and Efficient Visible Trajectories Planning for Dubins UAV model in 3D Built-up Environments," Robotica, FirstView, pp. 1-21 Cambridge University Press 2013 DOI: http://dx.doi.org/10.1017/S0263574713000787, [accessed February 2019].

[12] M. Haklay, D. O'Sullivan, and M.T. Goodwin, "So go down town: simulating pedestrian movement in town centres," Environment and Planning B: Planning & Design, vol. 28, no. 3, pp. 343-359, 2001.

[13] S. Karaman and E. Frazzoli, "Sampling-based algorithms for optimal motion planning," Int. J. Robot. Res., vol. 30, no. 7, pp. 846–894, 2011.

[14] N.Y. Ko and R. Simmons, "The lane-curvature method for local obstacle avoidance," In International Conference on Intelligence Robots and Systems, 1998.

[15] S. M. LaValle, "Rapidly-exploring random trees: A new tool for path planning," TR 98-11, Computer Science Dept., Iowa State University, USA, 1998.

[16] S. M. LaValle and J. Kuffner. "Randomized kinodynamic planning," In Proc. IEEE Int. Conf. on Robotics and Automation, Detroit, MI, USA, pp. 473–479, 1999.

[17] L. R. Lewis, "Rapid Motion Planning and Autonomous Obstacle Avoidance for Unmanned Vehicles," Master's Thesis, Naval Postgraduate School, Monterey, CA, USA, December 2006.

[18] C. W. Lum, R. T. Rysdyk, and A. Pongpunwattana, "Occupancy Based Map Searching Using Heterogeneous Teams of Autonomous Vehicles," Proceedings of the 2006 Guidance, Navigation, and Control Conference, Autonomous Flight Systems Laboratory, Keystone, CO, USA, August 2006.

[19] S. Okazaki and S. Matsushita, "A study of simulation model for pedestrian movement with evacuation and queuing," Proceedings of the International Conference on Engineering for Crowd Safety, London, UK, pp. 17-18, March 1993.

[20] P. Abbeel and P. Ng, "Apprenticeship learning via inverse reinforcement learning," in Proceedings of the twenty-first international conference on Machine learning, ICML '04, ACM, New York, NY, USA, http://doi.acm.org/10.1145/1015330.1015430, 2004.

[21] M. Kuderer, S. Gulati, and W. Burgard, "Learning driving styles for autonomous vehicles from demonstration," in Proceedings of the IEEE International Conference on Robotics & Automation (ICRA), Seattle, USA. vol. 134, 2015

[22] B. Ziebart, A. Maas, J. Bagnell, and A. Dey, "Maximum entropy inverse reinforcement learning," in Proc. of the National Conference on Artificial Intelligence (AAAI), 2008.